THE FALSE PROPHET

THE FALSE
PROPHET

CONSPIRACY, EXTORTION, AND
MURDER IN THE NAME OF GOD

CLAIRE BOOTH

BERKLEY BOOKS, NEW YORK

THE BERKLEY PUBLISHING GROUP
Published by the Penguin Group
Penguin Group (USA) Inc.
375 Hudson Street, New York, New York 10014, USA
Penguin Group (Canada), 90 Eglinton Avenue East, Suite 700, Toronto, Ontario M4P 2Y3, Canada
(a division of Pearson Penguin Canada Inc.)
Penguin Books Ltd., 80 Strand, London WC2R 0RL, England
Penguin Group Ireland, 25 St. Stephen's Green, Dublin 2, Ireland (a division of Penguin Books Ltd.)
Penguin Group (Australia), 250 Camberwell Road, Camberwell, Victoria 3124, Australia
(a division of Pearson Australia Group Pty. Ltd.)
Penguin Books India Pvt. Ltd., 11 Community Centre, Panchsheel Park, New Delhi—110 017, India
Penguin Group (NZ), 67 Apollo Drive, Rosedale, North Shore 0632, New Zealand
(a division of Pearson New Zealand Ltd.)
Penguin Books (South Africa) (Pty.) Ltd., 24 Sturdee Avenue, Rosebank, Johannesburg 2196,
South Africa

Penguin Books Ltd., Registered Offices: 80 Strand, London WC2R 0RL, England

The publisher does not have any control over and does not assume any responsibility for author or third-
party websites or their content.

THE FALSE PROPHET

A Berkley Book / published by arrangement with the author

PRINTING HISTORY
Berkley mass-market edition / February 2008

Copyright © 2008 by Claire Booth
Cover design by Steven Ferlauto
Book design by Laura K. Corless

ISBN: 978-0-425-21974-4

BERKLEY®
Berkley Books are published by The Berkley Publishing Group,
a division of Penguin Group (USA) Inc.,
375 Hudson Street, New York, New York 10014.
BERKLEY® is a registered trademark of Penguin Group (USA) Inc.
The "B" design is a trademark belonging to Penguin Group (USA) Inc.

PRINTED IN THE UNITED STATES OF AMERICA

10 9 8 7 6 5 4 3 2 1

THE FALSE PROPHET

ONE

Where are the Stinemans?

Nancy Hall drove up the quiet street and parked in front of her parents' house. She had brought her lunch and was hoping to eat with them during her noon break from work. She did this often, but today she had an additional motive: she wanted to check up on them. She had tried calling four or five times the night before and no one picked up. The answering machine wasn't even on, which was not only irritating but a little odd as well.

She got out of her pickup truck into the midday heat and walked up to the house. It was a modest, white two-story with a balcony over the garage and shade trees in the front yard. The neighborhood was a quiet one off Treat Boulevard in Concord, a bustling suburban city in the inland valley just east of San Francisco Bay. Her parents, Ivan and Annette Stineman, had lived there for thirty years. He was eighty-five, she was seventy-eight.

But this morning, they were not at home.

Nancy stopped and stared at the four newspapers littering the front step. "These people are retired. That's all they've got to do, is read the paper in the morning," she muttered as she let herself into the house. As she stepped through the entryway, she noticed that the door straight ahead, which usually closed off the kitchen from the front room and the foyer, was wide open. And there was a bowl sitting on the kitchen table. They always picked up their stuff, she thought. Since her mother did the cooking, her father did the dishes. And it was not a chore he usually left undone.

She kept looking around, and her gaze landed on the stove, where a pot still sat on the burner. Mold was growing on the leftover soup in the bottom. Nancy stared at the mess and felt her bewilderment turning to alarm. There was no way her parents would leave a pot in such a state in their pristine kitchen. No way. Her thoughts immediately turned to Ivan and Annette's most valuable possessions—their cats. She quickly went into the garage, where her parents kept the two cats when they left the house. Their beds, food, and water were all there, but Oreo and Twoy were not.

As she walked back into the house, Nancy caught sight of Oreo sitting outside, looking at her through the back glass door that led to a screened-in porch. "Well, come on in here," she said. As she let the black-and-white cat in the kitchen, she noticed there was no water bowl for him on the porch. With temperatures in the high nineties, that bordered on neglect. She watched as the thirsty animal streaked off toward the garage and his food and water. She thought briefly that perhaps her parents had asked her to care for the cats while they left town. She shook her head; she would have remembered them telling her that.

Nancy took another look around and then headed back to the living room. Annette, who entertained often, did not allow the cats and their dander into the front room or upstairs, where they might bother guests. But so many things were not right; Twoy could be anywhere. Nancy searched the rest of the ground floor and then headed upstairs. She was starting to panic.

The bedroom doors were shut, which also was out of the ordinary. She walked down the hallway and into the master bedroom, where everything still seemed to be in its proper place. Nancy opened the door to the master bath, which was split in two, with the sink in one area and the toilet and shower off to the side in a smaller room. She spotted a cat cowering behind the toilet. He had been so traumatized, she could barely tell it was Twoy. His eyes looked huge in his distorted little face. He just stared at her and refused to move.

Nancy started to cry. She had no idea how long he'd been trapped there, but the bathroom rug bunched in front of the shower was full of feces. He'd had no food, and because her parents always put the seat down, he'd had no water, either.

Who would do this? she wondered. She knew it wasn't Mama and Daddy. They would never, ever, leave their precious cats like this. As she looked through tears at Twoy hiding behind the toilet, a more disturbing question pressed forward in her mind. Where were her parents?[1]

————

Ivan and Annette Stineman were predictable, in that nice, reassuring way that everyone wants their parents to be— the result of spending more than half a century together. They met in 1945, while Ivan was still in the service. A mutual friend introduced the Coast Guard quartermaster second-class to the pretty USO hostess seven years his junior. When her mother laid eyes on him for the first time, she looked at his receding hairline in horror. "Oh, Annette! He's too old for you," she told her daughter.

The two hit it off so quickly they were engaged within three months. It came as no surprise, considering all the things they had in common. They'd both been born in the

Midwest, Ivan in Indiana and Annette in Oklahoma. Their
birthdays fell only a day apart. They had the same unusual
middle name—Lane. And their families had each migrated
to Southern California during the Depression.

Ivan had a compact frame and an easy smile that lit up
his face. He played football and lettered in track at Hunt-
ington Park High School. He finished in 1933 and went on
to Compton College, graduating in 1935. He found a job
with Standard Oil and worked with the company until enlisting in the U.S. Coast Guard during World War II. He
served on the USS *Burlington*, escorting convoys among
islands in the South Pacific. It was on a trip home on leave
that he met Annette Callender, a tall brunette who had
grown up in Downey, a town right outside of Los Angeles.
After attending the local high school, where she worked on
the yearbook and newspaper staffs, she had graduated from
Fullerton College.

The only hitch in the new couple's wedding plans—
aside from her mother's critique of Ivan's impending
baldness—was the clerk at the records office, who initially
refused to issue them a marriage license. Annette Lane
Callender and Ivan Lane Stineman, with birthdays only a
day apart? It sounded like they already were related and
should not be getting married at all, the clerk told them.
Eventually, they convinced the bureaucrat they were not
kissing cousins and deserved the proper paperwork. They
were married on September 16, 1945.

Annette's parents gave them property in the Southern
California area of Pico Rivera as a wedding present. After
Ivan's discharge from the Coast Guard, the newlyweds
promptly set about building a house. Ivan, his father, and a
friend did most of the construction, with Annette helping
at every turn. Since they had little money, she recycled
everything she could, including nails she would pound out
of boards and straighten one by one.

They were so proud of their little house. It had a living room and kitchen, an alcove for the bed, and a bathroom and dressing area. And it quickly became too small. In the space of one year, their family doubled in size. Daughter Nancy Lane Stineman was born in July 1948; Judith Lane came along only eleven and a half months later. Ivan and Annette gradually added on another bedroom, a dining area, and a living room.

It was a happy home. Ivan's playful sense of humor livened up dinnertime, as well as the many outdoor activities the family loved. He and Nancy would often just look at each other and crack up with laughter. With his round face and ever-receding hair, he was just a cute little man. He would tell stories, make noises, and delight his daughters.

"Oh, Ivan," Annette would sigh.

He would tell the same jokes again and again, until the whole family knew them by heart. He told one joke in particular whenever he felt the females in his family were not appreciating him as they should: A little boy's dog is hit by a car and killed while the child is at school. The boy comes home and his mother tells him that Laddie died. The boy, who loved Laddie more than anything, nods at her and skips out to play, much to her puzzlement. Later, he comes back to her and asks where his dog is. "Honey, I told you, Laddie died," the mother responds. "Oh," the boy says. "I thought you said Daddy." All Ivan had to do when he felt outnumbered by women was say, "Oh, I thought you said Daddy," and everyone would dissolve into laughter.

He loved garage sales and would come home with all sorts of tools and other contraptions. He prized a bargain, even if he did not need it. If he found he did not like what he had bought, he would turn around and sell it at his own garage sale. One weekend, he came home with a motorized scooter. His little girls ran out of the house as he was unloading it from the car and begged to ride it. Annette explained that it was just for Daddy, and he got to ride it first. Ivan climbed on with a smile and fired it up. He revved the engine and took off—straight into the side of the garage. His wife and daughters raced to pick him up out of the flower bed, and a sheepish Ivan never rode the thing again.

Annette was always there to dust everyone off when they fell. She ran her household with good doses of common sense and efficiency, but that did not diminish her innate kindness. She loved animals and always had a dog. That was never enough, however. Her family was always coming home with lizards and guinea pigs and turtles, including a perfectly ordinary fat round one that Ivan—with a twinkle in his eye—convinced Nancy was a genuine Texas racing turtle, faster than anything California ever produced. Annette accepted the false Texas import, as well as the chipmunk her other daughter somehow acquired and the spider monkey her husband brought home, despite her never-carried-out threats. "You can't have any more animals. When these die, we're not getting any more. Yep, when these are gone, we're not getting any more."

But they always did. Annette's younger daughter had wanted a cat for years, so when she finally thought Judy was ready to care for one, she relented. Ivan put an ad in the paper: little girl will give good home to a free Siamese or Persian cat. Someone called and offered a part Persian, and they said they would take Judy to see it. Annette watched her daughter get so excited she could not eat her dinner. When they arrived at the cat owner's house, they discovered the kitten was more tabby than Persian, but Judy did not care. They took the cat home that night, and Annette carefully took Judy through all the responsibilities of cat ownership. Her lessons worked; Taffy the tabby lived seventeen years.

In the early 1960s, Annette and Ivan got a cabin in the

mountains, where they would retreat from the bustle of Los Angeles each weekend. Annette joined Ivan at Standard Oil as the girls got older, and the cabin became a refuge for both working parents. They would load up the girls and the animals and spend a few days puttering around before heading back home, listening to the sounds of Ivan's favorite sports teams on the car radio. Summers they would pack up the camper and drive even farther, to places like Salt Lake City, the Four Corners, Hearst Castle, and Baja California.

Ivan had put in almost three decades at Standard Oil when the company consolidated its operations in 1970 and transferred its Southern California employees up to the Bay Area. Ivan, a credit-card supervisor, and Annette, who worked in accounts receivable, decided to make the move. Nancy went with them; she had started working in the company mailroom four years before. Judy, who by then had met the man who would become her husband, stayed behind.

The Stinemans loved Concord. They bought a lovely two-story house on a quiet street called Frayne Lane, and Annette delighted in its professionally finished niceties, so different from the ever-evolving rooms in the Pico Rivera house they had built board by board. She kept it immaculate, even with all the animals that were still such a part of her life. Ivan kept up his memberships with the Masons and the Shriners and became a passionate fan of the San Francisco 49ers.

Two years after moving north, Ivan took early retirement from Standard Oil. But the fifty-seven-year-old still had plenty of energy and he put it to use selling real estate for the next fifteen years. He certainly was not the area's highest seller, but he would work himself to the bone for the clients he did have. Annette left Standard Oil—now Chevron—in the mid-1980s. At that point, their true retirement began.

They took cruises, sailing the Mediterranean and the Caribbean and floating down the Mississippi on a paddle-boat. They got rid of their little camper and bought a motor home, deciding the time had come to take their creature comforts with them, instead of just the creatures. Doctors diagnosed Ivan with diabetes in 1990, so Annette started caring for his health just as she had everything else. She forbade him ice cream and made sure he took his insulin. It worked; he lost weight and felt better—just as she told him he would. After he had his gimpy knee replaced in 1998, he was truly ready to go. He and Annette had more of the world to see, more fun to have, and they wanted to get started.[2]

———

Judy picked up the phone in her Southern California home. It was her sister. "Hi," she said. "What's up?"

"Well, we may have missing parents," Nancy said.

"We do?" Judy asked, laughing. "Where'd they go this time?"

"I don't know where they are," Nancy said. Her worry and puzzlement came through the phone line as she described how she had found the house and her concern that she had forgotten whether she was supposed to take care of the cats. Judy's mind started racing.

"Can you find Daddy's insulin?" she asked. Nancy put down the phone and ran to check. The little kit he would take on trips was not there. Neither was one of their suit-cases. Maybe they had really gone off, and in the commotion of leaving, Mama thought Daddy had cared for the cats, and Daddy thought Mama had. After all, they were old, Judy thought as she hung up with Nancy. But as she was walking out the door to go to a meeting, something struck her: her mother's makeup. There was no way she would go anywhere overnight without it. She called Nancy back. Nancy raced upstairs to check; the makeup was there in its proper place. Now Judy was worried.

Nancy set down the phone and looked around the house. She had to do something, so she washed the moldy soup pan and cleaned the bathroom mat. Then she went to the neighbors, asking if anyone had seen her parents lately. The man who lived across the street said he had seen two guys on the Stinemans' porch one recent evening. Okay, Nancy said, tucking the information away for later. She told several people about the cats and the newspapers piled on the porch and asked what she should do. Call the police, they said.

She hesitated. What if her parents had just forgotten to mention that they were leaving town? Or what if they had told her, and she was the one who had forgotten? It would be so silly to bring in the police. But there was their calendar, with every date, every appointment, laid out in her mother's neat script. And for August 3, 2000, they had nothing to do. They should be home. Nancy picked up the phone.

The Concord Police Department sent Officer Mark Evans, who dutifully looked around the house and took down Nancy's litany of worries. These sorts of things usually turn out to be misunderstandings, he said. The supposedly missing people come home and everything is fine. Nancy nodded and watched him drive away. She stood in the house, feeling frustrated and panicky at the same time. "There's got to be something in this house," she muttered. "This is not right." She started going through everything— looking under tables, behind furniture, in between couch cushions. And then, in back of a chair cushion in the living room, her hand hit a metal object. She pulled out her father's watch, a Time Life freebie he had proudly shown her the week before. The metal band was twisted and torn apart. The evidence was getting to be overwhelming. She took the mangled watch next door and showed a neighbor, who said she needed to call the police back. She called Officer Evans, who told her to bring it down to the police station. Once he saw it and talked to the neighbor who had seen two young men at the Stinemans' house earlier in the week, Evans began to agree with Nancy. This was no misunderstanding.

————

Evans was now thoroughly concerned about the two retired residents of his city. He tracked down the detective on call that night and outlined the case. When Steve Chiabotti heard all the details, he agreed with the patrol officer. Put them in the statewide database of missing persons, he told Evans. Enter their missing van into the computer, too. And leave a photo of them on his desk so he could start investigating in the morning. He told the officer he would canvass the neighborhood and see what he could find.

The next morning, Chiabotti stared at the photo on his desk and did some thinking. Most of the time, adults went missing because they wanted to—a wife fleeing an abusive husband or a down-on-his-luck investor trying to escape his creditors. But the Stinemans did not fit any of the normal profiles. Chiabotti turned to the next cubicle and filled Judy Elo in on the case. The two had been partners on and off for more than four years and complemented each other well. Chiabotti needed to keep a certain emotional distance from a case to be an effective investigator. Just the facts, please. Elo, on the other hand, was known in the department for her empathy; she could not help but connect with victims and their families. Nevertheless, though they had different styles, they were typically on the same page—and this time was no different. With more than thirty years of police experience between them, they knew something was not right. They looked at each other and headed out to question the neighbors.

They spoke with a woman who lived at the end of Frayne Lane, who told them she had seen a short, fat, blond woman sitting in a pickup several days earlier, and with the man who lived across the street from the Stinemans, whom Nancy had spoken to previously. He told them that last Sunday he had seen two young men approach the Stinemans' house. They were dressed in suits and looked like missionaries.

The detectives noted all the information and kept poking around, but no breaks came until Sunday, when an Oakland police officer spotted the Stinemans' van in a bad section of the city. The white Chevrolet Lumina was parked haphazardly against a curb in an industrial area near the freeway. The keys were in the ignition, the driver's-side window was rolled down, and the radio was on and tuned to a rap station. The whole thing looked staged to Heidi Stephenson, the Concord detective called out to the scene. She had been a cop for fifteen years and had always relied on her gut. Right now, it was telling her that the situation was too strange to have a happy outcome.

"I just don't have a good feeling about this," she said over her walkie-talkie to Chiabotti. She explained the condition the van was in and mentioned the sawhorses and wood chips she had seen in the back. She began knocking on doors, talking to people in the few apartments in the area. No one knew much at all, although one man remembered that the van had been parked there since at least Friday. Stephenson sighed in frustration, then called in crime scene technicians to tow the van back to Concord.

Nancy went shopping Sunday morning, just to have something to do as she waited for word of her parents. As she turned down the street to her house, she saw Elo and Chiabotti coming toward her. They told her they needed to get

into the Frayne Lane house. She quickly unloaded her gro-
ceries and took them the short distance to her parents'
house and let them in. Then Elo sat her down in the comfortable family room.

"Nancy, they found the van," she said.

"They have?" asked Nancy hopefully.

"It was abandoned, with the windows rolled down and
the radio going," Elo said.

"They didn't find Mama and Daddy?" Nancy asked,
panic beginning to flood her body. She started sobbing.
Despite knowing how bad the news was, Elo tried to reassure her.

"That doesn't mean anything. That just means they're
not in the van," she said.

Nancy continued to cry. She knew her parents would
not have left the van in such condition.

"Do you have anyone you can call?" said Elo, who was
now quite worried about her. Nancy nodded. Her sister
needed to know what happened. But Nancy was still sobbing and could not do it. Elo picked up the phone. Through
her tears, Nancy told her to talk to Judy's husband, Fred,
first. She thought it seemed kinder to break the news to her
through him.

Judy had been sitting by her phone for the past three
days. She snatched it up as it rang. A woman asked for
Fred and she handed the phone over to him. Still on the
line, he turned to Judy.

"They found your parents' van and they're going to
close their house as a crime scene," he said.

Judy demanded the phone and spoke to Elo herself,
who explained that they'd found the van in a bad section of
Oakland near the airport. Judy grasped at a slim hope.

"Is it possible that they went on a trip with another couple, and they parked it wherever you found it so they
wouldn't have to pay the parking fee?" she asked.

"No," Elo said flatly.

That did it. Judy quickly made reservations for the next flight to Oakland. She and Fred threw clothes in a suitcase, picked up Annette's sister and her husband, and headed for the airport. When they arrived, they were forced to check in to a crummy little motel. Nancy's home was too small to hold them all, and their parents' house had been sealed by the police. It was now officially considered a crime scene.

TWO

A Quiet Night in Woodacre

The San Geronimo Valley was a sleepy place just north of San Francisco where people could, with effort, carve out unassuming rural lives amid the expensive hustle and bustle of the Bay Area. It was a stretch of rolling hills, redwood trees, and tiny towns where everyone knew one another, where residents who had lived there half a dozen years were still considered newcomers.

Jenny Villarin was not one of those people. She'd come to the Valley in the mid-1970s, and during the next quarter century became a fixture in the community. Everyone knew the soft-spoken woman with the long, dark hair and high cheekbones who was always willing to help anyone in need. Jenny took great care of her friends, a habit formed during a tough childhood.

Born in Salinas, California, in 1955, Jenny was the youngest of four children. Her parents split up before she reached kindergarten, and the siblings were separated as well. Jenny and her sister, Lydia, stayed with her mother, a waitress of Cherokee descent named Peggy, and brothers

David and Lucio left with their father, a farmworker and native of the Philippines named Guillermo San Luis Villarin.

Peggy soon moved in with a man who was just plain mean. To him, the little girls were just "Filipinas," and he allowed them no freedom. When Peggy had two more daughters with him, Jenny and Lydia were expected to take care of them and were beaten if they did anything wrong. They were not allowed to have friends over, go outside to play, or use the phone. The family moved around constantly, from Salinas to nearby Half Moon Bay, then to a series of other towns until finally settling in Sunnyvale, just northwest of San Jose. The girls' only joy came during the summer, when they would get to stay for a week or two with their real father in Salinas. They would romp with David, Lucio, and adopted brother Robert, who were all protective of their littlest sister—the meek, quiet one—but they could not do anything to defend her once she had to go back home.

It finally became too much, and when Jenny was twelve, Lydia convinced her that they needed to run away. It was a spur-of-the-moment decision, and the two girls literally took off running. Their parents screamed after them that they would catch the sisters and beat them. The girls thought no one would protect them if they did get away, so they stopped and went back home.

The aborted attempt did not deter Lydia, and it taught her a few things. She began planning her escape in advance and, when she turned fifteen, told the thirteen-year-old Jenny she was going. Jenny thought about it but was too scared to go with her, no matter how much Lydia tried to cajole her. She decided to stick it out and once Lydia left, struggled through with the help of a group of friends who also came from broken families and knew—at least a little bit—what she was going through. Jenny wanted desperately to fit in and would sometimes get a little too clingy, but her friends knew she meant well.

They were the first ones Jenny told about a man she met at a concert soon after she graduated from high school in 1973. She had a fake ID and sneaked into a bar to watch Elvin Bishop perform. She managed to meet the blues guitarist, and the two immediately became an item. She gratefully left Sunnyvale behind and moved in with him, first in San Francisco and then north across the Golden Gate Bridge, into Marin County and the Valley.

After always being the odd one out and trying to fit in, Jenny was now the center of her circle. But instead of lording her rock-star-girlfriend status over everyone, she shared it. Her friend Gloria and another pal moved up to Marin County, and Elvin helped them find a house. They would take limos to shows, fly to Los Angeles, go to different concert venues. Jenny got her brothers and sisters in backstage at shows.

It was a crazy rock-and-roll lifestyle—constant touring, staying up all night, easy access to drugs and booze. Jenny was in the middle of it all and took care of everyone in the Bishop retinue, especially Elvin. She drove him everywhere, pressed his clothes, made sure he had what he needed on and off the stage. The roadies and the guys in the band—and their women—loved her. So did Elvin. He wrote a song about her that would become his biggest hit: "Fooled Around and Fell in Love."

The couple's happiness only grew when Jenny got pregnant. Selina Grace was born in October 1977. She had a rounder face than her mother, but the same straight dark hair and arched eyebrows. Jenny kept touring with Elvin, but the lifestyle gradually began to take its toll on their relationship. The two drifted apart, and by the early 1980s, Jenny and her daughter were on their own.

Jenny chose not to leave the Valley. She drifted from

place to place and relationship to relationship. She scraped together enough to live on—working in schools, cleaning houses, making and selling jewelry. But she always found time for her loved ones, especially her family members, who had a tendency to drift apart under the weight of busy lives and different fathers. She never held her stepfather's abusiveness against her younger sisters, Olga and Yolanda. Although technically her half-siblings, they were just as much her family as anyone else. She called people all the time to find out how they were doing; relatives loved hearing from her so much they would accept her collect calls when she did not have the money to pay a long-distance bill.

It was difficult raising a child alone, but Jenny managed. As Selina got older, the two became best friends and depended on each other completely. Although they had a wide range of friends and family for support, it always came down to just the two of them, and they knew it.

Selina grew into a bright, sunny girl who was shy around most adults but bubbly and playful with her friends and cousins. She always did well in school, but as she neared high school in 1991, her grades began to fall, and Jenny decided it was time to get out of the Valley. She had met a man who wanted to move to Pennsylvania, and she decided she and Selina would go with him.

The relationship did not last more than a year, but by then Selina was settled in school, and Jenny had made friends. They stayed, even though making ends meet was just as difficult there as it had been in expensive Marin County. Jenny worked for a photography studio and as a grocery clerk, but she was broke a lot and took to calling relatives collect again. Selina did better in school, but decided in 1998 that she was done with Pennsylvania and wanted to go back to California. Jenny, determined to make the move work, stayed behind.

Once back home, Selina moved in with her aunt Olga's family in the Santa Cruz Mountains and started taking graphic arts classes. She was still quiet around adults, but loved to goof around with her cousins. The same held when she left to stay with her uncle David in Salinas. He did not put up with her natural teenage inclination to lie around doing nothing all day. Work or school, he told her. She took a few classes then began waiting tables at a Red Lobster restaurant. Then she moved into her first apartment with her cousin and a friend and bought a car, a little 1984 Honda she loved.

After years of moving around with her mother, Selina finally felt on stable ground. Her self-confidence grew; she was able to live on her own and take care of herself, yet she had family nearby for support and good times. Jenny could only watch from afar. Finally, she couldn't take it any longer. Despite talking to Selina almost every day, she missed her daughter too much. She could not afford to move back west, however, and found herself stuck in a place she no longer wanted to be until an old friend came to her rescue.

Jenny had known Jim Gamble for years. He was a great bear of a man, tall and broad, with a mustache and receding hairline. By 1999, the fifty-three-year-old's hair was almost gone, but his great laugh and generous nature remained. He drove back to Pennsylvania that year, packed up Jenny's stuff, and brought her home.[1]

Jim Gamble seized every opportunity life threw at him. He always had. He grew up playing with his little brother, Larry, in Sunnyvale, where the boys lived with their mother after she split from their father in 1955. As an adolescent, he loved all kinds of sports—baseball, football, golf. He struck out into the world even before graduating from high school, enlisting in the air force and getting his diploma while serving. Soon after, he married a woman almost twice his age. The marriage lasted six years; by then, he was out of the service and working at a computer firm in the Silicon Valley.

Jim quickly remarried and had two sons before his second marriage ended in 1983. He grew tired of the eighty-hour computer-industry workweeks and decided it would be more fun to semiretire. He became a man of leisure, dabbling in different interests and trying out new things. One of his favorites was mining. He had two claims with his brother, a turquoise stake in Nevada and a sunstone one in Oregon.

He married for the third time in 1988, but his wife traveled constantly, and he spent much of his time alone. Then in 1996, his mother, Fran Nelson, divorced her third husband and moved to a retirement mobile-home park in the Napa Valley. Jim, who had never really been welcome in her ex-husband's home, showed up with a bottle of champagne. "Now I can visit my mom whenever I want to," he said.

And he did, eventually moving in with her after he and his wife separated. He took care of Fran, and had a good time, too. The two loved cruises and sailed regularly—to Alaska, the Caribbean, the Panama Canal. He learned to scuba dive, took horseback-riding lessons on shore, and loved to spin the ladies around the cruise ships' dance floors. Life was fun, and he was going to enjoy it.[2]

With Jenny back in the Valley, Jim came down often to see her and their mutual friend Gloria. Selina moved up from Salinas, and she and Jenny lived with Gloria for several months in early 2000 while they got on their feet. Jenny did not have transportation and walked to work at Rancho

Nicasio, a restaurant and store near Gloria's house. When she eventually got a car, she took another job a few miles away at the Paper Mill Creek Saloon, a local institution. She had worked there before and was comfortable with it. And it helped her get together enough money to move out of Gloria's and into a house in the nearby city of Novato with a roommate.

Selina also was getting on her feet. She had a new boyfriend, a tall, handsome guy she met at a rave. She was enjoying her job at the Two Bird Café, one of the best spots to eat in the Valley, and she had just saved up enough in wages and tips to move into her own place. It was the first time she had lived without roommates and she could not have been more excited about the little studio apartment in the basement of a house on Redwood Drive in the Valley town of Woodacre. She invited everyone over to see it and offered to let people stay if they needed to. Her mother was one of the first to take her up on the offer. The situation with Jenny's new roommate was not really working out, and so she readily agreed to house-sit for Selina while she went on a camping trip to Yosemite National Park with her boyfriend. Jenny waved good-bye to her daughter and went to work at the Paper Mill, where Jim called her later that night. He was in town and offered to bring her dinner while she tended bar. He came with the food, and the two chatted with other customers until closing time. Then Jenny asked Jim, why not stay with her at Selina's? Jim didn't have anywhere to be; he said sure. They closed down the bar and headed up the hill the short distance to Selina's apartment.

They stayed up talking for a while before they fell asleep. And then, just before sunrise, the apartment door burst open.

THREE

The Search for Selina

The house on Redwood Drive turned, in the space of seven gunshots, from a typical suburban home into a horrific crime scene. Two people were sprawled dead in the studio apartment off the garage. The stunned homeowner stood on the lawn in his bathrobe as alarmed neighbors peered out their windows at the police cars roaring up the street.

Cops were everywhere in the early dawn light that Thursday morning. One of them was Marin County sheriff's detective Steve Nash. Dispatch had called him at home, even before the paramedics arrived at the scene, to tell him about the report of multiple gunshots and bodies. He was already awake when the phone rang, getting ready to go after a robbery suspect he'd just identified the day before. That quickly got pushed down on the priority list, and he set out for the normally sleepy hamlet of Woodacre shortly after 5:30 a.m.

Nash had been with the sheriff's department for twenty-one years, spending twelve of them as a detective. He loved investigations because it meant more interaction with people than a typical patrol beat. But even after all those years of viewing the worst humanity had to offer, the forty-three-year-old was not the least bit hard-boiled. He felt for his victims and took pains to be considerate while also allowing them to hear as much about his investigations as he could safely tell. It was a little old-fashioned, in the same way it used to be a given that people looked out for their neighbors. The fact that he regularly referred to those he was after as "crooks" only added to the impression. A cheerful and affable man, he was slender with the requisite cop mustache and short brown hair just starting to gray. His blue eyes usually twinkled as he talked. They were not twinkling now.

Murders were rare in the Valley; there hadn't been one in more than a decade. Now Nash had two on his hands. No one had any idea who would want to kill the beloved Jenny Villarin—or Jim Gamble for that matter. There was nothing new or unusual about either of their lives that could have caused someone to want them dead.

———————

Detectives learned Selina had recently started dating a man named Jordan. No one knew much about him, not even his last name. Then they found Selina's journal in her apartment. The pages inside the lavender cover made for some very interesting reading, especially several entries written as letters to Jordan.

"There is so much of your life hidden from me. What does it mean? Your name, your past, your wife, God knows what else. See, here is what happens. I start getting all happy, and then I think about long term and then I realize I don't know you from a can of paint." Her observations were making Jordan more, not less, mysterious to investigators. "I won't want to be with you when your big plan goes down. I don't want to be rich. I want to be comfortable . . . I won't be able to keep up with you and all of your big plans."

Big plans? What big plans? Nash read the diary and started to become concerned about Selina's well-being. She had not come home and no one had seen or talked to her recently. She knew something about her boyfriend's big plans, but he wondered whether she was involved or just trying to stay out of it.

This unknown boyfriend began to play large in the minds of Nash and other detectives and brought a sharp focus to their investigation. They therefore discounted the possibility that Jim Gamble was the intended target; the poor guy just seemed to have been in the wrong place at the wrong time. They also quickly ruled out robbery as a motive after finding $820 in twenty-dollar bills in a jewelry box and $1,000 in hundred-dollar bills—probably rent money—in a brown leather container, both safe on Selina's nightstand.

Nash and his partner, Don Wick, did consider the possibility that Jenny Villarin had been shot because the killer believed her to be Selina. But that theory never really took hold except as an extension of their belief that Jordan was somehow behind the whole thing. And that was before they learned of the phone call.

At 10 a.m., five hours after the shootings, a man claiming to be Jordan called the Two Bird Café.

"This is Selina's boyfriend, Jordan. I need to speak to Selina."

"Selina's on vacation," replied the coworker who answered the phone.

"I need to tell you what's going on. I need to calm down," he said. "I flaked on her. If she calls, tell her that I called, and if she cares at all, she can call me."

Jordan spoke forcefully and quickly. It sounded like he was using a pay phone, because the coworker heard a recording say "please deposit thirty-five cents."

The call was odd for several reasons. Selina was supposed to be with Jordan in Yosemite. If he was looking for her, they obviously weren't together. And by that time, news of Jenny Villarin's murder was all over television and the radio. But he made no mention of his girlfriend's mother. He didn't seem worried about Selina, either, just generally agitated.

As Thursday drew to a close, authorities continued to scour Selina's apartment for evidence and track down as many of Selina and Jenny's friends and family as they could. But try as they might, they got no closer to the true identity—or the whereabouts—of the mysterious Jordan.

———————

Early Friday morning, Olga Land pointed her big pickup north and started toward Marin County. The phone call had come the night before, but she had been in no state to go then, not right after hearing that Jenny had been murdered. She was barely better as she started the drive, but nothing was going to keep her from getting to her sister. As she drove north from her home in the Santa Cruz Mountains toward Woodacre more than a hundred miles away, she felt a bubble forming around her. It surrounded her, shutting out her emotions, cushioning the hard ride up Highway 101. Later, she would realize that it was shock, but for now, it just allowed her to focus on her mission. Get to Jenny.

The silence in the truck was intolerable. Although the radio was broken, the tape player still worked. She fished around the cab for the rock and blues cassettes she usually listened to, but there were none there. The only tape she could find was by a Christian horn player. She knew just one song on it, because her husband, a musician himself, was learning it for a show he was doing. She slid it into the dash. By the time she got to Marin, she'd listened to it so many times she knew every song on the tape. The repetition helped calm her down.

Normally Oggie, as her family and friends called her,

didn't need calming. Her open face, framed by long, lay-ered brown hair, often wore a warm smile. Her great bois-terous laugh could make those who heard it break into grins. She enjoyed a sunny outlook on life that was an-chored by her deep faith in the Lord.

For a brief moment, the bubble weakened and she thought of what had happened. The big sister who pro-tected her, loved her, and laughed with her was gone. "If Jenny really is gone, she's in a better place," Oggie thought. "She's not being tested anymore."

By the time she got to Selina's apartment, though, dis-belief had worked its way into her mind. No one in the world would want to hurt Jenny, she thought. It had to be a mistake. Someone else staying at Selina's apartment had been killed, not Jenny. She found the house, turned the truck around, and parked up the hill by some bushes.

Still in her bubble, she blew by the yellow police tape that circled the garage, yelling for Jenny and Selina. She ran into the garage and made it to the inner door that was the entrance to her niece's little studio. And then a man materialized out of nowhere and stopped her cold.

"Who are you? What are you doing here?" Steve Nash asked Oggie.

"I'm looking for my sister, I'm looking for my niece," she replied, a little out of breath.

"You don't want to come in here," Nash told her.

"I gotta find my sister," she said, still not really believ-ing that Jenny was dead.

"We found your sister," he said firmly. "We're looking for Selina now."

His words began to make it real for Oggie. As gently as he could, Nash let her know that the murder victim was in-deed Jenny. He led her out of the garage and to a police van parked in the driveway. Oggie hadn't even noticed it on her way into the apartment. He sat her inside the van and asked her name. As the morning air blew through the open doors, he tried to calm her down.

They talked about where Selina might be. Oggie asked if anyone had looked in Yosemite. Nash told her that authorities were already searching there, and then he asked the question the whole sheriff's department desperately wanted answered: Did she know Selina's boyfriend?

"No. I've never met him," she said. "I don't know anybody that's met him."

"You can't tell us what he looks like, or anything?"

"No, we hadn't met him. I'd just heard about him," she said.

And then, through the front windows of the van, Nash saw them coming. Television news trucks began to pull up, with people leaping out and grabbing cameras. "How do I get out of here?" Oggie asked in dismay. "I don't want to talk to them, and I don't want them coming up and talking to me."[1]

Nash looked at the distraught woman in front of him. He could only imagine what she was going through, but he knew she did not need the added trauma of an encounter with a pushy reporter. He told her he would take care of it by creating a diversion so she could slip away without a camera getting shoved in her face. He got out of the van and began to widen the crime scene perimeter with police tape. It worked like a charm. Every reporter rushed over to him. Oggie climbed out of the back of the police van, stumbled past the apartment where her sister's blood still stained the walls, and ran through the bushes to her truck.

She had told Nash that she would be staying with Gloria. She started the truck and drove to Gloria's house, where the rest of her shell-shocked family was already starting to gather. At that point, everyone's primary concern was finding Selina so they could tell her about her mother. They just wanted her to be with friends and relatives when she learned of the shooting.

Selina was supposed to return from Yosemite that Friday morning in time for a 10:30 a.m. shift at the Two Bird. Friends and sheriff's investigators joined her coworkers at the café, and everyone waited. But the scheduled start of her shift passed with no sign of her.

Now people really started to get worried. Authorities issued an all-points bulletin for the missing twenty-two-year-old and her gray 1984 Honda Accord, license number 4CQD822. And just in case she slipped past them and got home without anyone knowing, they taped a hand-printed sign to the front door of her apartment: "Selina, do not go inside." Call the sheriff's office instead, the note said.

One of the first things Selina's friends and family did was page her. She had always responded before. In the days before cell phones became the de facto means of instant communication, pagers were the gold standard for staying in touch. And Selina always carried her sleek, new model with all the latest bells and whistles. It had been a gift from Auntie Oggie, and she was never without it. But now she was not answering anyone's pages.

Later Friday morning, Nash discovered why. Selina had left her pager at work. Someone at the Two Bird called him and told him it was there. He rushed to the café to pick it up and gave it to another investigator to begin following up on the phone numbers it contained. Nash would not get it back until more than twenty-four hours later, its crucial information still locked inside.

———

Selina's loved ones fanned out and began searching for her themselves. Some who lived close to the Sierra Nevada joined in the search at Yosemite, almost two hundred miles east of Marin County. Cousins who had rushed to the Valley from throughout Northern California went to parks and hangouts and combed any back roads they could find. They didn't know where they were going, but they had to do something.

Their frustration was compounded by their inability to help the police figure out who Jordan was. Although Selina talked about him all the time, friends had never seen pictures of him or knew if he had a job. Some people did have tiny scraps of information, however. One close friend told Detective Erin Inskip that Jordan lived in Concord, and he had a key to Selina's apartment. Another said he had a brother named Justin. A coworker told her the couple would meet at Bison Brewery in Berkeley.

Inskip rushed to Berkeley. There she found Matthew King, a bartender at the popular bar. He identified Selina from a picture on a flyer Inskip had with her. He told her that Selina and a man who matched the description of Jordan were regulars at the bar. He had last seen them Wednesday afternoon, the day before the shootings.

All of this information went out to those working the case. The next day—Saturday—brought another nugget. Jordan lived with his younger brother, another witness told Detective Alisia Lellis. One of Selina's longtime friends then said something the detective found very, very interesting. Selina told her that Jordan was to receive a $125,000 inheritance, but if he deposited it in his bank account, he would lose the money. He wanted Selina to deposit the funds in her own name. In exchange for the favor, she'd keep $25,000.

That was a lot of money. It was also the first semiconcrete "big plan" detectives heard about. It did nothing to ease their worries about Selina's safety.

————

Saturday was the third day since Jenny's death—and the third day no one had heard from Selina. Loved ones continued to scour the hillsides. Sheriff's investigators, knowing that the odds of a happy outcome decrease exponentially as time goes by, pressed urgently on. The investigator to whom Nash had given Selina's pager hit nothing but dead ends, so the detective took it back and started working it himself. As he created a list of the phone numbers it contained, one leaped out at him. It had a 925 area code, which included Jordan's supposed city of residence, Concord. After some quick searching, he figured out that the number belonged to a GTE cell phone—good information he was ready to run with. But convoluted corporate bureaucracy would force his investigation to a screeching halt.

Just days before, the phone company GTE had merged with Verizon, a large East Coast–based cellular provider. Perhaps because of the upheaval caused by the merger, no one at the company office could help Nash get the subscriber information for the number in Selina's pager. The hours ticked by, and the normally composed Nash became more desperate, and more irate. "I am trying to save someone's life!" he yelled into the phone. He was certain by this point that Selina was being held hostage somewhere and had very little time left.

It was late Saturday afternoon by the time he finally got the name and location: Denise Anderson in Concord. He looked her up in a database and found her home address. Sergeant Barry Heying quickly drove across the bay to have a chat, but Ms. Anderson of Concord had no idea what he was talking about. Someone had used her name to get a cell phone and had obviously been using it without her knowledge.

Nash gritted his teeth and got back on the phone with the cell-phone company. He wanted Verizon to pull all of the calls made by that cell phone in the last two weeks. If Jordan had been using the phone, knowing who he had called could lead to a street address or other clue to his whereabouts. But officials at the phone company required a search warrant to turn over the phone numbers. He typed it up, fuming at the further delay. A Marin County judge approved the warrant in the early hours of Sunday morning. It took many more hours for the data to finally land in Nash's hands. While he waited, the frustration and the stress made the thought in his head beat more and more loudly, like a drum inside his skull: "I'm trying to save someone's life. I'm trying to save someone's life."

Once he finally received the necessary information, Nash pared down the list of calls so that each number appeared only once, then faxed it to Pacific Bell, the Bay Area's local telephone company. He had had people at the company's emergency center on standby for hours, waiting for the Verizon data so they could run the numbers and tell Nash whom they belonged to. Within an hour, he had the information he'd been waiting for all day. And it was the vital piece that would eventually crack the walls the mysterious Jordan had so carefully constructed around himself.[2]

———

That weekend, the sheriff's department finally finished processing Selina's apartment for evidence. Oggie knew Selina had a file box and thought it might contain information. She grabbed it and took it back to Gloria's, where the two of them went through every last piece of paper. They knew Jordan lived in Concord, so everything they found with an address in that city was carefully pulled out and set aside. They considered it evidence and so, just like in the movies, they sealed it all in plastic baggies to be turned over to detectives.

Then Oggie went back to Woodacre, this time accompanied by Gloria's daughter. They had access to the entire place—all of Selina's belongings, her stuff, her life. Oggie was adamant that her niece not have to come back to the place where her mother had been murdered. She wanted everything moved out so Selina would not forever associate her things with Jenny's death.

Selina's studio did not contain much. The room held a desk, double bed, and nightstand. The dresser, where the television sat, was pushed against the wall opposite the foot of the bed. The little kitchen took up about a third of the room, and the bathroom was off to the side.

The two women carefully picked through the mess— there was a pile of leftover evidence-collection waste in the middle of the floor, and the blood-spattered wall behind the bed had been cut out and taken by crime scene technicians. Oggie found a pair of little tongs and some gloves. Still in her bubble, she found it was easy to be sensible. She pulled on the gloves and picked up the tongs; there were a lot of things there still covered in blood.

She put everything bloody into bags and set them aside. Then she and Gloria's daughter bagged up all of Selina's clothes on the floor and in the dresser, as well as the stuff in the bathroom and the furniture, and loaded it all into Oggie's truck. It would stay at Gloria's house until Selina returned to reclaim it.

————

One of the phone numbers on Nash's tally was listed under the first name of Justin. And Justin's last name, Helzer, showed up under a different first name as well. Brothers, perhaps? Nash stared at the sheets of paper in front of him; this was the first real break in the case. He was starting to feel good.

He began a background check on Justin Helzer. Turned out that back in May, the man had purchased a gun—the same-caliber automatic used to kill Jenny and Jim. Nash felt even better.

Justin Helzer lived on Saddlewood Court, a cul-de-sac on the outskirts of Concord. Local police told Nash that they had previously contacted another family member at the same address. This one was older, a man named Glenn Taylor Helzer. "Now we're getting close," Nash thought as the adrenaline started to surge through his tired body. He began to think he would be able to save Selina.

But it was already Sunday evening, and the clock was ticking. The investigation took on an even more frenzied pace. Two detectives raced across the bay to Concord to stake out the Helzer home. Then Nash pulled Glenn Taylor Helzer's DMV photo. This guy was a piece of work, he thought as he looked at the picture. It showed a pale young man with dark hair pulled back from his face and several days of stubble covering his jaw. But that was ordinary compared with the expression on his face. He stared straight ahead with narrowed eyes, his tongue sticking out directly at the camera. It distorted his features, but hopefully not enough to make them unrecognizable.

———————

After Oggie finished cleaning out Selina's apartment, she headed for her sister's place. Jenny had been renting a room in a nearby town, and Oggie wanted to see it. Gloria's daughter asked her if they were going to empty it of belongings as they had done at Selina's.

"No," Oggie replied. She had thought about Selina's return for several days now, and she believed she knew what would be best for her grieving niece. "Selina's going to want to drink in her mom when she gets back. She can come here and curl up in Mommy's bed or whatever she's going to need to do to deal with it." So the two women cleaned Jenny's room—making the bed, straightening up—and turned it into a welcoming sight for the young woman who had just lost her mother and best friend.

Through motor-vehicle records, Nash learned that Glenn Taylor Helzer had a Saturn registered in his name. The detective remembered a small piece of information, one of dozens of facts turned up by investigators since the shooting—about a month before, a tow truck had been called to the restaurant where Selina worked so the driver could unlock Jordan's car. Nash quickly sent Detective Lellis to check it out.

Lellis learned that a local tow company had responded on June 16 to a report of keys locked inside a Saturn at the Two Bird Café. Now Lellis needed to track down the driver of that truck, Michael Small. When she finally found him, she was delighted to learn that he remembered the call. He said it stayed in his memory because the young lady was "very hot and beautiful." She showed him the driver's-license photos of Justin and Glenn Taylor Helzer. He identified Justin, but quickly called her back to correct himself. The man he saw when he unlocked the Saturn was Glenn Taylor Helzer. He was 100 percent sure.

Other Marin County detectives fanned out as the hours grew late that Sunday, knocking on the doors of Selina's friends, waking people up, showing them Helzer's picture. Many had not ever met her boyfriend. But Karen Novacich had. Selina's coworker and friend told Sergeant Gary Brock that she was 75 percent sure that the man in the photo was the man Selina called Jordan. The only thing that gave her pause was the fact that he was sticking his tongue out, and his complexion was a little darker than she remembered. That could easily have been the result of his beard growth, however.

As the minutes flew toward midnight, Brock took the photo to Ricco LaFranchi, Gloria's son. He also had seen Jordan, at the same rave where Selina first met him. Ricco positively identified Glenn Taylor Helzer as the same man.

———

While nearly everyone in the department was out pounding the pavement, Nash sat down and began to gather the investigation's threads together in a written request for a search warrant. He wanted to search 5370 Saddlewood Court, Concord, Contra Costa County, as well as the black 1998 Saturn and a white 1995 Nissan pickup, which was registered to Justin Helzer. He carefully listed what he would be looking for: a 9-mm semiautomatic handgun, copper-jacketed 9-mm ammunition, expended 9-mm cartridges, receipts and records pertaining to the Helzers, as well as what Selina was thought to be wearing the last day she'd been seen—a light-colored, short-sleeved shirt with small flowers and a pair of dark pants or jeans.

Nash laid out what authorities knew so far and wrote that he had very good reason to believe that one or both of the men living at the Saddlewood address had something to do with the shootings of Jennifer Villarin and Jim Gamble. He did not play down the urgency.

"It is now August 7, 2000, approximately 1:00 a.m., and Selina Bishop is still a missing person. She was to report for work at the Two Bird Café on August 4, 2000, at 10:30 a.m. and never appeared. No one has notified the Marin County Sheriff's Office that they have heard from Selina Bishop . . . an immediate search of the residence is needed in order to determine the location and safety of Selina Bishop."

He woke up the same county judge who signed the other search warrant, again in the middle of the night, and drove the new one out to her house so she could read it. She signed it immediately. Nash took off for Concord.

———

Once across the bay, Nash needed to borrow a SWAT team. The Concord police squad was quickly brought into the loop and dozens of officers from that agency and the Marin County Sheriff's Office quietly encircled the Saddlewood house. It was 6 a.m., Monday, August 7, four days—almost to the hour—after the murders of Jenny and Jim. Nash and Lellis, decked out in raid gear, took the back of the house. Inskip walked up to the front door and performed the "knock-and-notice," euphemistic policespeak for busting into a house. Almost immediately, Nash and Lellis saw a bedroom window fly open. A half-naked man hopped out and bolted over the back fence. Nash recognized him at once as Glenn Taylor Helzer—and thought to himself that only a guilty man runs. Nash drew his gun and ordered him to stop.

FOUR

A Prophet in the Making

Carma Lee Sorenson had been a devout Mormon all her life. She grew up surrounded by her family, her religion, and the fruit orchards and rice farms of a little town north of Sacramento in California's Central Valley. Her father was a commanding presence who prayed and preached eloquently and often to his large family. Her mother, who bore more than a dozen children, struggled with depression and was at times suicidal.

Carma became a seeker—always looking for new ways to think, to better herself, to understand life's greater truths. At nineteen, she did what good Mormon girls should and married a fellow Latter-day Saint. Gerald Helzer was a kind man, several years older and in the insurance business. They wed in November 1968 and soon embarked on two journeys: Gerry's climb through the ranks of the insurance industry and the raising of a family. They moved from Sacramento to Lansing, Michigan, and on July 26, 1970, they had a little boy whom Carma would come to believe

was a conduit for the word of God.[1] They named him Glenn
Taylor Helzer.

Taylor, as they called him from the beginning, was a
perceptive, outgoing boy who had an innate charm and
self-assurance that drew people to him from a young age.
That included his brother, who was born only eighteen
months later, after the family moved to Helena, Montana.
Justin Alan Helzer quickly became Taylor's greatest ad-
mirer and best friend. The two would play together constantly, riding their Big Wheels and, later, their bicycles off
on journeys of exploration, building elaborate scenes with
their plastic toy soldiers, or dashing around the house pretending to be superheroes. They would wrestle each other,
or use sticks to stage mock fights. And they occasionally
slowed down long enough to include their little sister,
Heather, born two years after Justin.[2]

After Montana, the family moved to Louisiana and then
Georgia. While living just outside Atlanta, the eight-year-
old Taylor was officially baptized into the Church of Jesus
Christ of Latter-day Saints. It was the age at which all
Mormons born into the church are baptized and Gerry
beamed at the occasion, hugging his tall, skinny son with
the mop of straight dark hair to his side in pride.

The family's next move, again spurred by a promotional
opportunity for Gerry, was back to Louisiana. There, Justin
was baptized into the church in another proud moment for
everyone. He was a much more reserved child than his
older brother, usually content to watch and listen as Taylor
took center stage. He never started a fight, but once came
home from elementary school after losing one to a school-
yard bully. Taylor stepped in the next day, and Justin was
not hassled again.

Throughout the siblings' childhood, it seemed to Heather
that their mother had an "illness" that prevented her from

doing any real mothering about half the time. As they matured, however, she began to realize Carma actually suffered more from her emotional state than any physical disability. She stopped worrying that their mother was going to die and she and her brothers took the days without her as golden opportunities to play, explore, and basically do whatever they wanted. They were compensated for the want of parenting during the times Carma was not "ill" and became an attentive mother who loved playing with and listening to her children. The children's self-sufficiency was cemented by Gerry's firm belief that men provided for their families and women raised them. He did not bother to notice his wife's ailments.[3]

In 1981, Gerry and Carma decided they were done moving from city to city for work. They wanted to live closer to family and moved back west to California. They picked Burlingame, in the Bay Area, and immediately became active in their local church ward. There, Taylor was ordained into the priesthood a week after he turned twelve. Called the Aaronic Priesthood, it is the preparatory priesthood for male Mormons and contains several offices of the church through which worthy members advance. Taylor first became a deacon, helping to pass the Sacrament during Sunday services and collect donations for the less fortunate.

He succeeded in carrying out those responsibilities, and so his parents agreed that he—and Justin as well—were ready to take on an additional job. They let the pair get a paper route. The boys shared the route for a few years, until Justin earned enough money to buy a bike he wanted. Happy, he quit the route. Taylor, on the other hand, never saved for anything. Money would slip through his hands almost as soon as he earned it.

A financial setback in 1983 sent the family to live with Carma's parents near Yuba City, close to where Carma grew up. The kids enrolled in school in the fall, but for Taylor at least, the far more pivotal education came at home. He became a willing student of his grandfather's lessons in LDS doctrine, soaking in more Scripture than those his age were usually ever taught.

It was impossible to avoid the constant preaching and prayer in the Sorenson household. Even family home evenings—a night set aside once a week for togetherness and fellowship that was supposed to be fun—turned into hour-and-a-half orations on Scripture. For Doyle Sorenson had seen the Savior and believed everyone needed to know it. His visit with Jesus Christ had happened years earlier; Doyle said it was the only time in his life he had ever been excited. He hugged and kissed Jesus and held His hand.[4] This religious fervor soaked into Taylor's spirit during the year he lived with his grandparents. It would soon come to permeate everything he did.

The family remained with Carma's parents until they were financially back on their feet, then the couple gathered their children and settled in an apartment in Concord. That year Taylor turned fourteen and became a teacher in the Aaronic Priesthood, and was allowed to help prepare the Sacrament and visit families to share lessons. His outgoing nature and boundless energy made him a natural at his new position.

As he grew older, Taylor's influence—within his family and his church—grew in ways not commonly held by teenagers. He was a dynamic force, commanding every situation and room he entered. He studied Scripture, knew it inside and out, and used it to make the points he felt needed to be made. His family treated him with deference. His cousin Charney Hoffmann thought obedience to him was something noble. When Taylor turned sixteen, he—like all worthy Mormon boys that age—became a priest in the Church of Jesus Christ of Latter-day Saints. He now had the authority to administer the Sacrament and perform baptisms.

   That same year Taylor received one of the most important affirmations of his life, his patriarchal blessing. Every
Mormon can ask for and receive such a blessing, which
usually includes recognition of special gifts or talents, as
well as counsel as to how he should use them to serve others. Patriarchal blessings are given only once in a lifetime,
and members treat them as sacred. The patriarch, a Mormon high priest, gives the blessing in person; it is recorded
so it can be transcribed and stored in the church's records.
A copy is given to the recipient, but Mormons are encouraged by the church not to share their personal blessings casually with others.[5]

   Taylor's blessing was pronounced on December 7,
1986. It acknowledged his already well-known leadership
talents and placed them in a very important context. In
Mormon theology, the spirit world began with God and
Goddess, who had innumerable spirit children who lived in
heaven with their divine parents. But the children were not
divine, and would not have the chance to be so until they
journeyed through the trials and tribulations of a mortal
life. These spirits-turned-humans would be gifted with
"free agency," the ability to make choices for themselves.
How they chose to live their mortal lives would directly affect whether they would be allowed back into God's presence after their deaths.

   The children would be helped in their travels by two elements of God—Jesus and the Holy Spirit. The Holy Spirit
would serve as a conscience, perhaps even as a ray of en-
lightenment, for those on their mortal journey. And Jesus,
the firstborn son, would become mortal but lead a life without sin before dying to atone for the wrongs committed by
all God's other children. His sacrifice would make up the
difference between the other children's imperfect mortal
lives and the requirements of godliness needed for entry
into heaven. Those mortals who conducted themselves

according to the Gospel would reenter God's presence. Those who chose to lead more sinful lives would be welcomed, but at lesser levels that did not include dwelling with the Heavenly Father.

Taylor knew all this as he listened to the patriarch intone his blessing that December day. The words confirmed what he already knew about himself. "You were among those in the spirit world who were chosen to be great leaders. Now you have the opportunity in your mortal life also to serve as a leader and an exemplar in the great work of God in bringing to pass the immortality and eternal life of His children. Your valiancy in the spirit world prepared you for a special place in this short but important phase of mortality as part of your eternal progress," the patriarch said.

The patriarch told Taylor he would be called upon to take up significant leadership positions within the church and to counsel others about their problems. He would receive the special guidance of the Spirit as he completed these tasks.

"You have been blessed with special spiritual gifts. You have the gift of discernment of spirits that permits you to distinguish that which is good from that which is bad in its ultimate effects. You also have the ability in this gift to understand the thoughts in the minds of other persons, and to understand their needs and their underlying attitudes. This gift will aid you greatly in rendering counsel and advice to those who come to you to seek guidance in their lives.

"You also have the special gift of revelation whereby the Lord will reveal to you His mind and His will both in a general way and in a detailed and specific way. You may feel His guidance and His presence and He will give you answers to your questions and to your prayers and will give you specific instructions in how to proceed in some of the more difficult matters with which you may deal."

The Heavenly Father recognized the potential Taylor had for service in his Kingdom, the patriarch said. The sixteen-year-old was well on his way to the top level of heaven, but his blessing cautioned that the special opportunities awaiting him were conditional upon his continued observance of all the principles of the Gospel.

———————

Taylor was on a fast track with spiritual matters and thought he should be with his education as well. He decided to withdraw from Concord's Ygnacio Valley High School and finish his schooling through independent study. He thought he could finish more quickly that way, but as it turned out, he did not get through his course work until about the same time he would have graduated had he stayed in school. His leaving meant that he never attended Ygnacio Valley with his little brother. Carma had home-schooled Justin for the eighth and ninth grades, and when he entered the public high school his sophomore year, Taylor was already gone. While he still worshipped his brother, Justin made a concerted effort to be as different from the popular and outgoing Taylor as possible. One of the tallest and skinniest kids in his class, he draped his naturally occurring shyness and bookishness over himself like a nerd costume, actively seeking out ridicule and harassment from fellow students, who—in the brutal class wars of high school—were only too happy to oblige. His outcast status extended to church as well. Adults realized he was more committed to the Gospel than others his age and were even impressed that he did not try to hide it in order to fit in with his peers. But those peers considered him too "churchy," and his pariah status grew.

Carma and Gerry did not realize how badly things were going for their younger son. His sister did, however, and would privately tell him he was being stupid for acting as he did while out in the world when he was completely normal at home. Luckily, their home life had grown more normal as they got older. For Gerry, the older his kids got, the more enjoyable they became. The family would take camping trips, watch movies, go to the library, and do other family activities that earlier would have held little interest for their father. They even sat down to eat as a family every once in a while after Heather learned how to cook.[6]

As Justin continued to dig himself into geek hell at school, Taylor decided to expand his horizons and enlisted in the California National Guard in November 1987. The next summer, he transferred to the Guard in Utah, where he also joined members of his mother's family on a survival trip into the wilderness. Many Sorensons took the traditional Mormon belief that the last days are near a bit further than most. They held that the Apocalypse would happen soon and they needed to be prepared for the collapse of modern technology that would force them to survive on their own. Taylor agreed that technology would fall away; he also believed that people would form groups that would be led by a new order of warrior prophets. Taylor and his cousin Charney were among those who went on the trip, which was a kind of trial run for the End of Days.

Charney and his brothers had been close to the Helzers growing up, and like everyone else, Charney revered his magnetic, fascinating cousin. Even when they were out having fun, Taylor provided guidance and counsel that Charney took to heart. Once, when the two spent a day at an amusement park, someone near them said something Charney thought was stupid. Taylor heard the comment and stopped his cousin from insulting the person. He told Charney he had hurt that person's feelings. Charney became embarrassed until Taylor finished. "I think you did that because you yourself were hurt. I want you to know, you don't have to feel that way around me because I accept you no matter what," Taylor said. It was an especially powerful lesson coming from one teen to another.

Taylor acted older than his years in most other social situations as well. At one church youth dance, a fuddy-duddy chaperone was not allowing the teens to dance too close together. Some of the dancers got upset with him, but Taylor did not agree. He appreciated that the chaperone was upholding the proper church standards and doing what was right. He walked up and told the man so.

His clear belief in his own special path next led Taylor back to the one who had helped him pave the way. After he received his high school diploma, he moved back to his grandfather's. He enrolled in Yuba College but lasted only one semester before deciding that he would rather work to earn money for what he considered a more important educational opportunity. He wanted to go on a mission.

Most men in the Church of Jesus Christ of Latter-day Saints serve on two-year missions when they turn nineteen. The church leadership decides where to send them, and the missionaries are responsible for the costs of their service. Mormons consider it one of the most spiritually fulfilling times in a young person's life, and Taylor knew with absolute faith that it would be so for him as well. He did not know where the Lord and church leaders would see fit to have him serve, but he wanted to be prepared. He took a job with a construction company and started actually saving his money.

———————

Taylor turned nineteen in the summer of 1989. It was going to be the best year of his life. Soon after his birthday, he was ordained as an elder in the church. This was the first step in the Melchizedek Priesthood, named after a high priest and king during Abraham's time. As an elder, Taylor now could do the things he believed he had been put upon the earth to do: bless the sick and others in need, participate in the sacred ordinances of the temple, and preach the Gospel. He was ready to go on a mission.

Before he left for training in Utah, a farewell party was held in Taylor's honor. About two dozen people from his family and church met to wish him well. This farewell differed from others, however, in the obvious effect Taylor had had on everyone in the room. They all spoke of insights they received when they talked about Scripture with Taylor. They were excited to share the knowledge he had given them and proud of their association with him. He had made everyone in the room feel good about themselves.[7] Taylor listened to the tributes and knew that his mission would only bring more opportunities to share the Gospel and enlighten others. He could hardly wait.

The church leadership had decided that Taylor should serve in Brazil. His first stop, however, was the Missionary Training Center in Provo, Utah. He arrived one morning with several hundred other missionaries, mostly young men, all dressed in white shirts and ties with carefully clipped hair. He was disappointed that his mother did not cry as he said good-bye to her.[8] After all, he was her favorite child, and she would not see him for the next two years. Though he didn't recognize it at the time, his mother's own lifelong quests for new and better truths had—and would continue to have—a profound impact on her son. As he bade her farewell, he realized with a little surprise how much he loved her.

The Provo campus could accommodate thousands of missionaries in a collegiate atmosphere. There were residence halls, meetinghouses, cafeterias, a bookstore, laundry facilities, and a gym. He was shown his dorm room and assigned a companion; the two teens would have to stay together all day, every day, for their entire time at the training center.

His days were long and strictly scheduled. He rose at 6:30 a.m., got a little personal study time, then headed to breakfast, class, and lunch. Afternoon class, dinner, and evening class completed the day, and it was lights out at 10:30 p.m. Bedtime was particularly hard for Taylor, who would often have to stop writing in his journal or to friends in order to be in bed on time. He kept telling himself he needed to "obey with exactness" all of the rules the training center set forth. That was the best way to become fully in tune with the Spirit.

Since he had been called to serve in Brazil, Taylor entered the center's language immersion program—a relentless barrage of instruction, six hours a day, six days a week. Teachers encouraged their students to use only the new language at all times. It was good practice, but one week into it, Taylor began chafing at the limitations. He lamented that he could no longer pray aloud as he had always done, because he did not know the right Portuguese words. Instead, he would lie in bed at night, praying silently in English.

Every morning he would wake with excitement, his energy propelling him out among his fellow students. All the missionaries were learning how to teach the Gospel to others, but Taylor—already an effective preacher by anyone's standards—used the knowledge to become a true force. He gave many well-received talks praised by everyone from peers to teachers. He credited the Spirit for his successes, but still proudly noted them all in his journal.

At the end of his first month at the center, Taylor had his wisdom teeth pulled. One minute he was lying in the chair talking to the dentist as his IV line was hooked up, and the next someone was shaking him awake and telling him the procedure was finished. He was disappointed; he had wanted to try to fight the drugs, but they worked on him too quickly.

"I guess it's sorta like Satan," he said to himself. "Unless you're fighting him all the time, he'll sneak up behind you and knock you out before you know it."

Taylor had no intention of letting the devil take hold of him. His faith in the Lord was too strong. He knew he was not perfect, however. He still struggled to obey with exactness, especially in his Scripture studies. What his teachers wanted him to learn was different from the way he had always chosen to preach. He thought about this and decided that he should at least know the readings the church wanted him to use. Whether he would actually use them was a question for another day.

The Spirit came to him constantly. It would awaken him at night, filling him with excitement and making him yearn for the mission work he would do in the field. One night, as his companion slept in the next bed, he began to wonder how successful he would be. Verses from *The Book of Mormon* floated through his head as he lay there, ones that offered glory to those who preached the Lord's word. He thought of Nephi, an obedient son and one of his favorite heroes in the Book.

Blessed art thou, Nephi, for those things which thou hast done; for I have beheld how thou hast with unwearyingness declared the word, which I have given unto thee, unto this people. And thou hast not feared them, and hast not sought thine own life, but hast sought my will, and to keep my commandments. And now, because thou hast done this with such unwearyingness, behold, I will bless thee forever; and I will make thee mighty in word and in deed, in faith and in works; yea,

*even that all things shall be done unto thee according to
thy word, for thou shalt not ask that which is contrary to
my will.*[9]

He continued to pray. He needed to know how many
people he would convert, and not in broad strokes, either;
he wanted an exact number. He prayed and prayed and
nothing came to him but a feeling of peaceful confirma-
tion. No tally of souls he would save. After an hour and a
half, he realized what the Lord was telling him. The number of people he would convert was innumerable, and it
was a goal possible for him to attain. Taylor leapt out of
bed and fell to his knees. Tears came to his eyes as he offered up a prayer of thanksgiving for such an answer.

FIVE

On a Mission

———————•———————

Taylor was fairly bursting with excitement as he boarded
the plane, Scripture in head and informational pamphlets
in hand. He flew first to Tampa and then to Miami, where
he waited for the flight to Brazil. All along the way, he bore
testimony to his faith to anyone he saw. Those who took
the time to talk he considered his instant friends. He urged
them to send for a free copy of *The Book of Mormon*. He
was sure they could feel his love for them.

He did not get through to two men who he thought
could certainly use some uplifting, however. He saw them
on the plane and noticed that they looked unhappy. He be-
stowed his megawatt smile on them and got no response. A
little while later, his companion came back with one of the
men's autograph. He was part of the pop duo Erasure on a
world tour. Taylor shrugged. "I hope I always remember that
it's not money, fame, or any amount of worldly things
that make a person truly happy," he said to himself. "I hope
that my priorities are always straight, clear, and in order."

The leader of his mission thought that Elder Helzer had

everything in order. He liked what he had seen and heard
about the young man and decided in early April to team
him with an experienced missionary and send the pair to
open up a new area in Tocantins, an area north of the national capital of Brasilia where Mormon missionaries had
never before worked. Taylor knew this was an enormous
responsibility, and he worried that he might not be up to
the challenge. He had been in the country for two days.

Taylor and his new companion boarded a bus for the
eighteen-hour trip to the little city of Miracema. Before
night fell, an idea popped into his head. He would stand up
and tell everyone on the bus about his work. He knew
this was completely out of the ordinary—even for a
missionary—but after hours of prayer, he was positive that
it was what the Lord wanted him to do. He looked around
the crowded bus as it traveled through the heat of the
Brazilian autumn night. Those people not asleep were en-
grossed in conversation. Now he was just unsure of the
timing. The Spirit did not offer any direction on that front,
so he settled back in his seat and decided to wait until
morning. He hoped he would still be blessed with the Spirit
when the sun rose.

As they approached their destination the next morning,
Taylor turned to his companion and told him what he
planned. He then rose from his seat at the front of the bus
and turned to face his fellow passengers.

"Attention, please. Everybody, attention please," he said
in Portuguese. "My name is Elder Helzer. I am from California in the United States. This is my first week in Brazil.
I only studied for two months the Portuguese language before I arrived here. I, and my companion, are going to
Miracema do Norte to teach the Gospel of Jesus Christ. We
are missionaries. My language is bad, but my message is
beautiful and powerful. It is about our Savior and His love
for us—for we are His children."

The bus was silent. Every eye was upon him.

"We are the first two missionaries to go to Miracema. I am so excited about being in Brazil and Miracema. God has given me a love for the people of Brazil. And the children I love, too," he said, looking down at a little girl he had made friends with earlier on the bus ride. He paused to smile and touch her head, then turned back to his new congregation.

"It is because of my love for my Savior and His children on earth that I have left my family, my friends, my work, my education in the United States to come to Brazil to share the Gospel of Christ. If you see me and my companion in the street, do this," he said, pausing to wave, "and call us. We would love to talk with you.

"I know that Jesus Christ is our Savior. I know that God has much love for us. In the name of Jesus Christ, amen."

The passengers began clapping. There were even a few cheers. Taylor stood at the front, happily swaying back and forth as the bus bounced along the road. The Spirit had not been wrong.[1]

————

Taylor threw himself into his missionary work with unabashed fervor. He came to love the Brazilians for their openness and hospitality. Still a growing boy, he also appreciated their food, which he would down in quantities that amazed his less-hungry companion. And he also noted the respect with which everyone—even the teenagers—treated their parents. He vowed to do better with his own mother and father, since he knew in his heart that he had often been ungrateful and unappreciative of their love and kindness toward him. He reminded himself of the commandment *Honor thy father and mother: that thy days may be long upon the land which the Lord thy God giveth thee.*[2]

There were cultural differences, however, that he had

trouble accepting. He grew frustrated at the tendency of
residents to agree with what he said and then proceed as if
he had not said it, or consent to meet at a certain time and
then not come. He figured that they were being polite to
him in person, and so did not consider it a lie to commit to
something with no intention of following through. He also
was appalled at some people's complete disregard for the
notion of chastity, which he thought one of the most important of all laws. Women openly lived with men without
benefit of marriage. This place was incredible, he thought.

The mission goal was to have twenty discussions a
week with prospective converts. He and his companion accomplished seventeen one week and the leadership was
pleased, but Taylor was not. He felt that he was not working to his full potential.

After four months in Miracema, the leadership called
Taylor back. He would serve in a different location with a
native Brazilian companion. He was excited at the thought.
The new guy would likely help him with his Portuguese,
and Taylor thought he would be more comfortable with
him than he was with his current companion. Although he
felt they got along well, Taylor considered him one of the
most conceited people he had ever met. Taylor had become, in his mind, more Brazilian than American during
his short stay in the country.

Taylor paired up with his new companion and began
spreading the Word in different areas. He became more
and more proficient in the language and in his preaching,
which he continued to hone by studying the Scriptures
daily. He would discuss them with his companion, but it
was not until another American arrived on the scene that he
truly had the opportunity to delve deeply into doctrine.
Church leaders sent Jonathan Taylor to be part of the four-

person team about sixty miles outside mission headquarters. He paired with a Brazilian who became friends with Taylor's partner; that left the two Americans as de facto companions and they quickly struck up a friendship.

Much of their talk revolved around the approaching Apocalypse. It was a favorite topic of Taylor's, and he was certain Christ's Second Coming was close at hand. He was not unique among Mormons in this belief; the church taught that mankind was soon to enter the final millennium—the Latter Days—when Jesus would reign and righteousness would prevail. But before Christ's return, the moral state of the world would deteriorate beyond measure.

While the church had no definitive timetable for the Savior's reappearance, Taylor slowly began to think that he did. He grew increasingly frustrated that Jonathan and others were not agreeing with his conclusions. His Scripture references shifted from those that glorified teachers of the Gospel to those that preached of the Apocalypse.

Let no man deceive you by any means: for that day shall not come, except there come a falling away first, and that man of sin be revealed, the son of perdition; Who opposeth and exalteth himself above all that is called God, or that is worshipped; so that he as God sitteth in the temple of God, shewing himself that he is God.[3]

He continued to look in distress at the way many of the people around him lived their lives; he felt they had forsaken God and were bringing on the end times. And no one was getting it. Jonathan did not understand, and was actually starting to look askance at him for sharing his interpretations with those they met on their mission. Taylor knew the church-approved curriculum did not include his conclusions, but the subject was too important for him to be bound by such restrictions. He became even more convinced of his truth as he tried to discuss it with the mission president and other church leaders. They would either disagree with him or misunderstand the points he was making. Were they just not revealing the truth to him? he wondered. Or did they honestly not see the truth of what he was saying? If that was the case, he obviously knew more than they did. How could he be accountable to people like that?

———————

His big brother might have been in a different hemisphere, but Justin still followed closely in Taylor's footsteps. He had joined the California National Guard as well, signing up just two days after his seventeenth birthday in 1989. Now it was the summer of 1990, and the Guard demanded more than one weekend a month. Three days after graduating from Ygnacio Valley High School, Justin reported for military-police training at Fort McClellan in Alabama. It was a nine-week course, and he did well, qualifying as a marksman with the M16 rifle, as a sharpshooter with the 9-mm pistol, and as an expert with the .45-caliber pistol.[4]

He was now qualified for what the army needed, which were MPs in a number of places. The 870th Military Police Company, with Specialist Justin Helzer, shipped out to Kaiserslatern, Germany, in December to support Operation Desert Shield, which the next month turned into Operation Desert Storm, the U.S. campaign to liberate Kuwait from Iraqi occupation.

The eighteen-year-old Justin was surrounded by a bunch of guys who had definitely not been raised in the Mormon church. They would drink and swear and talk about sex. He tried to avoid such things—which had some of his fellow soldiers referring to him as "Opie"—but he still fit in well, wandering from group to group and being accepted as a quiet listener. That did not keep his bunkmates from seizing the opportunity for practical jokes, however. When one learned that Justin was not supposed to be with a woman until marriage, he tore a page from an adult magazine and put it in a soldier's manual. He tossed the book to Justin and asked if it was the schematic for a certain rifle. Justin flipped it open and saw the photo of the nude woman. He slapped his hand over his eyes and walked away quickly, the joker's laughter echoing behind him.[5]

Justin could be almost too nice. His patrol partners would sometimes not allow him to approach a car because he could easily be talked out of issuing a ticket. His decency did not count against him, though. He received the standard National Defense Service Medal when released from his successful stint on active duty in June 1991.[6]

His obligations now returned to more familiar territory. He moved back to his parents' house near Concord and began preparing for his mission. He found out he would be called to serve in Texas, and he packed his suits and ties and headed off to the Utah Missionary Training Center in September.

————————

His mother saw him off. She then settled back to wait for the coming of her firstborn, who was expected to return from Brazil in November. Taylor had always been her favored son, and she could not wait for him to come home. Despite her irregular parenting, Carma had had an enormous influence on her son. Her constant seeking and openness to new ideas had led him to experiment as well. And she could not wait to share her most recent discovery—a kind of psychological training program that had made her feel wonderful. It broke down barriers and opened her eyes to the possibilities of life. She felt she knew herself better as a result and wanted her son to experience the same thing. Taylor arrived home by the twentieth of November, 1991, and the next day, he and his sister, Heather, began the four-day Impact seminar.[7] As Carma happily saw them off, she had no idea she was starting her idolized eldest child down a path that would twist his religion, and his mind, in ways beyond imagination. The Impact classes would begin to patch the holes he had come to believe existed in LDS doctrine and form a new faith that floated free of the confines of Mormonism.

Impact was a type of workshop commonly termed large-group awareness training. It took people through a step-by-step process, which some attendees reported first humiliated and degraded them in front of their classmates, then built them up again with positive imagery once they had broken through their emotional walls and found their "inner child." The classes usually started on Wednesday evenings and went until at least midnight. The next night was the same, and then Friday and Saturday were all-day and all-night sessions. The program seemed, to some, to be designed to induce sleep deprivation and emotional exhaustion.

Participants—who had paid hundreds of dollars for the privilege of being there—described how they were shown into a windowless room where the trainer began screaming at them. Staff members lined the walls, staring impassively at the abuse. According to some, anyone who deviated from the rules (not paying attention, not volunteering quickly enough for activities) was berated mercilessly. Ultimately, no one was spared. After encouraging people to share their deepest secrets, the trainer would make fun of them. People's physical disabilities, their financial troubles, their backgrounds, their feelings—nothing seemed to be off-limits. The trainer would call people everything from sluts to thieves as they stood trembling before the group. Anyone who talked back or tried to leave was cheating the group and considered worthless.

Once everyone knew everything about their fellow participants, they opened up even more. Trainees reported that they were grouped into several semicircles. One person at a time would go from circle to circle, where fellow classmates would give "feedback," highlighting what they saw as negative aspects of the person's personality, based on what people had shared about themselves earlier on. Many of these people had known one another only hours, so much of the insulting was off the mark—but no less hurtful.[8]

Another activity some endured was called the red/black game. The group was split into two teams and given a red-and-black board. If a team voted for black, both teams got points. If a team voted for red, the opposing team lost points. If both teams voted for red, both teams lost. As players debated how to vote, the trainer and staff would circle the teams, observing how individuals played. Some were generous and wanted everyone on both teams to win. Others were paranoid and tried to figure out how to stick it to the other team while winning themselves. Regardless of how they did, most players were derided for their performance after the game.

Then they were symbolically left to drown. The lifeboat activity tasked groups with deciding which three or four people among them deserved to get off a sinking ship. Each person got a minute to explain why he or she should live. Then the others decided, giving those they thought should get on the lifeboat one of several small sticks. Those with the most sticks at the end got to sail off. Everyone else went down with the ship. Taylor did not collect enough sticks for a seat and "drowned" along with most everyone else.[9]

It seemed like the organizers knew exactly what emotional impact all of this would have on participants. They heightened the effects with well-chosen music and mood

lighting. They also knew to supply a generous number of
trash cans for people to vomit into when they became so
emotionally overwhelmed that throwing up became their
only recourse. And then the trainees got to let loose. Who
in your life has held you back? the trainer asked. What has
kept you from being the person you should be? People
were encouraged to rage against everything that had ever
limited them. They screamed and cried, they beat on walls
and chairs, they collapsed on the floor, and they needed
plenty of trash cans.

This was supposed to break down all the barriers that
had formed throughout the trainees' lives, walls that prevented them from knowing the perfect inner child that existed within. Once they reunited with their child, many
trainees would fall to the ground weeping. It was billed as a
cathartic group experience, and the trainer intensified it
with peaceful guided imagery and words of love and support. People could attain anything as long as they were authentic to themselves. There was no right or wrong, only
what worked. Taking care of oneself was the way to show
love for others.

These good feelings were what participants, including
Taylor and Heather, took away from the three weekend
trainings they attended. Heather equated it with what it
must be like to have a near-death experience, something
horrible that makes you appreciate life more afterward.
Taylor loved it, and with his sister recruited many friends
to the program before gradually phasing out and going
back to his normal life. But the Impact training never really
left him.

———

One night at the movies, Taylor ran into an old classmate.
Ann had also gone to Ygnacio Valley High School, though
she had been in a class ahead of him and they had not re-

ally seen each other since they had been schoolmates. She was pretty, with light brown hair and an oval face. He became taken with her as he renewed her acquaintance. There was just one hitch. She was not Mormon. She was willing to convert, though, and by September had joined the church. Taylor eagerly proposed. This was what he had always wanted—a wife and a family. It was one of the basic tenets of the church and one of the best ways he could honor his faith. Still on a spiritual high from his mission, he worked for the Lord in other ways as well. He became an even greater presence in his church ward than he had been when he left for Brazil. He was the center of attention at any gathering, and knew that people came to him for insight into the Scriptures. People felt that he was enlightened; some even wondered if he really did have a special link with God.[10]

Carma knew that he did. Her son had always been special, and she and everyone else in the family happily deferred to him. It was so nice having him back at home. They started doing activities as a family again. Gerry genuinely enjoyed his grown children and had found a hobby that they all loved. He became a river-rafting guide and traveled the American River almost every Saturday. Some days they would raft the upper fork of the popular river that ran down from the Sierra Nevada and some days the lower. If they did the upper fork, they would pull over after making it through the biggest stretch of rapids and have lunch. They would scramble up on the rocks that covered the riverbanks and watch other rafts navigate the swirling waters, then jump off into calmer pools for a swim. It was a wonderful way to while away the months until Taylor got to start his own family.

Taylor and Ann were married at the end of April 1993 at the Mormon temple in Oakland. Since only church members could witness the ceremony in the temple, considered

the holiest of buildings, the couple also held a "ring ceremony" at a church meetinghouse near Concord that anyone
could attend. Taylor looked tall, dark, and handsome in a
tuxedo with Ann by his side in a long-sleeved white lace
dress and cascading veil.

Taylor had quit a dead-end telemarketing job earlier
that month.[11] Ann's uncle worked for Dean Witter and
arranged some interviews for his new nephew, who impressed company officials enough that they hired him as a
financial adviser trainee. The job required a certain talent
for salesmanship—advisers had to recruit clients—that
suited Taylor's outgoing nature perfectly. He quickly became known in the office for his clean-living Mormon values and boundless enthusiasm. Colleague George Calhoun
would shake his head in wonder as Taylor came into his office and plopped down in a chair. "George, I love you. I
love you. This is a great job. I love being here. This is just
an absolutely wonderful place. This is a great day. I'm
thrilled."

His inexhaustible zeal extended to his new home life. It
was the first time he had the freedom to do many things he
had always wanted to do, and he took full advantage. He
stayed up all night watching television, amazed at everything he'd been missing. "There's just always interesting
stuff on," he told Ann. "It just never ends. There's always
something great. I couldn't go to sleep."

His ability to focus, always a bit tenuous, became even
worse. For the longest time, he could not even remember
his new home phone number. Ann would write reminders
on sticky notes and plaster them everywhere. They did not
work. She would call him at the office just before he was to
leave at five o'clock and ask him to pick up things at the
store. When he still wasn't home at eight, she would go
searching. She often found him playing games at arcades.
He just forgot the time, he would say.

The obligations and pressures of a home and family continued to build. Slowly but surely, Taylor's almost manic enthusiasm dampened. This was not what he had envisioned as he lay in bed at night during his mission, thinking of the promised adult utopia of married life. Taylor began to feel that he was owed more—more freedom, more fun, more happiness. So he turned to what had made him almost blissful once before. If group awareness training helped him once, it could do so again.

———

Justin returned home from Texas to find his brother married and out of the house. He did not feel the same spiritual high Taylor had experienced after his mission; it had been a difficult job, and his reserved nature made it even more of a challenge. Still, he was glad he had gone and considered it a rewarding experience.[12]

He plunged back into church activities, hanging out with fellow members in their early twenties who found him to be an endearing goofball, cracking jokes and telling stories when they would get together for outings or to read Scripture. He started rafting with the family as well, which gave him the opportunity to spend time with Taylor, still the biggest influence in his life.

He started listening to Taylor extol the virtues of the group trainings. His older brother began going again in 1994 and loved them. He soaked up everything the trainers said and did, and recommended the program to everyone who would listen. The trainings played perfectly into Taylor's shifting mind-set: they highlighted his life's shortcomings and made him see what he was missing. Of course, the trainings were not actually fixing Taylor's problems, just highlighting them. He continued to chafe at his work responsibilities. He began to think that his home life was cheating him out of everything he deserved. For one thing, his wife would not give him sex whenever he wanted it. She tried to schedule his time and limit his desire for new experiences in the bedroom and everywhere else.

He had been a good Mormon for so long, and now it was not paying off with the rewards he thought he had earned. He was so special—after all, his patriarchal blessing had gone on and on about his exceptional spiritual gifts—that this ordinary existence in which he found himself could not be what the Lord intended for him. He needed to break free of the church's restrictions if he was to truly reach the potential everyone believed him to have.

But then he began to think that perhaps it was not he who was falling away. Maybe it was the church itself. There had been a series of prophets chosen to lead the church after founder Joseph Smith was killed in 1844. They, Taylor thought, had led the Mormons astray from Smith's visions as the true prophet. Their revelations had no more merit than anyone else's did—certainly no more merit than his own. And with what he knew to be his powerful grasp of Scripture and understanding of the Gospel, he slowly began to convince himself that he actually had more divine authority than the rightfully chosen prophet who claimed charge over the world's nine million Latter-day Saints. He could lead the Mormons. He could save them. He could be the true heir to Joseph Smith.

SIX

Drifting Away

Joseph Smith Jr. first spoke with God and Jesus in a forest in western New York state in 1820. Seven years later, he received a set of golden plates from an angel named Moroni that told—in a language Smith called "reformed" Egyptian[1]—the stories that became *The Book of Mormon*. Smith translated the plates, published the book, and began to attract followers.

It was a heady time in America. The Second Great Awakening had swept across much of the Eastern United States and was especially prominent in the region where Smith grew up. Unlike previous revivals, this one began to advocate social activism, fostering movements such as abolitionism and temperance. It also contained a strong evangelical element that stressed proselytizing and conversion.

Prominent Protestant denominations like the Baptists, Methodists, and Presbyterians grew in strength and influence during this period. Other sects were founded, gained some success, then faded away. The notable exception was the one founded by Smith. The reasons have as much to do with the man as with his message, which was certainly engaging but not unique. Smith was a natural preacher, a tall, handsome, broad-shouldered evangelist who drew people to him with his optimistic outlook and a theology that was both comfortingly familiar and breathtakingly new.

Smith harkened back to the very beginning of Christianity for his authority. He taught that the death of Christ's last apostles meant there was no longer anyone who held God's keys to the earthly kingdom. Until him. The period of darkness and disarray, the "Great Apostasy" that followed, lasted almost two thousand years, until the apostles John, James, and Peter returned to bestow the keys of the Melchizedek Priesthood upon Smith and one of his followers. That act, Smith said, returned Christ's true church to earth. He came to call it the Church of Jesus Christ of Latter-day Saints and went on to lead it for fourteen years. And although he appointed two chief counselors and later a quorum of twelve to advise him, he made it quite clear that there was only one prophet who could receive the word of God as it guided the church.

> Behold, verily, verily, I say unto thee, no one shall be appointed to receive commandments or revelations in this church excepting my servant Joseph Smith, Jun., for he receiveth them even as Moses. And thou shalt be obedient unto the things which I shall give unto him, even as Aaron, to declare faithfully the commandments and the revelations, with power and authority unto the church. . . . For I have given him the keys of the mysteries, and the revelations which are sealed, until I shall appoint unto them another in his stead.[2]

Smith was not infallible. Many of his ideas did not work, including turning the church into a true communist

society with only community property and the establish-
ment of a bank that issued its own money.[3] But enough
initiatives were successful that Smith—guided by his revelations from God—built an organization with true staying
power. The church, and Smith himself, survived years of
persecution. Mormons were chased from settlements in
Ohio and Missouri before he founded a hoped-for safe
haven in Illinois called Nauvoo. He and other leaders were
arrested numerous times on charges ranging from disor-
derly conduct to treason; at one point, he was actually
tarred and feathered.

And still the converts came, inspired as much by the
presence of the founder as by the religion itself. But when
Smith died at the hands of an anti-Mormon mob in Carthage,
Illinois, in 1844, the mantle had to be passed. Brigham Young
was chosen the next prophet of the church; most church
members accepted him and the faith continued to grow as its
adherents settled in the Utah Territory. Fourteen other
prophets followed through the years, continuing the tradi-
tion that while individual Latter-day Saints could receive
personal revelations from God, only the prophet could lead
the church as a whole through revelation from God. But
there were always a few Mormons who believed that the
church had drifted from Smith's true purpose, that the later
leaders did not truly hold the keys to Christ's church on
earth.

After repeated pleas from his wife, who had watched with
dismay as he shrugged off his religion and his responsibilities, Taylor finally agreed to go to counseling and saw a
psychologist through his health insurance in the fall of
1995. He told the doctor that his wife had basically tricked
him into thinking she was much more sexually adventur-
ous than she really was and now was not fulfilling her end

of the deal. He wanted what he saw in the porno films he had started watching, and Ann was not cooperating. He did not dwell on the fact that she had given birth to their first child only weeks before. During his five sessions with the therapist, he admitted that he was thinking about other ways to satisfy his needs. He explained one plan so outlandish it led the doctor to diagnose him with "narcissistic personality features." He explained that he wanted to find women who would have sex daily. To do this, he would advertise in Brazil and get a pool of between eighty and a hundred women. From that, he would choose thirty-five and then date them in order to winnow down which ones he wanted to enter into two-year contracts with for daily sex.[4] Like someone who returns to his hum-drum life after a nice vacation, Taylor could not stop reliving his mission experiences—making them better than they really were and turning Brazil into a paradise that existed only in his imagination.

As he explained himself, Taylor could see that the doctor was not getting it. He decided to stop the therapy. The only conclusion it helped him reach was that to end his marital misery, he had to leave Ann. But he hesitated for two reasons. He knew it would disappoint her, and he knew the church would be extremely displeased. Mormons did not get divorced; Mormons also did not do any of the other things he was contemplating. He wanted to try alcohol, cigarettes, sex with other women—and even though he knew the church would disapprove, he did.

Taylor began to experiment with marijuana and booze[5] and continued attending awareness trainings. The combination eventually gave him the nerve to finally leave his marriage; in the summer of 1996, he walked out on Ann and their year-old child for the lifestyle heretofore denied him. He started having sex with other women, doing harder drugs, and drinking more. His metamorphosis into a hard-partying Lothario was tempered a bit, however, when he was forced to move back in with his parents.[6] He did not yet have the means to get his own place; his mother and father were pretty much the twenty-six-year-old's only option.

Carma and Gerry had both sons living under their roof once again. Justin had never left after returning from his mission. He took advantage of his rent-free circumstances to take classes at Diablo Valley College and volunteer in the physical therapy program at a local hospital. He enjoyed both, especially working with therapy patients since he was considering a career in the field. It was obvious that he was having a good time, smiling quickly and often as he helped the therapists tend to their duties. He asked smart questions and wanted to learn as much as he could.

But gradually, Justin began to see his life from the outside, and he did not like the view. He was twenty-four years old, and he still lived at home. He did not have a real job, any money, or a girlfriend, and his few community-college classes were not exactly the fast track to a successful career. He did not tell his big brother what he was feeling, but he leaped at the chance to escape the bonds of his situation when Taylor finally moved out of Carma and Gerry's in December 1996. Justin went with him—breaking away, but by no means breaking free.

Taylor decided his little brother needed more training and had him enroll in a group awareness program similar to Impact. On an early spring evening, Justin waited in another brightly lit, windowless room deliberately kept as cold as an icebox. Mystical music played softly in the background. Two easels stood in front of the rows of chairs. Trash cans lined the walls. He knew what to expect as the doors slammed open and the trainer entered the room. The abuse began.

Participants were given nicknames based on what they had confided to the group—Daddy's Doormat, Mommy's

Play Toy. They did the feedback exercise. They were assigned pages of homework. They were told that there were
no such things as victims—they created their own circumstances and that meant they must have chosen to be victim-
ized. They were informed that there was no right and
wrong, just what worked for each person. They needed to
shed their baggage and connect with their inner child. Once
they did, the feelings of peace and joy were overwhelming.

Justin started out subdued, but slowly became more lively
as he gave himself permission to really participate in the
program. But he still took a backseat to Taylor, who wasn't
even taking the class. He hovered at the edges throughout
the training, casting a shadow over his little brother that was
seen by everyone.

One person who saw the gathering darkness in Taylor
and Justin was their sister. Heather returned from her own
mission in the spring of 1997. She had heard that Taylor
had started sinning, but now she discovered that Justin—
the kind brother who had always been happy to be there for
her—was following along. And Taylor had changed the
way he related to his brother. Heather took Justin aside.

"Can't you see Taylor's turned mean?" she asked.
"Can't you see he doesn't treat you very well?"

"No. I have so much to learn from Taylor," Justin said,
proving that at least his position in their relationship had
not changed.

───────

Mostly because he and Justin needed money to pay rent for
their new place, Taylor kept working at Dean Witter. He
had about a hundred and fifty clients and at one point was
considered a rising star in the Concord branch. But his
sunny outlook had darkened considerably. He told a
coworker once that he would rather be flipping burgers. He
began to avoid the people and personal service that went

with the job, once going so far as to turn out the lights and hide under the desk in his office so he would not have to deal with a client who stopped by to see him.

It was getting to be too much. He needed a paycheck, but was weary of having to work for it. He pondered how to fake a slip-and-fall that would get him on disability. But that was a temporary measure, at best; he would eventually have to heal. Getting sick in the head, on the other hand, was a lot more difficult to fix. And it might be a lot easier to fake, if he could get it right. As luck would have it, the perfect tutor had just moved in.

Taylor and Justin's maternal cousin Chi was actually on disability for mental illness. He identified himself as bipolar and suffering from a schizophrenic personality disorder and had been hospitalized in both state and local mental health wards.[7] He was a well of information for Taylor. Once Chi started living with him, Taylor questioned him about his hospital stays. What were the other patients like? How did they act? What specific little things would they do? Chi tried to remember as much as he could. Although he was roughly the same age as his cousin, Chi admired Taylor just like everyone else did. He wanted to please him.

But there was another aspect to their friendship that made it unique among Taylor's associations. Taylor actually looked up to Chi, who had lived a rougher life, and esteemed what he thought was Chi's criminal past. He thought his cousin knew useful things, and during the months they lived together, he began talking about some of his ideas, using tough-guy Chi as a sounding board.

The warped thoughts that had been flitting through Taylor's head about saving the world were finally starting to coalesce into solid plans. The feeling that began during his mission—that the world was sliding into moral decay—had only intensified. He knew he had the power and skill to stop the descent, to bring back peace and love to the world,

but he needed a place where he could work unfettered by
existing laws or governments. He had to start his own
nation-state, and that was going to take some money. But
he certainly was not going to roll up his sleeves and work
for it. If it took a few illegal actions to raise cash for his
purposes, then so be it. The glaring hypocrisy of saving the
world from moral decay through immoral means was conveniently swept aside.

Taylor pondered his options as he and Chi sat around
and got high. His mind kept returning to one of his favorite
activities—sex. Everyone liked sex, and many guys would
probably be willing to pay for it. He could start an escort
service. Chi would be the muscle, protecting the women
and the profits. He asked if his cousin had ever killed anybody. No, Chi said. Would he be willing to do whatever it
took to protect the business? Chi stared at him. Taylor patiently explained what his Impact trainings had taught him:
that right and wrong did not exist; they were primitive so-
cietal beliefs that he had evolved beyond. If in the course
of business, certain impediments needed to be swept aside,
well then, that was the way it went.

"People get in the way," he said. "I wouldn't have any
problem killing someone who got in my way."[8]

———

Although Taylor left Ann, the two had not yet gotten divorced and still maintained some kind of relationship, one
that in March 1998 produced a second child. But even a
new baby was not enough to induce Taylor to return to
hearth and home. Now, however, he was not the only one in
the family to have abandoned a marriage. After almost
thirty years with his father, his mother, Carma, filed for di-
vorce. She told Gerry she did not know why she was leaving, but leave she did. He was stunned. He had always been
stable and reliable, a good provider for her and the children.

He was a good person. She had to be out of her mind.[9] Carma, however, felt at peace with her decision to live with another man even though she knew full well this violated Mormon tenets.[10]

She had gotten into a variety of New Age activities over the years, and kept finding new ones to enthusiastically try. One—a retreat that featured a type of massage designed to release toxic emotions from the body—had a particularly profound effect on her. As she sat in a sweat lodge during one retreat session, it came to her that she should be called "Teonae." She thought it was an Indian name and accepted it gratefully. But that was not all she took away from the program. She met a man named Don, and when she decided to leave Gerry, it was to begin living with him.

She did not intervene in her son's new lifestyle. She had, years before, decided that she would not ask her children questions. She would listen if they came to her, but she would not give them advice. And what, really, would she have said about Taylor's escort-service plan if he had told her?

Taylor kept at it, talking with Chi late at night, when Justin was not around. He made up business cards, but had not yet recruited any women when one night he stopped for dinner at a Concord restaurant. The waitress was cute, with long blond hair and a wholesome cheerleader look to her. He had come from work and was still in his suit and tie, looking businesslike and successful. His told her his name was Taylor. She was Keri, she replied. He'd like to take her out, he said. She did not accept the offer, so when he paid the bill, Taylor left her his credit card. He wanted her to buy something nice for herself, he said.

This was intriguing, Keri Furman thought as she looked at the credit card and business card he left behind. He was older, good-looking, charming, and had to have it together financially if he was willing to hand over his credit card without a care. That put him far above guys her own age, the twenty-two-year-old thought. She gave him a call. She would not use his card, but she told him that he was welcome to buy her something if he wanted. They made plans to go out.

Of course Taylor was not the least bit stable, financially or otherwise. But his front worked with most people, and it certainly won over Keri. She moved in with him that summer, and he quickly sent her through the latest group awareness training, a program called Harmony. He also started her on ecstasy, one of his favorite drugs. He figured she would not take it outright, so one day when she had a headache, he said, "Here, honey, take an aspirin." She did, and not only did it get rid of her headache, it made her feel wonderful all over. "How do you feel?" he asked her. "You feel great? Yeah, that's ecstasy."

Taylor had not been able to convince Justin of the pleasures of ecstasy. Justin would smoke a little pot now and then, but otherwise was uninterested in the drug buffet his big brother seemed to have going all the time. He had a job at a Black Angus Steakhouse, which he took more seriously than Taylor did his brokerage career. It was in Justin's nature to apply himself to the task at hand, so even though he was still struggling to find himself, he continued to accept his responsibilities. But his quest for the meaning of life, coupled with the constant bombardment of Taylor's philosophies, left him exhausted. He decided he was just too stressed to travel to Utah that summer for his sister's wedding.

Taylor did go to the wedding. Relatives had heard rumors of his deviation from the family religion; his smoking during the celebration only confirmed their fears. He took a walk with an aunt between the wedding and the reception. He had a copy of *The Book of Mormon* with him, which she latched onto. When was he going to start going to church again? He looked at her. He was thinking about it, he said vaguely, but wasn't sure exactly what he wanted to do. She told him she had heard about his breakup with Ann. How was he taking care of his family? He tried explaining his new outlook on life but could tell that his aunt did not understand. They walked back to the reception. Taylor wandered off with his *Book of Mormon*. His aunt began to think he might need to see a psychologist. He had always considered the feelings of other people; now it seemed as if he felt entitled to something big without having to work for it or care for others along the way. She was very concerned.

———

Heather thought about what she should do. Her brother's soul was in danger, and the more he sinned, the worse the ultimate consequences would be. The Church of Jesus Christ of Latter-day Saints believes in different levels of heaven based on people's actions during their mortal lives. And those who are Mormons—who know all the tenets and how to live life according to the Gospel—are held to a higher standard than those who, for instance, never have the opportunity to accept Jesus Christ as their Savior while on earth.

Taylor the Mormon was breaking his covenant with God. And he knew better. There was one thing Heather could think of that might save him. She sat down and wrote letters to his local church leaders about his sins, knowing what the drastic result could be. They ex-communicated him. He no longer had any official agreement with God, and would hopefully not be held to the higher Mormon standard. He was on his own.[11]

———

Taylor shrugged off the church's dismissal and continued to study his new religion—the large-group awareness trainings. He was learning so much, it was incredible. How to give proper feedback to people, how to instruct them properly about their failings, how to make them "be authentic." He knew how to shed the outmoded paradigms of right and wrong. It was only about what worked.

So there was nothing wrong with leaving Dean Witter for reasons of mental disability after he felt he had perfected how to act like he was mentally ill. Chi had initially laughed at him as he faked crazy, but then as Taylor practiced, his cousin admitted that he had it down.

The real test came on September 1, 1998, when Taylor went in for his first appointment with a psychologist. Keri went with him. He was highly distraught and looked scared as he sat in front of Dr. Jeffrey Kaye. His words poured out in a rush as he tried to explain that he was having problems functioning at work. He could not concentrate and was irritable and paranoid. Kaye thought he was in a manic phase and diagnosed him as bipolar. He enrolled his new patient in an intensive outpatient program that involved group therapy. Taylor went once and decided it was not for him; he preferred to keep meeting with the doctor individually.

Taylor met with the psychologist several times during the fall and winter. He slowly began to talk about conversing with Spirit, his new, shortened name for the element of God he believed himself to now be on familiar terms with. He acted so disorganized that Kaye finally offered to help him with his disability paperwork, without which Taylor would not get his checks. Kaye also warned him that he needed to stay on his drug therapy in order to keep those financial benefits. Unfortunately for Taylor—who would much rather have stuck with the ecstasy and methamphetamines he had grown to love—that meant a laundry list of actual medications that included an antipsychotic drug, a pill similar to Valium, an anticonvulsant used to treat epileptics that also helped to calm manic symptoms, and lithium.

The lithium was the kicker; it had to be monitored with blood tests to ensure a patient was not getting too much, so it was quite easy to tell when someone was not following the treatment. That meant Taylor had to take it at least occasionally, which he did not like doing. It and all the other medications made him sick to his stomach. But if that was the price to pay for his free ride on the disability gravy train, then he would do it.

———

Justin was spending a lot of time thinking about his life. The group trainings had made their mark, and he decided he needed a wider range of experiences than what the Mormon church allowed. He had always followed the rules, and look where it had gotten him. He still had no girlfriend, no money, and no happiness. What was the point of continuing to be a good Mormon boy? He decided to start sinning. He was curious about what would happen. Would God still love him, or would the Holy Spirit leave him? Would his spiritual decline be rapid, slow, or nonexistent?[12]

He looked at his new path as one similar to that chosen by Adam and Eve. Mormon theology teaches that the first couple was immortal and unable to multiply when they first walked the Garden of Eden. In order to fulfill God's commandment to have children, they had to become mortal, which meant consciously choosing to fall from grace by eating the forbidden fruit. Their choice, their exercise of free agency, was heralded by Latter-day Saints as a heroic decision.

And they would have had no children; wherefore they would have remained in a state of innocence, having no joy, for they knew no misery; doing no good, for they knew no sin. But behold, all things have been done in the wisdom of him who knoweth all things. Adam fell

*that men might be; and men are, that they might have
joy.[13]*

So to know joy, Justin resolved to begin sinning. Unlike
his brother, however, he hedged his bets. He was not en-
tirely sure that the church would turn out to be wrong in the
end, so he figured it would not hurt to have a little insurance. He went to his church leaders and asked to have his
name removed from the records. That way, he would not be
held to the higher standard of Mormons when it came time
to enter the afterlife. It was the same course of action his
sister had taken on behalf of Taylor. If Mormon doctrine
should prove to be the truth, it could offer him some pro-
tection later on.

Although released from the church's strictures, Justin
did not plunge headlong into Taylor's pool of sin; instead,
he stuck a toe or two in to test the waters. He was trying to
improve himself and wanted a full-body experience. He
kept eating the healthy food he had always enjoyed. He
read self-help books and carefully recorded their advice.
He thought about bettering himself constantly, even when
he got high (which was one sin of Taylor's he adopted
quickly and found quite enjoyable).

Justin tried all sorts of things with colors, exercises,
thought patterns. He scribbled mantras in his journal—
platitudes about not judging, expanding the mind, living in
the moment. "Limiting paradigm: It's too hard!! New Paradigm: I easily and joyfully fulfill my dreams!!" But as he
filled page after page, he never noted any actual successes
on these self-improvement laundry lists, no examples of
putting his extensive research into practice.

———

Taylor had a good thing in Keri—she worked two jobs,
brought in a decent amount of money, and looked good on

his arm—but that did not stop him from pursuing other possibilities. He found one at a Harmony training he attended with Keri. Lina was a beautiful eighteen-year-old blonde who immediately caught his eye. After the Harmony weekend, he began calling her constantly. He showed up at her apartment several times and left his card in the door. The attention was flattering, and he had a girlfriend, so Lina felt safe. The three of them went dancing a couple of times, and then one night Taylor invited her out with them again. But he showed up alone.

Lina reluctantly went along. They stopped to eat before going to the club, and when they finished, they wandered outside and sat on the curb. Taylor was up, excited, speaking fast. He started talking about spreading peace and love. He had refined his plan a bit by this point and decided that he would run his own trainings to spread his gospel, instead of trying to start his own country. He explained that he had been a stockbroker but was taking some time off to work on his plans. Then he went even further, telling this teenager he barely knew that he had himself declared insane so he could collect disability and have an income while he plotted his next course of action.

They left for the club, and Taylor did not stop talking all night. He was having breakthroughs just being with her. He loved her. He did not notice—or care—that he was completely overwhelming Lina. She grew very quiet and withdrawn; there was no room for her. Taylor simply took up too much space. When they finished dancing, Taylor decided to spend the night. Lina drew the line, though: they did not have sex.

The next morning, Taylor relaxed with a cigarette on the balcony. Lina came out and they listened to some music. She looked as if she wanted to say something, and eventually she worked up the courage to do so.

"You know, Taylor, I can't be around you. Your energy's

dark, you know. Your energy is in many ways really evil. You know, it's just the color black," she said.

She took a breath and told him she couldn't see him anymore. Taylor started crying and then asked her to pray with him. They prayed for the highest good for both of them and to let the situation go and move on. Then Taylor gathered his things and left, his pursuit over—for now.

———————

Taylor and Chi were heading south in Taylor's older-model Cadillac. They were on their way to Mexico, where Taylor was sure they would find women more than willing to work for his as-yet-nonexistent escort service. They might even be able to smuggle the girls across the border in the trunk. Taylor was excited about the possibility. They got the Caddy painted and toured around south of the border, looking for prostitutes but not picking up any. Then they stopped to visit Taylor's aunt who lived in the San Diego area. Taylor did not think that he needed to put on the good Mormon act around her, even though she had seemed so worried when they talked at Heather's wedding months earlier. He bragged about almost getting into a fight while down in Mexico and then started talking about buying drugs. He continued to deliberately push all of her buttons, telling her he wanted to go out and get drunk. His uncle finally had enough, and the two exchanged heated words before Taylor and Chi left the house.

Taylor was far beyond offering apologies for his behavior. If people did not see his worth, his superior grasp of universal truths, his brilliance—well then, they either needed to leave his presence or be properly educated so they would be capable of appreciating him. He sent more people to Harmony, and at one session, he ran into Lina again. She had been lonely and sad since she had parted ways with Taylor. She decided to spend more time with him and see where it led.

Taylor had known she would. He told her he was glad she had come around. He had not forgotten her parting assessment of him, however. He brought it up, telling her patiently that the dark energy she sensed in him actually meant that she was concealing dark energy within herself and was just not evolved enough to see it.

Now properly chastened, Lina began dating him. She knew he was still seeing Keri, but he told her he didn't love Keri anymore; besides, he said, Keri knew he was seeing Lina, so there was no betrayal. Lina bought the line he fed her, and they started spending a good deal of time together. Taylor was as intense as ever. He would talk nonstop for hours on end. Lina would feign sleep, but he would keep talking through the night. Several times he felt he was on the verge of an emotional breakthrough and, not unlike in group training, would go to the center of the room and yell and cry, working himself into such a state he would almost throw up.

But the things he talked about began to disturb Lina. He spoke often about trust and loyalty. It was very important that he have complete faith in his inner circle. He stressed this again and again and decided she needed examples to illustrate how serious he was. He brought up his relationship with Keri. If he killed someone and brought the body home, she would cut it up and hide it without asking a single question. This was too much for Lina. Not only was he talking about killing, he kept bringing up his other girlfriend. She broke up with him for good.

———

Girlfriend problems were not Taylor's only concern. Dr. Kaye had decided that he would be fit to return to work on

March 1, 1999. The date was approaching and Taylor had
no intention of putting a suit back on and selling stocks. On
February 23, Kaye noted in his records that a woman iden-
tifying herself as Keri called and said Taylor was off his
meds. She told him it was because they were reacting
badly with a drug he was taking for recently diagnosed
genital warts. That set the stage for two days later, when
Taylor walked into the emergency room of a local hospital
and asked to be committed. He correctly told the doctor
questioning him that the day of the week was Thursday, but
said he did not know the date. He haltingly went through
other questions and even admitted that his current distress
had been precipitated by a denial of disability insurance
earlier that day. But he became evasive when the doctor
asked whether he was hearing voices. "All I can tell you is
that there is a spirit world out there," he mumbled. The
doctor had seen enough. He packed Taylor into an ambu-
lance for transport to another facility that had inpatient
psychiatric services.[14]

   The hospitalization scheme worked. Taylor's return-to-
work date was pushed back at least six months. He could
continue with his plans.

SEVEN

Exerting Control

———————◆———————

Taylor surveyed the room. He had not been to a church event in a long time, but this one intrigued him. It was a murder-mystery dinner put on by a church group, where actors play out scenes while the audience eats. He walked in and sat down at a table. Justin followed. They quite obviously did not belong. They were both dressed all in black. Taylor had long, flowing hair and a beard, and wore a scarf tied around his head, as if he needed that little extra something to really stand out among the clean-cut Mormon singles who were warily eyeing him from afar.

Taylor continued to look around. No one was coming to talk with him, but a woman did keep glancing his way. She was short and overweight, but she had an open, welcoming expression. She kept looking over at him, trying to decide what to do. Taylor waited. Finally, she approached. She wanted to say hello and make sure he felt welcome, so she thought she would introduce herself. Her name was Dawn Godman.

———————

Dawn was from the foothills of the Sierra Nevada, a rural stretch of Northern California dotted with tiny towns and abandoned mines popularly known as Gold Country. She grew up in a devoutly Pentecostal family that lived an hour from the nearest school. She was isolated in other ways as well. She did not have a knack for easy friendships and quietly put on weight until she turned from someone who was ignored to someone who was ridiculed. She never stopped harboring hope, however. She made big plans for a sweet-sixteen birthday party, and many people said they would come. No one did.[1] She joined all manner of organizations—the local volunteer fire department, a teen anti-drug-and-alcohol program, the high school student council. Nowhere did she feel any real sense of belonging. She decided that she really needed to be on her own to figure things out. She transferred from the high school to a continuation school and graduated in 1991 at age seventeen. She moved out of her parents' home and with their approval, filed for emancipation. She wanted to run her life without limitations.[2]

Dawn wanted to go to school to become a registered nurse. She got a job as a certified nurse's assistant at a convalescent facility in the small foothill town of Jackson and discovered that she enjoyed the work. But her plans changed when she got pregnant in early 1992. The news quickly derailed her career plans and she gladly threw herself into the role of new mother, overjoyed with the prospect of someone who would love her unconditionally. She was devastated when her little girl died soon after birth. She needed someone to love her.

Two months after her baby's death, the eighteen-year-old thought she found it. Patrick Godman was tall, with brown hair and brown eyes. He was five years older, and as she stood beside him in the quickie wedding chapel in

Lake Tahoe just before Christmas, Dawn was positive that he was the answer to all of her unrequited longings.

Dawn immediately got pregnant again. The Godmans' child was born in the late summer of 1993, but family life was not idyllic. They fought and Patrick would threaten to take the child if she ever left him. One February morning, they argued and he stormed out of the house to go to work, but quickly came back. When he did, he found Dawn packing her things. He smashed some dishes and a window, then grabbed one of the seven rifles they kept at the house and walked outside. He emptied ten rounds into his wife's 1986 Chevy Sprint and then left, a shaken Dawn told authorities when she called the sheriff's office; deputies came out and helped her meet up with her parents. They also impounded the rifles and the Godmans' handgun—just for safekeeping.[3] Three days later, Dawn asked for a restraining order against her husband, but they quickly made up and she had the order withdrawn.

The reconciliation did not last. Within a year they divorced, and Dawn slid straight into the pit of unhappiness that had always been just at her feet. She moved into a house in the small town of Jackson with a few acquaintances and started using marijuana and methamphetamine. Eventually even that tenuous stability ended and she found herself living out of her car. She could not seem to get it together. -She no longer had full custody of her kid. The man she had married did not want her. What was the point of it all?

Two days before what would have been her fourth wedding anniversary, she drove her car/home to a local lake and parked it. She looked at the note she had written and then put it aside. Then came the pills and booze, liberal quantities of each. She was so upset, she could not even keep herself together as the combination started to work. Suddenly there was a cop outside the car, peering through the fogged windows. He pulled her out and called for medical help.

Dawn spent three days in a mental hospital before doctors were sufficiently assured that her suicidal thoughts had diminished enough that she was not an immediate danger to herself. Her circumstances had not changed, however. She moved from her car to a homeless shelter. She did not know what she was going to do next. Then she remembered someone who had tried to introduce her to a new religion. At the time, she had brushed the whole thing off; growing up in her family's Bible-centric household had given her quite enough strict dogma.

But now she had nothing. She looked up her Mormon acquaintance and said she was interested in learning more. Her friend was only too happy to provide her with a *Book of Mormon,* along with the other Scriptures and church literature. Dawn liked what she read and started to study obsessively. If this was going to be her salvation, she was going to seize it quickly. She moved back in with her parents, but her February 1997 baptism into the Church of Jesus Christ of Latter-day Saints proved too much for them and she had to leave.

She moved into her grandmother's house in Martinez, a small city just north of Concord in the Bay Area. Her grandmother permitted her Mormon metamorphosis and Dawn immersed herself in the church. She attended Sunday services, went to weekly meetings, helped with event nights, wore the special temple garment under her clothing, and did anything else she possibly could within the Martinez family ward. Church leaders soon transferred her to the local singles ward, where not-yet-married Mormons worshipped and socialized together with the obvious aim of finding a spouse among their fellow Saints.

Dawn was still working minimum-wage jobs, and the Bay Area was expensive. She went to her bishop and got goods and money to help her through rough patches. The assistance gave her the boost she needed. A year after moving in with her grandmother, Dawn was able to afford her own apartment, a little place on a busy avenue in Martinez. She had a roommate—a friend!—also named Dawn. Dawn Kirkland was impressed with Dawn's determination to better herself. So was her bishop. Her physical health and spiritual wellness were improving, and her future held nothing but promise.

———————

Dawn Godman was ecstatic. She was going on a date with Taylor. He had looked into her eyes and said he wanted to take her somewhere, and now here he was, knocking on her apartment door. She opened it and beamed at him. Taylor smiled. He thought after meeting her at the mystery dinner that she would be easy to influence, and her shining countenance confirmed it. But he needed to disabuse her of this notion she had about a date. They were going into San Francisco with some other people, he explained as he led her down to a van waiting in the parking lot.

Dawn's dream date ended up being an introduction to the Harmony program. Taylor told her it would be a very good idea if she signed up for the training, and she agreed. Tall, gorgeous men did not usually pay attention to her; she was certainly going to listen to one who did. Taylor—who liked what he saw in Dawn more and more—decided to try out the training techniques he had learned through the program on her. And they worked. Within a month, she was shoehorning his philosophies into her Mormon faith, eagerly accepting his sometimes nonsensical musings as logical values. This was particularly true of a list Taylor formulated from all of his group training experiences. He called it the Twelve Principles of Magic:

1. I am already perfect and therefore can do nothing wrong.
2. There is no such thing as right and wrong.

3. I am all-powerful and therefore the creator of, and accountable for, everything that occurs in my life.
4. Life is always right, I embrace all of my results.
5. All of my results I have created, to learn from, at some level.
6. I know nothing; I believe nothing; I simply perceive without fear.
7. It is of no concern to me how accurate, or inaccurate, my perceptions are, and therefore I am always right.
8. Unconditional fearless love is the most powerful force in the universe.
9. Spirit knows.
10. I gain total control by losing all control.
11. Life is such a precious gift. And when I give back to life, immediately life gives more back to me, and therefore I am forever in its debt. What goes around comes around.
12. There is a higher power than mine, and that is my Savior, Jesus Christ, the son of my Father.

Dawn eagerly accepted the new doctrine, despite its flagrant inconsistencies. "I am all-powerful" and "I believe nothing" did not exactly mesh with "There is a higher power than mine and that is my Savior, Jesus Christ." But it was a fluid list, and Taylor would add to it as he saw fit, telling people the principles had been revealed to him by God through Spirit.

Dawn believed Taylor was helping her find the peace she knew she lacked within herself. She was now fully prepped for Harmony. She endured the days of treatment that humiliated her as she took in the trainer's words about her inner child. Before she was allowed to find it, however, the trainer targeted her weight in front of everyone. She was made to wear a cowbell and crawl around the room on all fours, mooing for forgiveness.[4]

Then came the real agony. Dawn was forced to choose

between leaving the training or stripping off her temple garment—the special underclothing Mormons believe protects against temptation and evil. She was such a good Mormon. She loved wearing her garment—it made her feel like she belonged. But Taylor made her feel that way, too. And she knew she would never be able to bask in his attention again if she did not complete Harmony. She stood in front of all those people and sobbed. And then she made her choice. She took off the garment. And Taylor knew he had her.

———

Dawn was not the only planet orbiting Taylor's sun during this time. His household was expanding and he was establishing himself as its head. He, Justin, and Keri moved into a house on Oak Grove Road in Concord with another man named Brandon Davids. Taylor made it quite clear that the Twelve Principles of Magic were the house rules, and they must be followed. He made Brandon and his girlfriend, Olivia Embry, go through Harmony. And, just like in the program, he gave everyone the benefit of feedback. He would press and press his points, winding Scriptures no one else knew through his talks. If people did not agree with what he said or had independent thoughts about it, they were wrong. "Ah, pride and arrogance. Go back and look at that, and you'll get it," he would say. Sometimes he would literally send Keri to her room. "Maybe you should be by yourself to think about what I've told you until you come into agreement with me." He told people repeatedly that he was the only one who cared enough to give them the real truth. "Are we clear? Is there anything else that you need to talk about? Are you clear?"

But his domination was cloaked in "unconditional love." If he was just a jerk, his roommates and the other friends he carefully cultivated would not have stayed. His rock-solid belief in himself overwhelmed those around him, and since they were often in need of affirmation as it was, Taylor's effortless aplomb seemed even more inspiring. His energy was a kinetic force that radiated through crowds. When he entered a room, people noticed immediately. He cemented their attention by greeting everyone with hugs and smiles. The world was great, everything was great, and Taylor was slowly gathering followers to him with words of God's blessings and his own backhanded praises.

His talents worked especially well on women. Their emotional defenses had been erased by the group trainings, and Taylor just walked right in with no resistance. It was hard to resist someone who looked straight into your eyes, his long, lean face inches from yours as he said, "I love you." He would hold friends like Dawn for hours, stroking their skin and listening to them recount their hopes and fears. He had seen all the holes in their souls when he first met them and knew this was the way to fill them.

And did he ever love a captive audience. Not only would he share his philosophies with his lucky disciples, he deigned to reveal the plans he was preparing for the rest of the world. He wanted to start his own group training and have everyone in the country go through it. His program would rescue their inner children, freeing them from their self-constructed emotional prisons. It would save everyone from themselves, and deliver joy and peace to them. Taylor would transform America. And that was what he decided to call his plan: Transform America.[5]

This was the duty given him by God, he told Brandon. As the Lord's earthly representative, however, he was bound by practicalities. He needed money to practice outreach in schools and businesses, lobby politicians, and otherwise promote his plan. He figured it would take $20 million to spread his message, and that was certainly not an amount he was going to earn legally.

He decided to turn a hobby into a business and began dealing ecstasy, with seed money provided by Keri. He would sell it at raves, with her keeping an eye out for security and Dawn holding the merchandise until he was ready for it. At twenty dollars a pill, he could make a thousand dollars on a good night. His success led him to believe that his entrepreneurial knack was so great, any idea he came up with would work. He started putting more and more thought into the escort service he had talked about with Chi. He would bring women up from Brazil, or maybe use runaways. He ran through his plans with Brandon and Keri, each of whom shrugged them off. But Brandon—fearful Taylor did not trust him completely—kept quiet when Taylor said his mission from God was so important, he was not only willing to break drug and prostitution laws, but also would kill people if necessary.

Justin took a page from Taylor's playbook and started spending a lot of time with Dawn. He would stare into her eyes, tell her he felt her love and acceptance, hold and stroke her endlessly, and talk with her for hours. She loved his attention, although it did not make her tremble like Taylor's interest in her did. But Justin kept at it, and the two became good friends.

Still the responsible one, Justin remained gainfully employed throughout 1999. He decided he had had enough of food service and took a few courses that gave him the skills he needed to become a cable installer. It was a job where he did not have to sit behind a desk, which suited his increasing focus on the purity and well-being of his body. He concentrated on his posture, his breathing, and various kinds of exercises that were supposed to improve his appearance, sexual attractiveness, and overall health.

He took great care with what he put into his body. He

refused foods that were not organic and still turned down
most of the drugs others were using at the Oak Grove
house. He considered eating a singular experience and
took his time. He would chew slowly, loudly, and with his
mouth open, like a child intent on a new dish and oblivious
to those around him. He did not limit his eating to the
table, either. A visitor to the Oak Grove house caught him
in the kitchen one night eating food off a plate on the floor
like a dog.

His existence was almost spartan. He slept on the floor
and owned few clothes or other things common to single
twenty-seven-year-old men, such as CDs, video games, or
a television. One of his few luxuries was a juicer. But sim-
plicity did not mean stress-free. He would on occasion shut
himself in his room and scream and yell obscenities at the
empty space. He became obsessed with trying to complete
five hours a day of a certain exercise that was supposed to
put him in a meditative state.

Justin's chief stressor, Taylor, would not let him be. Big
brother kept talking about all sorts of different things, and
now told Justin that Spirit was speaking to him more often.
He said he was a prophet of God. Justin needed to think
about that one.

———

Everyone had to be quiet. Taylor needed complete silence
when Spirit was talking to him. He would announce that
Spirit was speaking and shush whoever was in the room.
What Spirit told him would sometimes make him weep.
He would listen intently and, when finished, share the
revelations. After all, his plans to save the world came
from somewhere. He said Spirit was guiding and inspiring him.

People, especially those accustomed to the prophet-rich
history of the Mormon church, did not see this as too out of

the ordinary. One was Kelly Lord, a young woman whom Taylor met at the same mystery dinner where he found Dawn. He led her down a similar, if slightly less intense, path. He completely captivated her with his attention, sent her through group training, and started talking about himself as a prophet. But the trainings had not completely obliterated Kelly's capacity for critical thinking. She told him that if he was destined to be a prophet, God would see to it. She pointed out that in Mormonism—which is led by a man officially chosen to be the church's prophet—such Saints traveled through the leadership ranks before being called to lead the church. Taylor disagreed with the way this was done. It was not necessary to work one's way up the spiritual ladder in such a way in order to receive revelation on behalf of the whole world, he said.

Dawn was not showing such irritating flashes of independence. Taylor decided that instead of having her take the third level of Harmony, he would become her trainer. She lapped up everything he espoused. There was no right or wrong, only what worked. She created all of the results in her life. Control was an illusion.

That last one was a nice notion, but it did not apply to Taylor. He exerted more and more of it as the summer of 1999 went on. People needed to know who was in charge. Kelly and Dawn were chatting one day when Taylor interrupted. "I want both of you to understand you are not to talk about anything that I talk to you about to each other. You are to keep it completely separate and never discuss anything that I have told you."

It was a hot Sunday morning in August, and, inexplicably, Taylor felt like going to church. It was the day of the month for bearing testimony, when congregants stand before their fellows and speak about things that inspire them or blessings they receive. People certainly noticed the tall man with long dark hair and a beard who came into the church wearing a long black trench coat and small spectacles. As he approached the pulpit to bear his testimony, silence fell. No one moved and all eyes turned toward him.

Taylor faced the congregation. He had not been to church in some time, but now he felt he had been spiritually prompted to come back, he said. And he knew this was right because shortly after he decided to return, he said he received a call from church leaders about ex-communicating him, which was something he said he wanted to avoid. The audience was riveted. People did not usually bear testimony about getting kicked out of the church. But no one except high-level church officials knew Taylor had actually been ex-communicated a year earlier. In reality, anything he chose to say that Sunday was not going to reverse that.

Standing at the pulpit in front of all those people was too excellent an opportunity to pass up, and Taylor began to preach. Did people know how to live without sin? He had lived without sin for some time, he said, making only a single mistake. Spirit told him his only transgression was not smiling at a grocery-store clerk.[6] Again, his words were far from the truth, but he did not seem bothered by it and took a breath to continue. The bishop, who had never seen Taylor before and thought his testimony incoherent, stopped him. He asked that Taylor be excused to make room for the next person.[7]

Within a few weeks, Taylor and Justin began holding meetings in the LDS meetinghouse parking lot. They would talk about Scripture and Taylor would preach to the fifteen to twenty people who gathered around him instead of attending their normal Sunday-school classes. Dawn Kirkland watched the meetings from inside the church.

She had moved out of Dawn Godman's apartment shortly before and had not seen her former roommate much since. Now she was worried about her friend. One Sunday, when Dawn came inside the church to use the bathroom, Dawn Kirkland stopped her in the hallway. Everyone was concerned about the parking lot meetings, she said. These were not the right people to spend time with, and Dawn needed to be careful. Dawn smiled. "They're nice, and they're my friends. And thank you, but I'm fine." Dawn Kirkland tried one more time. She really was worried about Taylor, who had made her feel almost ill with his earlier testimony in church. "He's not hearing the Spirit," she said. "He might be listening to the adversary or the wrong spirit." Dawn paid her no heed, but Dawn Kirkland did not give up. She and other concerned Saints went to the bishop about the parking-lot meetings, and the gatherings quietly ended.

———

Kelly Lord had concerns of her own, but she was still so enthralled with Taylor that she pushed them away and kept spending as much time with him as he would permit. She took another New Age seminar with him, Carma, Justin, and Dawn. One session, she was startled to find Dawn wearing a tiny shirt with see-through netting. "How are you doing?" she asked the friend who used to be the picture of modesty heralded by the Mormon church. "Taylor is teaching me to embrace my sexuality and be okay with everything," Dawn said.

Other red flags went up as well. Another night at the seminar, Kelly and Justin were hanging out when Taylor came up to where Justin was sitting, knelt down, and stuck a cup in his brother's face. "Just look at that. Look at that. Do you see that dirt?" He waved the cup, which had dried liquid in the bottom. "I brought this cup from home. This is why the roommates don't like you." It was deliberate humiliation in front of a room full of people. Justin just hung his head.

Taylor was constantly pushing people, testing them to gauge their loyalty. He was always measuring Justin, Keri, and Dawn. He needed to see where Kelly stood, too. They were together one afternoon on the lawn outside the LDS meetinghouse when Taylor turned to her. "What would you do if you saw my picture on the front page of the newspaper, and I was in jail for something that they said I did, but I didn't do it?" he asked her. "Would you come get me?"

"Absolutely," Kelly said.

"Good," Taylor said.

They walked over to a fast-food restaurant to eat. After they got their food, Taylor started talking about carjacking people and robbing businesses. "If we did something like rob a small place like this, would you be open to it?" he asked. Kelly did not know what to say. She thought he was testing her devotion. She loved him, but all this talk of illegal activity was just too much.

———

Keri continued bringing in money through waitressing and other jobs, but she was about to make a big career leap, at least as far as Taylor was concerned. She got a job stripping at a San Francisco club. He loved the fast lifestyle associated with her job, and the status that having a girlfriend with a stripper-worthy body conferred. Keri's motives were more practical. Taylor had convinced her to get breast implants, and she needed to pay off the $5,000 in loans she had taken out to get them.

Her new line of work inspired Taylor, who thought he could use Keri's contacts with other dancers to start a new business. He modified his escort-service plan, thinking he could lure some of Keri's colleagues into working as prostitutes at high-end parties he would arrange. He called it the Feline Club, but Keri never got around to recruiting anyone, and the idea fizzled.

The ideas that actually did coalesce into action usually did not involve Taylor at all. The most significant was Keri's decision to submit photos of herself to *Playboy* magazine. They took pictures in the backyard and sent them off. Taylor initially was quite supportive—having a stripper girlfriend was nothing compared with how he would look dating a *Playboy* model.

But as 1999 drew to a close, their relationship began to sour. Taylor began to think that Keri was not treating him well, and she was not following the Twelve Principles, either. She refused to let go of right and wrong. She would not acknowledge that she—not anyone else—created the results in her life. She had no unconditional love. She did not realize her life was already perfect, and she had only to learn from it.

He was so upset, he sat down and typed out a five-and-a-half page letter to her, shouting off the pages in all capital letters as he berated her and professed his love in dizzying alternation.

> *You are ungrateful. You are selfish and self-centered. You are fake and superficial. You are delusional. You are blind. And you are weak. You are a victim to everything and everyone around you. Mass amounts of people in this world are literally struggling and dying from exposure, hunger, or war, and you are in the mirror 24/7 freaking out and despondent about your zits and other compartativly [sic] small things."*

Three pages later he called her his "angel heart" and his best friend.

You are a good person. You are intuitive. You are cre-
ative. You are gentle. You are fun. You have such a
bright, sunshiny, natural personality. You are warm.
And when you love, it is like a blanket I want to wrap
myself in forever. And you are stunningly, amazingly,
perfectly beautiful. You are so gorgeous!!!

He wrote that he had always said he would support her
if she decided to stop stripping. Then he accused her of not
being sincere when she said she wanted to earn a lump-
sum amount to bankroll one of his ideas so they could go
into business together, and she would then not have to strip
anymore.

You will create drama, in one form or another, that al-
lows you to only work 3–4 days out of a month, which
barely pays living expenses and bills, and does not al-
low any chance of creating any meaningful amount to
capitalize on any idea I have ever had. Your dumb-ass
boyfreind [sic] has been sitting on his ass waiting wait-
ing waiting wanting for you to come through, always be-
lieving that next month you would, and he could start
bringing in an income.

Yet he struck a magnanimous tone later on in the letter,
writing that he hoped she quit for her own sake and that he
did not need her money, even though he quite clearly did.

He spent pages trying to wrest scraps of power from her.
He turned the $4,000 he lent her to buy a car into a gift.
"You don't owe me. Your obligation has been removed.
You have not fulfilled it." And he once more told her how
to think. "You know exactly how you're treating me, and,
frankly, everything else I've written in this letter you already know in your heart too. And you are blaming and
shaming and judging and condemning yourself for it. And

it's killing you. Litterally [sic]. You look and act like you have nothing to live for."

In what would become the final nail in the coffin of their relationship, Keri told him she was not interested in Transform America. Taylor never spoke of it to her again. Keri slowly began to drift away.

EIGHT

Transforming America

The Mormon temple in Oakland sits where the flatlands of the southern section of the city gradually begins to rise into the hills. The building itself is not so subtle. Blinding white with five golden spires, the temple overlooks immaculately kept gardens and graceful walkways lined with palm trees. It is not used for regular Sunday worship, but instead is reserved for special religious education classes and ceremonies. Only church members in good standing and with official recommendation can enter. For Latter-day Saints, it is among the holiest places in their religion.

In 2000, the temple was the only one in Northern California, a natural place for a local Mormon to go when he or she wanted to be closer to the divine. Few, however, would think they needed God for the type of conversation Taylor wanted to have in January of that year.

He parked in the temple's lot and looked at the woman next to him in the car. It was not Keri, the beautiful blonde he planned to have join him and Justin as the third person in his trinity, the inner circle he needed to implement

Transform America. No, Taylor had found it necessary to lower his standards. He turned to Dawn Godman, whose pudgy face was turned toward his with rapt devotion.

Spirit told him it was time she knew everything. He explained that being near the temple allowed angels to guard them so that Satan and his minions couldn't overhear his plan. And it was one as grand as the temple in the background. It reached to the highest echelons of the Mormon church, a place he said he deserved to be. To get there, he told Dawn, he would recruit Brazilian orphans and train them as assassins. He would smuggle them into the United States and then into church headquarters in Salt Lake City, where they would kidnap the fifteen top leaders of the church, including the prophet. Some might be killed during the kidnapping, but those who survived would be taken back to Brazil and forced to write letters calling for a new prophet to lead the world's 11 million Mormons. And that prophet would be Taylor.

For Taylor's ambitions were rapidly becoming more and more grandiose. He was no longer content to just bring harmony and love to the world through his own group awareness program. Now he said he had the power to turn two thousand years of Christian theology upside down by personally bringing forth the Second Coming of Christ peacefully and preventing the chaos and darkness of the Apocalypse prophesied in the Bible.

To bolster his plan, Taylor picked certain biblical verses that exalted the glory Jesus would bestow on chosen followers, but blithely ignored surrounding text that preached of humbling oneself before the Lord and warning of what would happen to those who sin. Those writings had no place in his plans. He needed money for Transform America, and if actions that the Bible deemed sinful—like those pesky commandments against murder and theft—were necessary, then so be it. In fact, he was able to twist his

quest for funding into a divine mandate, just as easily as he
had manipulated everything else in his life.

Taylor loved reading about Christ sitting at the right hand
of God. He decided he would ask to sit at the right hand of
Christ. He was not the first to make that request. Two of Jesus' greatest apostles, the brothers John and James, had
asked that they be allowed to sit at His right and left hands.
Although Jesus told them only God could grant that honor,
he took John and James in and made them, along with Simon Peter, the inner core of his apostles. Jesus named the
brothers the Sons of Thunder.¹

The brothers also had great importance in the Mormon
faith. They and Simon Peter were the ones given the keys
to Christ's ministry, which then were lost until the apostles
appeared to Joseph Smith, gave him those keys, and returned the ministry to earth.

Now that Taylor had appointed himself the one to usher
in the Second Coming, he was most certainly as important
as John, James, and Peter. Taylor had created his own special inner circle, which now needed a name. Factoring in
Dawn's gender, Taylor changed the biblical appellation
slightly. They would call themselves Children of Thunder.

The household on Oak Grove Road was breaking up. Brandon and his girlfriend moved out around the beginning of
2000. Keri and Taylor found an apartment in Martinez, but
that lasted only a month before Keri finally left for good.
Playboy was interested in her; suddenly she had options
that did not include a controlling boyfriend who spouted
Scripture, got her involved with drugs, and wanted her help
to start a prostitution ring. She decided to move to Los Angeles and start a modeling career. On her way out of town,
she paid the following month's rent on the apartment. She
knew Taylor had nowhere else to go.

That left Justin, who had just turned twenty-eight, on his own for really the first time in his life. He packed up his sleeping bag, radio, and scant wardrobe and rented a room in a house in Concord. He did not change his habits, eating as he always had and continuing to perform his odd body-contorting exercises in plain view until the landlady told him he needed to shut the door to his room. He still had his temper tantrums, yelling and screaming behind his closed door, and made little effort to converse with his room-mates.

This baffled Johnette Gray, a work colleague who moved into the house about a month after Justin did. Johnette had worked with him since he started at AT&T the previous summer and thought he was cute, sweet, and quiet, if a lit-tle naive. He was fond of her as well, cheerfully giving her rides to and from work and occasionally cooking her meals. Sometimes, however, she was just too chatty for Justin to take.

"Just because I come in the house doesn't mean I want to be said hi to," he told her at one point.

"What?" Johnette said, astonished.

"Well, just because I'm in your presence, just because I happen to be near you, doesn't mean I want to converse, you know, converse and talk," he replied.

Justin did not generally like intimate conversations, so it was unusual one night when he began talking about poems he had written. Johnette also wrote poetry and was eager to see his work. But what she heard frightened her.

Justin read her a poem that started with a lover seducing a woman. But as the verses continued, the focus changed from just the sacrifice of innocence to the sacrifice of life itself. The imagery reminded Johnette of gory movies. By the end, it was clear that the writer was asking the woman to give her life for some greater good.

It was a theme Justin thought about often in the spring

of 2000, because it was something Taylor talked about a
lot. He had decided that they would have to kill at least a
few people in order to steal the money needed for Children
of Thunder to succeed. He would save billions of lives by
preventing the horrors of the Apocalypse. The few deaths
he would cause were small prices to pay to save humanity.

Besides, killing was sometimes excusable; the Scriptures said so. Taylor picked two passages and quoted them
again and again to bolster his argument. In the Bible's First
Book of Samuel, Samuel tells Saul that the Lord anointed
Saul king of Israel and ordered him to destroy the town of
Amalek. But Saul spares the town's king. The Lord, through
Samuel, reprimands his mercy and has Samuel kill the king
himself.[2] Taylor explained that the story proved that God
must be obeyed and that killing was justified if the Lord so
ordered.

Another defense of bloodshed could be found in *The
Book of Mormon*'s First Book of Nephi, narrated by a righ-
teous man who understands God's will. Nephi steals into
Jerusalem by night to find a man named Laban. He finds
his quarry drunk in the street and is told by the Spirit to kill
him. *And it came to pass that the Spirit said unto me again:
Slay him, for the Lord hath delivered him into thy hands . . .
It is better that one man should perish than that a nation
should dwindle and perish in unbelief.*[3]

But Taylor, the master of Scripture, had conveniently
omitted a crucial element of both stories. Both the Amalek
king and Laban had wronged others first. The king had
harmed Israelites fleeing Egypt. *And Samuel said, As thy
sword hath made women childless, so shall thy mother be
childless among women.*[4] And in *The Book of Mormon*, Laban had tried to kill Nephi. *Yea, and I also knew that he
had sought to take away mine own life; yea, and he would
not hearken unto the commandments of the Lord; and he
also had taken away our property.*[5] But these details were

not as important as the ones that fit Taylor's plans, so he excluded them.

———

After Keri's month of prepaid rent ended, Taylor had no money and nowhere to go. He decided to move into Dawn's apartment in Martinez. Except for the gorgeous-girlfriend part, she more than filled the void left by Keri's departure. She had a job, which meant steady income, and now she was putting a roof over his head as well. She was also a good girl Friday, always running errands and taking notes about his ideas, which was useful because he still had trouble remembering things—even the amazing plans he kept devising. And the best part was that he knew she would stay. There was no possibility of a modeling career in Dawn Godman's future, no threat of a sudden rise in her self-confidence. This time, he had chosen well.

Dawn continued helping Taylor with the one money-making scheme that was actually bringing in cash—dealing ecstasy. Although he was liberally using his own product, Taylor still had the wherewithal to create a business plan to more efficiently distribute the drugs. He wanted to be at least three levels above the street pushers. He thought dealers could pick up the drugs from some drop spot like a fitness-club locker, and leave the money, so he would never have to meet them in person. He obsessed over different ways to make his ecstasy business boom, filling pages and pages with figures, estimates, and to-do lists. One hundred pills at ten dollars a pop would mean $10,000 a month if he had ten people working for him. He hoped to eventually pull in close to a million dollars a year by having forty people work for him. But he was stymied by the fact that he did not know how to make ecstasy himself in order to lower his costs, so his dealing stayed small-time.

As he stood at raves, watching the dancers move to the

techno music and occasionally come to him for an ecstasy
pill or two, his mind would wander once again to his
favorite scheme—prostitution. The plan was now called
"Intimacy = Into Me See," but still suffered from a lack of
willing women. These people dancing in front of him
might be good ones to approach. But even Taylor knew he
could not just ask someone if she was interested in becoming a whore. To be more subtle, Children of Thunder created a questionnaire and passed it out at raves. It asked
seventy questions ranging from the mundane to the sexual
to the spiritual.

It asked whether respondents got along with their parents and whether they were religious, what their family's
income level was, how much money they wanted to make,
and what drugs they used. Sprinkled throughout the list
were questions about sex. True or false: "I hate one-night
stands," "I love one-night stands," "I love sex."

Then there were the philosophical questions. Many
came straight from the Twelve Principles of Magic. They
were presented as true-or-false questions.

"Spirit knows."

"There is no such thing as right and wrong."

"Unconditional fearless love is the most powerful force
in the universe."

Taylor also added a few practical questions; when
screening women as potential prostitutes, it made sense to
find out whether they were law-abiding citizens. More
true-or-false questions asked whether prostitution, murder,
lying, and stealing were wrong. Many questions had a third
answer option, just in case—like Taylor—the respondents
had a more complex view of such things: it depends.

Taylor was sure that if he could just recruit some
women, he could not only make money, but help them as
well. He would be a generous employer. Every dollar a
woman brought in would earn her one point. Women would

get medical, dental, vision, and retirement plans for themselves and their dependants when they earned 3,500 points. For 7,500 points, they would receive their choice of permanent makeup, electrolysis, or breast augmentation. And with 10,000 points, they would become salaried Intimacy models, and also receive an annual paid vacation for two.

———

While Dawn helped Taylor deal ecstasy and pass out questionnaires at raves, she also tried a few things on her own. She had been dabbling in witchcraft and magic for some time and began casting spells in the spring of 2000, under the guidance of a thirty-eight-year-old friend named Debra McClanahan.

Debra met Dawn in 1997 at a Mormon church dance in Danville. Debra joined the church in 1998, but that didn't stop her from practicing witchcraft, which she had done since her early teens. She saw no incompatibility between the two. She knew her Mormon church elders would, though, so she wisely chose not to mention it.

Debra thought of Wicca as the positive healing nature of the planet, as well as a practice that involved love potions, protections, and rituals. She showed Dawn rituals and incantations and lent the younger woman books, including *Good Magic* and *Helping Yourself with White Witchcraft*. Dawn took the teachings to heart and tried several spells, including one where she waved a sword over her head and chanted. On another occasion, she invited Taylor and Justin's mother over for an evening of gathering rainwater and "connecting" with its energy. Dawn hoped the incantation would make her more attractive. She inhaled the steam from hot rainwater mixed with amethysts, but Carma Helzer certainly did not see any physical change in her son's roommate. She thought the whole thing was just a sweet way to spend an evening.[6]

Debra was there for the rainwater spell. She might have directed Dawn's interest toward witchcraft, but that didn't mean she wasn't looking for a little guidance of her own. Debra McClanahan was searching for people and beliefs that would help anchor her life. She instantly volunteered her time, her money, her body—anything asked of her, or anything she thought might help a friend. She lived a somewhat chaotic life, sharing an extremely messy apartment in Concord with her ten-year-old daughter and a ferret named Cosmo.[7]

Debra began to fill many of the voids in her psyche when she met Taylor in late 1999. When Dawn introduced them, she quickly became as mesmerized as her friend was. Soon she was allowed to witness his conversations with Spirit; she could feel the light and love when Spirit spoke through him.[8]

He plied her with his full bag of tricks—cuddling shirtless for hours on end, crying with her, making her feel like the only person in his life. Once, after she went to a Berkeley rave with Taylor and Dawn, they dropped Dawn off, went back to Debra's apartment, and had sex. It was the only time they did so, and Debra insisted she was not in love with him; the two were just friends. But no one was as special to her as Taylor, and despite her protestations, she acted more like a love-struck girlfriend than a hang-around pal.

She began participating in the Scripture tutorials Taylor conducted with Dawn. As he taught both women, he also wedged himself deeply into their friendship. Before he moved in with Dawn, Debra would casually drop by her friend's Martinez apartment. Once he was in residence, that was no longer permitted; visits had to be arranged and approved. Neither woman seemed to mind.

———

Despite having some success finding women at raves to actually fill out the questionnaires, Taylor had not been able to put together any prostitution parties. So another idea began to slowly take shape in his mind. He decided he could make money more quickly through extortion and blackmail. And he knew a place where there were deep pockets—Dean Witter, his old employer. He would recruit underage girls to open accounts with a male stockbroker at the firm and convince the man they were of legal age. The girls would seduce the stockbroker and catch the whole thing on tape. Then Taylor would claim that the broker forced the girls into sex and get the firm to pay a large sum of money to keep the whole thing quiet.

Taylor's belief in his own power of persuasion was so strong that he planned to give the girls the blackmail money in the belief that they would then donate it all to Transform America. He would graciously set aside a portion, however, for the actual duped stockbroker whose life he had ruined.[9]

Before they ensnared the stockbroker, however, the girls would need a little training—in how to be compliant and in how to have sex. Taylor thought a group training course would accomplish the first requirement. The second he would take upon himself. He told Dawn he would take the girls somewhere and teach them how to please a man. Considering his years-long preoccupation with sex, this aspect of the plan was likely just as appealing and deliberate a goal for him as the blackmail.

As he batted around the brokerage blackmail idea, it began to evolve into a straight extortion scheme without the complication of sex. He would need someone to launder the stolen money, someone who could then be easily gotten rid of once her task was finished. He started looking around for a suitable target.

———

Kelly Lord continued taking the New Age seminar with Taylor and his family. It was a wonderful opportunity to

spend time with him, until the night she found out about
the drug use he had carefully tried to hide from her. Kelly
could not abide anyone who took drugs, and was shocked
and agonized when a mutual friend told her of Taylor's
pharmacological pursuits.

She had to say something. Taylor guided her out to the
lobby of the hotel where the seminar was being held and settled in for one of their standard chats. "What do you need?"
he asked gently. She looked really upset. "I know all about
the drugs," she said. She looked at him and thought for a
minute. Then, in a moment of startling clarity, she went further. "You're going to be the next David Koresh," she said.

Taylor stared at her. She was comparing him with the
Waco cult leader? He did not need anyone trying to deci-
pher his modus operandi. His mood changed instantly, and
his anger seemed to make him grow in size as he sat in his
chair.

"If Kelly gets in my way, she's fucked!" he snapped at
her in the third person. "Are we clear?" Kelly hurried back
into the seminar room. Taylor thought about what he had
said and rushed after her, yelling her name. He skidded to
a halt when he realized she was now in a room full of people. There would be no opportunity to continue their conversation that night.

He did not really talk with her again until she invited
him over for dinner a while later. He accepted the invitation, needing to see where she stood.

"I know you won't do anything illegal, but would you
help me afterward?" he asked. Kelly's mind was racing. If
he had good intentions, there were ways to do things without breaking the law, she thought. But she did not say anything. Taylor then began to get a message from Spirit. He
became very emotional and ran outside into the rainy evening. Kelly stayed put. When he noticed she had not followed him, Taylor ran back inside and stomped his feet.

"Will you come out here with me?" he demanded. Kelly got up and walked after him. She just stood quietly and watched as he raised his arms to the sky and started ranting. He felt his audience's deliberate unresponsiveness, and his revelation fizzled. He dropped his arms and slouched back into the apartment.

Out of the rain, he gave it one last shot. "Let me hold you," he said. Kelly, who had invited him to dinner in order to see what kind of power he still had over her, now proved to herself she had finally broken free. "No," she said. "It's time to go. You need to go."

Taylor looked at her. "I'm very clear now," he said. "If people aren't loyal to me, then I'm just going to have to kill them."

Kelly was speechless. "I think you have to leave now," she finally said, sending Taylor out again into the rain, this time alone.

———

Losing Kelly was only one of Taylor's frustrations in the spring of 2000. Now Dawn was giving him problems. She quit her job at the alarm company where she had been working as an entry-level dispatcher. Taylor was furious—they needed her salary. And to add insult to economic injury, she had not asked his permission before handing in her resignation. She told him that she felt she had learned all she could from the job and Spirit was guiding her to do something different.[10] She was perhaps more honest with her boss, telling the woman that she and some friends had the chance to make a lot of money by going into business for themselves.[11]

Right now Children of Thunder's only marginally successful entrepreneurial effort was the ecstasy dealing. Taylor kept going to raves, where he used the alias "Jordan" as he hovered on the edges of the dancing crowds, waiting for people to approach him for a few pills. One night, he trekked all the way up to Guerneville, a tiny town more than eighty miles away, for an underground rave. He wore his customary dark clothing, which separated him from the throng of partygoers whose deliberately bright outfits caught the black lights that illuminated the dance floor. A woman walked up to him. She was short and chubby, but had beautiful long dark hair and a sweet smile. Taylor's radar prickled. She seemed very innocent and trusting. He smiled and introduced himself as Jordan. Hello, she said. Her name was Selina.

NINE

Children of Thunder

Taylor began seeing the bubbly twenty-two-year-old Selina Bishop soon after meeting her at the rave. He was quite pleased with his find. And so was Selina. "Jordan" was handsome, kind, and totally interested in her. She knew he was an ecstasy dealer and that Jordan was not his real name, but things were light and fun and she did not take those details too seriously. Jordan protected her, too. He said he did not want her knowing where he lived or anything else about him just in case she was ever asked anything about his drug dealing.

His real motives for secrecy were, of course, much different. Children of Thunder were about to move on to the next phase of their operation. For that, they needed a head-quarters, someplace where they could live and plan without interference. So they turned to Justin, the only one of the three still employed and able to pass a credit check. On April 29, 2000, he signed a one-year lease for a nondescript three-bedroom, two-bath house on a cul-de-sac at the far eastern edge of Concord. He put down a $2,000 security deposit and agreed to pay a monthly rent of $1,650. He also lied and said he would be the property's sole tenant. It was certainly the least of the many lease violations to come.

Taylor, Justin, and Dawn settled into the house on Saddlewood Court. Justin continued working and living a mostly clean life. Taylor and Dawn, on the other hand, did methamphetamine almost daily and spent most of their time talking about Transform America and what they needed to do to make it work. They would bring Justin up to speed on things during weekly Children of Thunder meetings. It was all very organized.

All three had also finally decided that Taylor was indeed a prophet of God. Spirit had been communicating with him for years, but there had been some hesitancy on Justin's part to fully accept that Taylor's ideas were coming courtesy of divine revelation.

Just as with every other task he took on, Justin approached the prophet question methodically and deliberately. There could be other reasons for Taylor's revelations. Was it the drugs? He decided that was not the case because Taylor had ideas and plans even while sober. That conclusion made sense. But then Justin's critical thinking began to slip. He concluded that Taylor was not crazy because his ideas were logical and rational, although any outsider could plainly see that was not the case. And he knew Satan had not possessed his big brother—the Transform America plan would heal the world, which obviously was not one of the devil's goals.[1] Justin turned to the Scriptures of the church he had abandoned and found what he needed.

And it shall come to pass that I, the Lord God, will send one mighty and strong, holding the scepter of power in his hand, clothed with light for a covering, whose mouth shall utter words, eternal words; while his bowels shall be a fountain of truth, to set in order the house of God.[2]

Taylor was glad to have Justin fully on board. The main reason he wanted his little brother to be part of the group was to have access to his money, but Justin also fit in nicely with Taylor's interpretation of the Bible. The Sons of Thunder were two brothers, and Taylor's millennial Children of Thunder should be the same. As the summer wore on, he convinced Justin that martyrdom would be a worthy end if it became necessary. That also fit in with his scriptural antecedents. James was generally considered the second Christian martyr, after Saint Stephen. James's brother, John, took a much different path, however. In LDS Scripture, he asked to remain on earth until Christ came again.

> *And the Lord said unto me: John, my beloved, what desirest thou? For if you shall ask what you will, it shall be granted unto you. And I said unto him: Lord, give unto me power over death, that I may live and bring souls unto thee. And the Lord said unto me: Verily, verily, I say unto thee, because thou desirest this thou shalt tarry until I come in my glory, and shalt prophesy before nations, kindreds, tongues and people.*[3]

If John would live until Christ's return, and James would give his life for the cause, which apostle was it more likely Taylor thought himself to be? Certainly not the one dying early.

———

Justin walked into the sporting-goods store and took a look around. He needed to buy a gun, and he wanted a 9-mm. It was what he had used in the service, he told the clerk. He chose a Beretta that cost $599.99 and added some boxes of ammunition to the purchase. He signed the California dealer's record, honestly stating he was not a felon or mental patient precluded from owning a firearm. He was not required to give his reason for wanting the gun. "Ushering in Christ's Second Coming" probably would have made the clerk think twice about selling it to him.

Justin not only bought the gun, he financed many of Children of Thunder's other necessities as well. Taylor had debt collectors hounding him and had maxed out his credit cards. The state was even after him for unpaid taxes from three years before. And Dawn was little better. She had skipped out on her Martinez landlady without paying her last month's rent[4] and no longer had a job. That meant she did have time, though, which she put to use shopping for everything from handcuffs to ski masks to stun guns.

She also needed plenty of construction materials. Taylor had not decided on the exact way they would get rid of the bodies of the people they would kill. He had a couple of ideas and needed to see what would be the most viable. Dawn thought they could dump the bodies down an abandoned mine shaft; they went up to the foothills near where she had grown up, but all the sites she remembered had been filled in. She suggested just going out into the woods and digging a hole. Taylor dismissed this—it would take too long. He thought it might be possible for dogs to eat the bodies. He instructed Dawn to build a dog run in the backyard. When she finished, they adopted three dogs from the county animal shelter: a Rottweiler, a border-collie mix, and an Australian-shepherd mix. They fed the canines huge bones with the meat still attached. The dogs loved them, but Taylor decided they did not eat enough for the body-devouring idea to work. Justin took Taylor's two dogs and told Dawn he released them in a rural part of the county. She did not want to do that to her dog, the Rottweiler named Jake, so he stayed at Saddlewood with her.

Children of Thunder's target list was evolving. In order to pull off the Dean Witter scheme, they needed start-up capital, and Taylor had grown tired of trying to raise the cash by attempting to set up a prostitution ring and selling insignificant amounts of drugs. He decided it would be much easier to just steal the money from people who already had it. And he had plenty to choose from. When he left his brokerage firm, he had taken his client list with him. He had helped many of the people on the list plan for their retirements, and he knew exactly what they were worth. He picked five people, and he and Dawn scouted out where they lived.

They would choose one, kidnap him, and force him to turn over his assets to Taylor. Then the person would be killed. Since the unemployed Taylor could not just deposit hundreds of thousands of dollars into his bank account without raising suspicions, the money would have to be laundered. And that was where Selina came in. Taylor had marked Selina for death even before he moved into Saddlewood, but her part in the plan had now crystallized. She would deposit the money for him. Then he would get rid of her.

No one was surprised when Selina and Jenny arrived late at the Villarin family reunion. The two had always been inseparable and were always late. Selina was delighted to see her cousins that hot day in June and had much to tell them. Her life was going so great, she just couldn't believe it. She had just moved into her own apartment, and she had a new boyfriend. He was great and fun and handsome and she really liked him, even though he had a few quirks. He would not let her take a picture of him, she did not know his real name, and he sold ecstasy. Her cousins Lusha and Amber thought that a bit strange, but Selina seemed so happy. She also was excited about an assignment he had given her; she would be helping him out and making some money at the same time, she told Amber and Lusha. Jordan was inheriting hundreds of thousands of dollars that he needed to hide from the wife he was divorcing. Selina would deposit the money in her bank account, and in exchange for hiding it, Jordan would give her a cut. She wasn't asking a lot of questions about the scheme, and Lusha thought that made sense. If your boyfriend offered to give you money, well, who would argue with that?

Off in another section of the San Jose park where the Villarins had gathered, Jenny was also talking about Selina's boyfriend. She had not yet met him, and it was starting to bother her. Come on, her sister Lydia said, who wants to introduce a boyfriend to their mom so soon? But she and her daughter were so close, she always knew all of Selina's friends, Jenny said. And Selina had been dating this guy for a couple of months now. It was time to meet him.

Jenny did not know the details of Jordan's money plan, and she certainly did not know about the drug dealing. But despite both questionable activities, Selina pressed on with the relationship. On June 30, she opened a new account at Cal Fed Bank; it would be a safe place for Jordan's inheritance.

The same day, she sat down and wrote a letter to her friend Julia Bernbaum, who was away at college in the far north of the state. She was so happy, she had to share.

Dear Jules, I'm just chillin' in my new place. It's going to be so cute when I get some shelves and some furniture. I can't wait to see you again. We'll be neighbors. You can stay here whenever you want. I have a pool in the backyard and the people here are super nice. I also can't wait for you to meet them—or meet Jordan. I've never met anyone like him before. I don't know what's going to happen with him, but I hope he stays with me. He's going to be busy in the next couple of months so we'll have plenty of time together."

She was going to a rave soon, but otherwise told her friend she did not feel much like partying.

> *I have everything I need here. I'm finally home again. I can actually afford to live in the Valley by myself. I'm so proud. I don't know when I've ever been happier in my life.*

———

Taylor still needed to come up with a way to dispose of all the bodies he soon would have on his hands. It struck him that he could cut them up and dump them somewhere. If he did it in the Delta, no one would ever find them. The Delta was a tangled web of rivers and islands that drained into San Francisco Bay. Children of Thunder could take out a boat—or even better, a Jet Ski—and toss the weighted remains overboard. No one would ever know.

He thought it would be a good idea to practice on the watercraft first. He and Dawn drove up to Lake Berryessa, a popular resort area north of Napa Valley, and rented a Jet Ski. They took Selina with them. Taylor told Dawn he thought it would be a fun outing for her. He did not mention to Selina that the next time she was on a Jet Ski, he planned for her to be in pieces.

Selina was beginning to sense, however, that her Jordan was not altogether committed to the relationship. He never called when he said he would, and her hopes of meeting him often went unfulfilled. And all the big plans and riches that he talked of were too much for her. She just wanted a normal life in a comfortable house, a few kids, and simple happiness.

The truth was, Jordan most often disappointed her. She was still in love with him but was desperately trying not to let him walk all over her. She knew he did not want her to come to his house in Concord, but one day she went anyway. Dawn opened the door. Selina could see the sympathetic look on her face. "It's really okay. This is so hard for you," Dawn said as she brought Selina inside and hugged her. Then Jordan came home, and he and Selina went to his bedroom and cuddled before he sent her home.

The cuddling was part of yet another restriction he placed on their relationship. "At first we had this great sex life, and everything was great, but now he doesn't even want to sleep with me. He wants to hold off on the sex for six months and see where our relationship goes," she confided in Rosanne Lusk Urban, one of her mother's closest friends.

If that were not enough to make Selina doubt her attractiveness, Jordan also had casually mentioned that his exgirlfriend was going to be in *Playboy,* she told Rosanne. The older woman thought this was just too much. "Maybe he's trying to tell you something. Maybe you should just back it off," she said.

Well, he did want to take her camping in Yosemite, Selina said. Rosanne thought for a minute. "You guys could still be friends, you know," she said. "I mean, why not? There's nothing wrong with being friends. And if he's willing to foot the bill . . ." Rosanne trailed off. She had always loved Yosemite; it would be wonderful for Selina to experience it. "Honey, everybody needs to see Yosemite at least once before they die."

———————

Things were starting to come together. Taylor needed to make sure everyone was on board. He stressed complete loyalty, telling Dawn that anyone who betrayed him would get hurt. He told Debra, who continued to hang on his every word, that if she violated his trust, he would fix her car so that something happened. Then he drew a circle in the air that encompassed her daughter, who was sleeping in a nearby chair. Debra got the point. She did not protest when Taylor and Dawn brought a portable safe over to her apartment and said they would be leaving it with her. She knew they dealt drugs and were likely storing them in the safe, but she still kept her mouth shut. She did not want to sacrifice her friendship with any of the three of them.

She loved getting invited to Saddlewood and playing chess or canasta into the early hours of the morning. She would even occasionally get to go out with Dawn. One night, they went to a local bar with a man Debra was dating. Dawn picked up some guy, and they all went back to Debra's apartment. Dawn and her new acquaintance messed around in the living room, and then Dawn joined Debra and her date in the bedroom. It was the only time the two women had sex, but their close relationship would continue.[5]

Dawn continued to use meth almost every day. Taylor kept using it as well because it helped him concentrate and stay awake. But he gave up his favorite hallucinogens—including mushrooms, peyote, and LSD—because they were too distracting.[6] He needed every brain cell focused on Transform America. It was going to happen soon. He thought Sunday would be the best day of the week, when more former clients were likely to be home and available for kidnapping. He decided on July 30, the first Sunday after his thirtieth birthday. Christ began his ministry at that age, and Joseph Smith was thirty when he dedicated the first Mormon temple. Just as Smith laid the cornerstone for the church, Taylor this day wanted to lay the foundation for all that would come as the result of his actions. He had his disciples, his list of targets, and he was ready to go.

He and Dawn began including Justin in every Children of Thunder meeting. Each one would begin with all three on their knees in prayer. Taylor continued to remind his team that Samuel and Nephi had killed. It was all right for them to do so as well. Justin listened again to all of Taylor's spiritual rationales and examined them critically—in

his own mind, at least—one last time. He came to the conclusion that what Taylor had planned would be done with
God's permission, but not necessarily on His orders. The
Lord was not commanding that Children of Thunder
kill these people. But the Lord was giving Justin the
opportunity—the choice—to become a hero by saving the
world. It was certainly more than Justin had achieved in his
life so far. He would do it.

Just to make sure that Taylor was getting his signals
right, they prayed to Spirit for a sign to stop the plan. They
got no response. Then Taylor tried one more thing. He
called an old friend of his mother's and asked if she had
$5,000 to invest in a business opportunity he was putting
together. She said she had $1,000, but not the full amount.
She offered to call around and see if she could raise more,
but Taylor told her to forget about it. He hung up the
phone. If the woman had given him the full $5,000, he told
Dawn he would have taken that as a sign not to go through
with the plan. Since she did not, that meant Children of
Thunder would go forward.

———

It was almost the end of July, and Jenny still had not met
Selina's boyfriend. It was time to take matters into her own
hands. She and Rosanne had breakfast at a little restaurant
outside the Valley and cooked up a plan over blueberry
pancakes. Jenny knew that Jordan had stayed at her daughter's apartment the night before. They needed an excuse to
stop by. Jenny decided she would say she needed to borrow
a blouse for work. They hopped in Rosanne's car and
headed for Woodacre.

Jenny went into Selina's as Rosanne—who did not have
an excuse to go in—settled down to wait in the car, figuring
that there would be an extended chat as Jenny made Jordan's
acquaintance. But her friend was back within five minutes.

"He's kind of cute, I guess," she said. It was too brief a meeting to really judge, but overall, she was not impressed. She felt like she had been shooed out of the apartment far too quickly as she and Rosanne drove away.[7] But she held her tongue when she talked to her daughter later. She told Selina she liked her boyfriend and left it at that.[8]

Selina continued to worry about where she and Jordan were headed. But she had so much fun when they actually spent time together that she just could not walk away. She was excited about going to Yosemite the following week, where it would be just the two of them. She wanted to write and draw and take pictures while they were there.

––––––––––

The thirtieth was only a few days away and everything was almost ready. Taylor thought they all needed a night out. There was a reggae band playing in Berkeley and he, Justin, and Dawn decided to go. He even took Selina. She seemed to have a great time. They made out in the car while Dawn and Justin were inside.

On Saturday, Taylor passed on the chance to go river rafting with his father and cousin Charney, who was visiting from out of town. He had been putting Gerry off for a while now. He had lost interest in the slower class-three river trips his father enjoyed; he would only do the hard-core classes four and five. Plus, Gerry always seemed to be asking questions, trying to find out what was going on and wondering what he planned to do with his life. He had not even seen his father more than two or three times so far that year, although they lived minutes away from each other.[9]

Charney had been hoping to see his favorite cousin, though, and called Taylor when they got back from the rafting trip that evening. Taylor was his usual upbeat self, but he told Charney he was busy and would be out of town the next day, so they would not be able to see each other.

Then Taylor reconsidered. He, Justin, and Dawn had settled in for the night with the board game Risk. He got on
the phone with his father. Why not? "Me and Justin and
Dawn are playing Risk right now. Come on over, Dad, and
play it," he said. And bring Charney, he added.

Gerry was so surprised at the invitation that he almost
fell out of his chair. He thought about it but decided he was
just too tired after a full day on the river to go. He went to
bed. It was July 29.

TEN

The Day the War Began

This was it. After all the planning, all the praying, all the preparation, July 30, 2000, was the day. Taylor, Justin, and Dawn got up that Sunday morning and wandered around the Saddlewood house. They came together, just as they had so many times before, to talk about Children of Thunder. Only this time, they went a step further and officially declared war on Satan.

They prayed and prayed. For her part, Dawn got to work. She packed the boss's briefcase with what they thought he would need for the day: handcuffs, a gun, a Taser stun gun, and a pair of gloves. She also threw in a pipe prepacked with meth and a pencil torch. She figured Taylor could use it to light the pipe when he needed a smoke. It also would come in handy if he needed to threaten anyone.[1]

Taylor figured it would be useful to have an alibi for later that day. He thought of everyone in his orbit and decided that Debra was the most practical choice to manufacture one for them. He knew she was flighty, but also that she was in enough awe of him to pull herself together and follow his instructions. What's more, she never asked questions.

He called her about ten o'clock and asked if she was interested in seeing the new X-Men movie that evening. Sure, she said. He phoned again a few minutes later and told her he wanted her to go to a specific theater in the nearby town of Pittsburg and buy four adult tickets for the 8:10 p.m. showing. She didn't have any money, however. "We'll drop it off," he said.

Dawn had other errands to run; while she was out, Taylor told her to take Debra a hundred-dollar bill for the tickets. He wanted to make sure she had enough money to get to the theater even if her car broke down or something else unexpected happened.

Debra was sunbathing at her apartment-complex pool when Dawn arrived. Her daughter was playing in the water, and she was chatting with neighbors. Dawn went straight up to her, looking decidedly out of place in a big reddish-purple shirt dress and stretch pants as she stood on the bright pool deck. Debra looked up at her.

"When will I see Taylor?"

"You won't," Dawn said. "Things have changed."[2]

Debra had wanted to spend time with Taylor, but she didn't question Dawn's dashing of her evening's plans. It wasn't unusual for Dawn, Justin, or Taylor to abruptly cancel or switch arrangements. She shrugged, and Dawn went upstairs to leave the money in Debra's apartment. They each told the other "I love you" as Dawn walked away.[3]

Dawn still had plenty of cash left for her other errands. She swung by an adult novelty store in the neighboring town of Pleasant Hill and picked up ninety-nine-dollar leg irons, then stopped at a liquor store, where she bought some cheap cigars and Merlot and a fifty-dollar bottle of Chateau Ste. Michelle wine.

The fancy wine was a prop, necessary to begin the action that evening. Taylor had to start things off by talking his way into the house of his target, an elderly man who used to be one of his brokerage clients. He thought an offer of celebration would do the trick. He planned to go to the door with the wine and a briefcase in hand and spin a story. "Hey, I'm with a new company. I just made a bunch of money. This bottle of wine was for a customer down the road that I was seeing, but they decided they didn't want it. Have a drink with me, let's celebrate, and I'll tell you all about it." It was a good line, Taylor thought, and it would work to get him and Justin in the door.

Before they put the plan in motion, however, Taylor needed to solidify things with Debra. He called her and made sure Dawn had dropped off the money, which was a lot more than she needed to buy four movie tickets.

"Well, I wanted to make sure you had enough money to get there," he said, trying to stress the importance of her task. "I mean, if you break down, I want you to take a taxi so that you can get there and get these tickets."

Then he said she also needed to buy four dinners, maybe at McDonald's. Then he paused.

"No. Forget that," he said. "Go wherever you want."

Just make sure to get the meals, he said. And keep the receipts.[4]

————

Children of Thunder left their Saddlewood headquarters in two separate cars as the sun slowly slid toward the western hills and the heat began to relent. Justin and Taylor were dressed in dark suits, with their hair carefully pulled back into ponytails. They had the briefcase and wine in Taylor's Saturn as they pulled up to a house in a quiet residential neighborhood. Dawn followed in Justin's truck and parked a short distance away.

The brothers got out and walked up to the door. They agreed they would be able to subdue up to five people; if there were more in the house, they would talk their way out and leave without implementing the plan. They knocked. Their adrenaline was flowing. Taylor was pumped full of false charm and stories, Justin was ready as backup.

And no one answered the door.

They knocked again. Then they walked around the house, calling out.

"Bob? Hey, Bob! Bob?"

But Bob White was not home. And Taylor was not happy. White was perfect—a single, elderly man who lived in an easily accessible section of Walnut Creek, the city next to Concord and a quick drive to the house on Saddlewood. He also had the assets that Children of Thunder needed, which Taylor knew because White had been a client at Dean Witter. The retired air-force pilot had once switched brokerage firms but returned at Taylor's urging, partly because he thought the stockbroker was a nice fellow.[5]

Now that nice fellow needed someone else to kidnap. He and Justin walked back toward Dawn as she sat in the truck. They would have to move on to target number two.

———

Debra and her daughter got into the car for the longish drive to the Pittsburg movie theater. There were several others much closer to their apartment, but Taylor had been specific. They got there just after seven o'clock, and as they stood in line, Debra started thinking. And getting nervous. The reason for her task was finally starting to pierce her usually impenetrable wall of obliviousness. Her friends were up to something. Maybe it had to do with the drugs. She knew she had always shrugged that off before; this time, though, she was uneasy.

They got to the front of the line and she purchased four

tickets for the 8:10 showing. Then she got two more, for the 7:20. She could not explain why she bought tickets for the earlier show, too. Perhaps it was an attempt to insulate her and her daughter from what she knew in her heart were the undeniably questionable intentions of her friends. But after buying the two extra tickets, Debra chickened out. Taylor had told her in no uncertain terms to attend the 8:10 showing. So she did.

Since Bob White was not cooperating, Taylor was forced to move to the next name on his list, a couple who also had been brokerage clients. Although his second choice, they actually presented a better set of circumstances than White had. Even older than White, they lived much closer to the Saddlewood house. And they had a relationship more friendly than professional with their former stockbroker, which would likely make it much easier for Taylor to talk his way inside. So Taylor and Justin got back in the Saturn and, followed by Dawn in the truck, made their way through the warm evening to the Concord home of Ivan and Annette Stineman.

When they reached Frayne Lane, Dawn parked on the corner so she could keep a lookout in all directions. It was a quiet area a few blocks off one of the city's main thoroughfares. Older, well-kept homes were bordered to the east by Lime Ridge, public parkland the July heat had cooked to a caramel-brown swath that loomed in sharp contrast to the watered greenery of the neighborhood's lawns and trees. Dawn lit a cigarette and looked around.

Justin and Taylor parked the Saturn and walked up the street. Taylor pulled about ten feet ahead of Justin, walking quickly and smoking, with his brow furrowed in thought. They stopped in front of the off-white two-story with a little balcony over the garage and shade trees in the front yard. He felt sure the Stinemans would let them in; after all, he had been their financial adviser for years and even socialized with them, taking them river rafting and showing off his daughter just after she was born. He hesitated only briefly and looked around. There was a car in the driveway. The Stinemans were home.

The war was starting.

Justin put his hand on his brother's back and nudged him toward the door. They went up the walk and knocked. The Stinemans opened the door and welcomed them inside.

Dawn sat and waited for what seemed like a very long time. She smoked, paid attention to the people driving by, and read her book. She was in the middle of *The Four Agreements: A Practical Guide to Personal Freedom,* a book by a Native American shaman outlining a code of personal conduct focused on dreams and visions. It had been highly recommended by Taylor, and no wonder. Its "agreements" dovetailed perfectly with his philosophies— the lack of absolute right or wrong, and a mandate to disregard outward perceptions.

Inside, the Helzers' visit had started with nice chitchat. The guests were unexpected, however, and Annette was a bit put out. When her daughter called about 8:30, she couldn't quite hide her annoyance. They had company, Annette told Nancy, so she couldn't talk. She'd have to call her back later.[6]

The "visit" continued for quite a while. Finally the gun came out. The brothers handcuffed the Stinemans at gunpoint and escorted them out to their own minivan.[7] Taylor called Dawn's cell phone to tell her they were coming out. A moment later, the minivan pulled up beside her. Dawn could see Taylor, as well as three other people silhouetted inside the van.

"I got it," Taylor said as he pulled the van alongside the truck.

"Okay," Dawn responded. "I'll be right behind you. I have to do something real quick."

She had noticed several people sitting on their front porch, watching her. She thought about what to do and decided that Spirit was guiding her to go talk to them. After the minivan pulled away, she got out of the truck and walked over to the house.

The couple who lived there and a friend had watched the woman in the truck for about an hour. It was hard not to notice a fidgety, nervous, chain-smoking, two-hundred-pound blond woman parked outside their house. She came over and explained that her friends had been down the street buying some weed and had asked her to keep a lookout. The explanation sounded completely off-key to the neighbors; theirs was not a street where such things happened.

The fidgety, nervous smoker got in the white pickup and drove off. She made the quick trip back to the Saddlewood house, parked outside, and went in the front door. Taylor had already pulled the minivan into the garage and lowered the door. He and Justin led the handcuffed Stinemans inside.

ELEVEN

The Point of No Return

───────────────●───────────────

Taylor and Justin led the Stinemans into the house and settled them on an old tan-colored couch in the living room.
The room was narrow, with one end opening into the
house's entryway and the other occupied by a small brick
fireplace. Although it had vaulted ceilings, the room's dark
blue carpet made it seem small and enclosed. Light came
from several cheap standing halogen lamps, the kind often found in college dorm rooms. A potted plant sat in the
corner.

Taylor told Ivan and Annette that he had things he
needed to do, and he would be back with them shortly. He
handed them the television remote, and he and Dawn left
the room. Justin remained, sitting silently in a nearby chair
with his handgun hidden behind it.

Back in the bedroom, Taylor showed Dawn the brokerage statements and Social Security cards he had taken from
the Stinemans' house. Now that they had the old couple
and their financial particulars, they could start collecting
money in earnest. Taylor paused. He knew the Stinemans

had daughters; they might get worried if they didn't hear from their parents. They'd have to ask their captives some questions. Dawn grabbed a piece of notebook paper and started scribbling: What are your top three vacation spots at least two hours north of here? Where do you go? What commitments do you have during the next three days, for yourself and for each other? How do you spell your daughter's name? What is her address and phone number? Do you own a cell phone? Do you have one in your purse? If you were going on vacation, would you call both of your daughters to let them know? Who would you call to say you were going on vacation for three days?

Satisfied that this would cover their bases, Taylor got Ivan and brought him back to his bedroom. Dawn took Annette into the den, and they each went through the list of questions. They brought the two back together in the living room after two rounds of interrogation. Taylor told them they needed to cancel a hair appointment for Annette and then let their daughter know they were going on a mini-vacation for a few days. The Stinemans—scared, unsure what would happen, and knowing Justin sat there with the gun—agreed.

Finally, Taylor gave his prisoners some sort of explanation for their situation. It wasn't the truth, but he thought it might keep them quiet and compliant. He had gotten into some trouble, he told them, and needed money to get out of the country. He would empty their retirement accounts and then leave. They would need to stay restrained in the house while he got away, he said. After three days, he would call and let someone know where they were.

Annette didn't like this at all. How were they supposed to eat or use the bathroom? Taylor had not expected resistance, even in the form of perfectly reasonable questions. He stalled Annette, saying he would try to figure something else out. In the meantime, they should get some sleep. He and Dawn hauled his mattress into the living room and had them lie down.

He now needed to think about how to get to the Dean Witter accounts. He did not want to be interrupted, but Debra was paging, and he knew she wouldn't stop until someone talked to her. And he did want to find out whether she had completed her mission. So he called her back.

"Did everything go okay?" he asked.

"Yes," Debra said, all set to launch into a recitation of her evening at the movies and dinner at Denny's.

"Good. Don't call back again," he said, and hung up the phone.

He turned his focus back to the money. There was no way he trusted the old couple to actually help liquidate their own assets. Dawn would have to do it over the phone by pretending to be Annette. He stayed up all night coaching her—what to say, what was in the accounts, how it all worked. Justin mostly just listened. All three took enough meth to stay awake until the sun rose. Then Taylor and Dawn headed out just after 6 a.m. and found a pay phone. Taylor knew the markets were already open on the East Coast and there would be someone on duty at Dean Witter. Dawn fed change into the phone and dialed the number.

She did her best old-lady impersonation as she explained to the brokerage manager that she had a family emergency and wanted to liquidate her entire portfolio. She made it sound urgent. "I've been up all night. I've got to catch a flight," she said hurriedly.

The manager, believing he actually was talking to Mrs. Stineman, tried to explain that cashing out hundreds of thousands of dollars in retirement funds would mean stiff early-withdrawal penalties. Dawn didn't want to hear it. Taylor was hanging on her every word and quickly getting impatient.

"Hurry, we have to go," he told her.

"Just take care of the trades. Liquidate the account. I have to go," she told the broker, and hung up the phone.[1]

The pair went back to the Saddlewood house and woke up the Stinemans. Taylor took Ivan out to make pay-phone calls canceling their appointments for the week. He warned the older man that Annette would be hurt if he didn't cooperate and kept a cell-phone connection open between him and Dawn while they were gone.

When they returned, Dawn asked if her captives wanted anything to eat. Neither one could summon much of an appetite by that point, although Ivan thought it wouldn't hurt to ask for some coffee. Dawn said sure, and ran down to Starbucks for drinks for him and herself.

Taylor began to panic. What if the broker at Dean Witter didn't buy Dawn's impression of Annette Stineman? What if the accounts weren't liquidated? They needed the cash, and they needed it now. What other ways did he have to get his hands on some? He thought of the ever-helpful Debra and picked up the phone.

Did she have a rich uncle or somebody from whom she could get $50,000? he asked. No, she said. But she did have a figurine, a nice piece of art she had inherited from her stepfather that she had been told was worth $30,000. She could see about selling it. Great, Taylor said. Do it. Debra called a San Francisco auction house and found out that the process of getting something appraised and then actually sold at auction could take months. That would not meet Taylor's needs at all.

But after Taylor and Dawn reviewed the numbers she'd gotten from the Dean Witter manager, he became more sure of their success. He called Debra back and told her to forget it. He hung up and turned to Dawn. It was time the Stinemans' real purpose came into play.

But Taylor started to get ahead of himself. Instead of immediately making Annette and Ivan start writing checks, he

decided to spin another tale first. He went out to the living
room and looked them in the eyes. He said he had decided
that Dawn would stay with them after he fled the country.
She would be there for two of the three days they had to
spend as hostages—but because she had to sleep, they
would need to take pills in order to sleep as well. He didn't
want them escaping while Dawn snoozed. And, now that he
thought about it, why not just get started and take a few
right now? He made Ivan and Annette each take six Rohypnol, a sedative known as a date-rape drug for its ability to
completely knock a person out.

Drugging the eighty-five-year-old man and his seventy-
eight-year-old wife was, essentially, the point of no return.
There was now no explaining away the extortion as a misunderstanding or the kidnapping as a friendly visit gone
wrong. All three Children of Thunder were in it, and they
were in it for good.

Taylor did not hesitate. He ordered that Annette be
shackled with leg irons and handcuffs in the kitchen. Then
he took Ivan back into his bedroom, waiting for the old
man to hobble down the hall. He handed Ivan his Dean
Witter checkbook and told him to make out a check to
Selina Bishop for $33,000. Ivan carefully wrote the name
he'd never heard before in block letters, filled in the
amount and signed it "I. L. Stineman."

Then Ivan, by this time certainly woozy, was shackled
to the kitchen chair. His wife was being led down the hallway. She kept nodding off, but Taylor needed her to write a
check. He hollered for Dawn to bring him the meth pipe
and lighter. He had Annette inhale from the pipe. It didn't
work. He took a hit and blew smoke in her face. That didn't
work, either. Finally, he managed to get her to make out a
check to Selina Bishop for $67,000. Even though she was
drugged, Annette's script was as elegant as always, the

only sign showing when her signature slipped a bit below the line as she tried to control her hand.

Her usefulness now finished, Annette was left in the bedroom. Taylor then got Justin, and together they carried Ivan into the bathroom. Then they retrieved Annette and lugged her in to lie beside her husband on the floor. Taylor knew what was coming. He ordered his brother and Dawn to strip down to their underwear. The less to clean up, the better.

Justin stared at the couple. This was God's work, he told himself. God wanted to transform America, and Taylor said this was the way to do it. You did not disobey God, and you certainly did not disobey Taylor. As he stood there in the stark white bathroom in only his underwear, he felt like a soldier—reluctant to kill, but bound by duty to do so.[2]

The Rohypnol was not doing the job. Dawn was monitoring the Stinemans' blood pressure with a blood pressure cuff as they lay on the bathroom floor, and it did not appear that the drug would be killing them anytime soon. Taylor got tired of waiting and put his hand over Annette's nose and mouth. She began to fight back. He ordered Dawn to get plastic sheeting out of the garage. They would use it to smother them. But that didn't work, either.

He was trying to be merciful, Taylor thought, but his victims would not lose consciousness.[3] He started banging Annette's head against the floor with such force that he cracked her skull. Justin quickly did the same to Ivan, but the brothers couldn't even knock them out. Both of their captives kept struggling, the thuds and scrapes of the fight bouncing off the walls of the little bathroom.

Taylor had had enough of this. These were old people, and they should be dead by now. He lifted Annette up and slung the upper half of her body over the bathtub. He grabbed Justin's hunting knife and slit her throat. But Annette would not give up. She continued to struggle against

him. Taylor picked her head up and held it so that instead
of pooling in the bathtub, the blood running out of her
throat flowed back down and into her lungs. She slowly
drowned, half suspended over the bathtub by her former
stockbroker.

Dawn stood motionless in the doorway. She couldn't believe this was actually happening. She just wanted them to
die, to have the whole thing done with. Justin was still beating Ivan's head against the floor. He was conscious and putting up a fight. Dawn came over and sat on him as Justin
kept pounding.[4] Soon after his wife went limp, Ivan stopped
moving. His eighty-five-year-old heart just couldn't take it
anymore. Justin stopped banging his head against the floor.
The room went quiet.

The three members of Children of Thunder caught their
breath and walked out of the bathroom. They had just done
God's work. The Lord had sanctioned their plan for world
peace and love, and the Stinemans had been willing to sacrifice their lives for the cause.

Even if they had put up a struggle.

———————

Taylor started thinking about the money again. He had an
idea he should have come up with a half hour before. He
would distract the police from his and his accomplices'
real purpose with a decoy check. Annette could write one
to Ivan, and it would be deposited in the couple's regular
savings account. Since Annette was now dead, he had
Dawn get a pen. Still stripped down to her bra and panties,
she wrote out a check for $10,000 without really attempt-
ing to disguise her own girlish handwriting. She also didn't
bother to look at the preprinted Stineman name on the
check itself—making it out to "Ivan Stinman" and signing
it "Annette L. Stinman."

Now she needed to go someplace farther away to deposit the money, in order to keep up the ruse for police. Taylor told her to get dressed and go to a branch of the Stinemans' bank in Petaluma, a town about fifty miles away across San Francisco Bay. He picked a lime-green pantsuit out of a selection of clothes she had bought earlier at a thrift store for just this purpose. And he told her to use the wheelchair; it would hide her height and make it more difficult to identify her. Dawn topped off the unflattering outfit with a straw cowboy hat, loaded the wheelchair into Taylor's Saturn, and drove off. Taylor and Justin turned back toward the bathroom. They had a lot of work to do.

Still practically naked, they set up the reciprocating saw in the bathroom and decided they would do Ivan first. They grabbed his right arm and worked at tearing it out by the socket. It was heavy, sloppy work and it took forever. Justin and Taylor looked at each other. There had to be a better way to do this. On the second arm, they decided to go for a straight amputation. Instead of pulling it out by the socket, they simply sawed through the bone.[5] Much better. Quicker, too, although the blood was everywhere. Justin held black trash bags open as Taylor put body parts inside.[6]

After Ivan, they started in on Annette. And they went a little further with her. Not only did they cut her in half, they removed her liver, intestines and a kidney. Then they dug into her chest cavity and took out her heart and lungs, neatly packaging them all in the trash bags.

Dawn finally pulled into the Petaluma bank and hefted herself out of the car. She got the wheelchair out of the back, climbed in, and wheeled herself inside, cowboy hat still perched on her head. She had no problems depositing "Annette L. Stinman's" forged $10,000 check and happily wheeled herself back out to the sunny parking lot.

On her way back to Saddlewood, Taylor called her cell

phone and told her to stop and pick up some firewood. He
wanted to burn evidence. She filled the backseat and trunk
with wood and drove home. Once she had unloaded it, she
went inside. Full, black garbage bags were neatly lined up
on clear plastic sheeting in the hallway. She glanced into
the bathroom. Justin was wiping down the countertop and
walls, but he couldn't get the blood to stop seeping out
from the seals around the faucets. They would need to be
replaced, so Dawn headed for the local hardware store,
again with a hundred-dollar bill in hand. She didn't bother
to use the wheelchair.

———————

The phone rang. It was Selina. Taylor did not have time to
talk to her, let alone see her. They still needed her for the
plan, though, so he hedged a little bit, putting her questions
about the camping trip off with vague assurances. He hung
up the phone and walked past the black bags in the hallway.
Selina hung up the phone and sighed. She'd just have to
figure out something else to do in the meantime.[7]

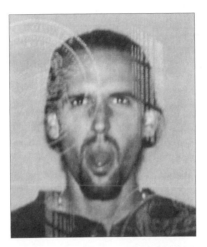

Taylor Helzer's driver's license photo, which police showed Selina Bishop's friends during their search for her. Several identified Taylor as the same person they knew as her mysterious boyfriend "Jordan."

TOP LEFT:
Jenny Villarin and daughter, Selina Bishop, snuggle in the late 1970s. Jenny soon split from Selina's father, blues guitarist Elvin Bishop, and the two set out on their own.
Courtesy of the Villarin family

BOTTOM RIGHT:
Jenny Villarin always placed family above all else. Here she proudly holds her niece's newborn daughter, Kiana, in 1999. Her many relatives could always count on her to remember birthdays and special occasions with cards and phone calls.
Courtesy of the Villarin family

ABOVE:
Selina Bishop, having fun in a fallen tree in 1999 while on an outing with her cousins. She loved nature and the giant redwoods that grew near her home in Marin County, California.
Courtesy of Olga Land

LEFT:
Jim Gamble poses in a field of flowers in the mid 1990s. He traveled to Pennsylvania in 1999 to help good friend Jenny Villarin move back to California.
Courtesy of Frances Nelson

Annette and Ivan Stineman
in 1945, while Ivan was
serving in the U.S. Coast
Guard. The two married
that year and would have
celebrated their fifty-fifth
wedding anniversary in
September 2000.
Courtesy of Nancy Hall

The Stinemans on a camp-
ing trip in the mid-1950s.
Annette, Ivan (back row),
a fellow camper, and their
daughters Nancy (center)
and Judy (right). The
family loved camping and
would always find a place
where Ivan could fish.
Courtesy of Nancy Hall

After retiring, Ivan and Annette Stineman loved to travel. They had timeshares in Hawaii, Mexico, and Walker River, California. This trip took them to Puerto Vallarta in the late 1980s.

Courtesy of Nancy Hall

The Stinemans combined their loves of travel and animals during this trip to Hawaii in 1997. Just three years later, their daughters would initially think they had gone on another trip when the two disappeared from their Concord home. Instead they were found murdered after being kidnapped as part of their former stockbroker's extortion scheme.

Courtesy of Nancy Hall

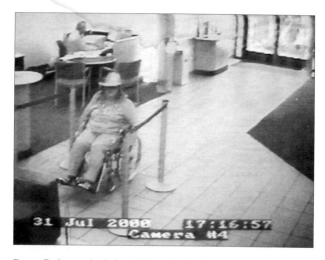

31 Jul 2000   17:16:57
Camera #4

Dawn Godman wheels herself into the Petaluma branch of the Stine-mans' bank on July 31, 2000. She will deposit a $10,000 check written from Annette Stineman to Ivan Stineman as a test to see if the extortion scheme she and the Helzer brothers were committing would work. Taylor chose her outfit and had her use the wheelchair, saying that appearing eccentric would make her less conspicuous while committing the crime.

Dawn Godman was arrested August 7, 2000, and booked into the Concord Police Department jail.
Courtesy of the Concord Police Department

Justin Helzer was arrested August 7, 2000, and booked into the Concord Police Department jail.
Courtesy of the Concord Police Department

Taylor Helzer was arrested August 7, 2000, and booked into the Concord Police Department jail.
Courtesy of the Concord Police Department

Justin Helzer (left) and Glenn Taylor Helzer are led into Contra Costa County Superior Court in Martinez, California, for the start of their preliminary hearing December 3, 2001.
Bob Larson / Contra Costa Times

TWELVE

Logistics

———◆———

Dawn was back in costume. She had the lime-green outfit and the cowboy hat on again. Her hair was in pigtails this time and she'd added a pair of big sunglasses. She squeezed herself into the wheelchair and rolled into the Walnut Creek branch of Selina's bank, not noticing that she was not using the handicap entrance.

Since the previous day's trial run had gone so well, Taylor had decided to continue using Dawn instead of bothering to have Selina deposit the checks. The two had prepared for what they thought was every contingency. The story would be that Selina needed surgery and had no insurance. The Stinemans were her grandparents and were going to pay for the operation, which was why their checks needed to be deposited in Selina's account as quickly as possible. Dawn was just a friend running the errand for them.

As was her habit, Dawn had taken notes as they went over things, this time typing up a list of responses to possible concerns the bank people might have about her bogus transaction.

"[Ivan] never goes out of the house, and frankly I'm more mobile in my chair than they are. I don't know him very well, Selina is one of my closest friends and I have a good relationship with Annette."

"I didn't that think I would have to remember the name of the hospital and the only way I have of getting the message to Annette and Selina that you want to talk to all three of them before you can do this is through Ivan."

With her script fresh in her head, Dawn rolled up to a teller and asked for the bank manager. She was shown over to a woman named Vicki Sexton and introduced herself as Jackie. Dawn told her tale about the operation, throwing in that it was open-heart surgery—more serious-sounding—and that Selina needed the funds right away. She handed over the two checks the Stinemans had signed.

Sexton looked at the two checks that totaled $100,000. This woman with a raspy voice and very bad taste in clothing was quite odd, but if the story was legit, she certainly wanted to help expedite things. But it was a lot of money. She reached for the phone and dialed the number preprinted on the $33,000 check.

Dawn watched her in horror. They had rented a pager and had recorded a message on it that was supposed to be from the Stinemans. That was the number the bank manager was supposed to call, not the one to the Stinemans' actual house. She had not thought the woman would do that.

"Hello. This is the Stineman residence. We are unable to come to the phone right now, but if you will leave your name and number at the sound of the beep, we'll get back to you as soon as possible." Perfectly ordinary greeting in an elderly man's voice, Sexton thought. She left a message.

"Hi, this is Vicki at Cal Fed bank, and if you could give me a call as soon as possible," Sexton said, listing her phone number. "I'll be here until five-thirty and I'll be here all day tomorrow, so I look forward to hearing from you."

Dawn tried to think fast. "Oh," she said, trying to sound casual. "The Stinemans have moved, and they have a new number." She rattled off the number, and Sexton wrote it down on the check and dialed. This time, it was a younger-sounding male voice saying pretty much the same thing as the first greeting. Sexton left the same message and then called Dean Witter to see if there were sufficient funds in the Stinemans' brokerage accounts to cover the checks. She was told that Dean Witter needed the Stinemans' Social Security numbers in order to give her that information. She looked at the woman in the wheelchair expectantly.

For all her careful preparation, Dawn hadn't anticipated this, either. She didn't have the numbers with her. She would have the Stinemans call Sexton with the information, she said. Sexton said that was fine; she would put a hold on the deposit until she got the numbers and spoke directly with the Stinemans. Dawn said she understood and then quickly wheeled herself out of the bank before anything else could go wrong. Sexton watched her go. That's funny, she thought. The woman didn't use the handicap entrance.[1]

Dawn wheeled out to the parking lot. She was not looking forward to telling Taylor what had happened at the bank, but she knew she had to admit her mistake with the phone numbers. Taylor was not at all pleased. Now he would have to clean up her mess. She suggested they get the answering-machine tape from the Stinemans' house. Taylor drove there—rather cavalierly—in the Stinemans' own van. Dawn met him and waited while he went inside and stole the tape with Sexton's message on it.

Justin, who had not found it necessary to disguise himself in ridiculous clothing, was also completing important elements of the plan. He needed to get his truck ready to haul the Jet Skis they intended to use to dump the bodies. He took it to Pep Boys auto service and bought a chrome trailer hitch that would haul 3,500 pounds. It was going to take a while to install, so he called a cab to take him back home.

He couldn't believe it when the taxi pulled up. Of all the unlucky coincidences, he knew the guy behind the wheel. They had served together in Germany, and now he wanted to talk all the way home. That's all Justin needed, someone who would remember him later. Finally, they arrived back at Saddlewood Court. Justin tried to pay with one of the trio's ubiquitous hundred-dollar bills, but his army buddy couldn't make change. Justin ran inside and found enough cash to pay and tip the guy and get him on his way.[2]

The trailer-hitch installation took forever. Justin got more and more frantic because it had to be on the truck before he could get the additional insurance coverage the Jet Ski rental shop had demanded. And the insurance agency closed at 7 p.m. Finally, they finished, and Justin paid the bill with only ten minutes to spare.

He and Taylor got to the insurance agency just before the agent was scheduled to leave for the day. The agent took a Polaroid of the truck and then set about completing the paperwork. Justin and Taylor took the opportunity to try out their story, chatting in front of the man about a camping trip they planned to take with the watercraft. The agent finished the paperwork and gave Justin proof to show the rental company. Justin made a quick cell-phone call to say he was on his way and left. Dawn was waiting.

After renting a Yamaha WaveRunner that would suit their purposes nicely—it could carry 350 pounds—Justin and Dawn headed home. They walked in with food from Burger King and found Taylor already there; he had hitched a ride home with the insurance agent. All three sat down to eat.

Taylor was still worried about the money situation. From what Dawn had said about her trip to the bank, the manager did not sound very cooperative. They might not be able to get the cash at all. Dawn had already called the branch and left a message with the Stinemans' Social Security numbers. But they needed to do more, Taylor said. Dawn must leave an outgoing message on the pager in her old-woman voice. Make it sound like Ivan and Annette were busy and the message got cut off in the middle of the recording. That would suggest urgency and help convince the hesitant bank manager the transaction was legitimate, Taylor said. Dawn wrote it down: "Hi. This message is for Cal Fed . . . Okay, hon, I'll do it later. I'll be right there."

Even if they were not going to be able to get the money out of her account, Taylor knew he still needed to keep track of Selina. He gave her a call. Something had come up and he couldn't come see her tonight, he said. But it should all be taken care of soon, and they would get to spend time together. She suggested a trip to Great America, but Taylor said no. He had something better planned.[3]

They both hung up pleased. Selina hoped that whatever it was, she would have a nice time. And Taylor was reassured that he still had her on the hook, at least for long enough to finish her part in the plan.   •

———————

Vicki Sexton arrived at work Wednesday morning to find a message on her desk with the Stinemans' Social Security numbers. The note said Mrs. Stineman had called about 6 p.m. Tuesday with the information. She checked, and the funds had cleared and would be available in Selina Bishop's account whenever Vicki decided to remove the hold. But she didn't want to do that just yet. Something about this whole thing was strange. She tried to reach the Stinemans again, first through the number "Jackie" had

given her. The recorded message from the day before was
gone; instead she got some weird recording that sounded
like it had gotten cut off. She left a message, then decided
to try the number printed on the check again.

"Mr. Stineman, this is Vicki at Cal Fed Bank. If you
could please give me a call today, I'd greatly appreciate it."

But she didn't hear from Ivan Stineman. Instead,
"Jackie" called and inquired about the status of the money.
The funds were available, Sexton said, but she still needed
to talk directly to the Stinemans before she could release
the hold.

Dawn said she understood and hung up the phone. This
was not good at all. The Stinemans obviously were not going to be talking to anybody. Children of Thunder were not
going to be able to get the money. They had to cover their
tracks and fast. Taylor had to meet Selina quickly and get
her back to the Saddlewood house. All three agreed that
she would not be allowed to leave.

———

Keri called and wanted to chitchat with Taylor. The issue
of *Playboy* with her as the centerfold was hitting news-
stands, and she was excited about all the possibilities that
could result from it. The ten-page spread showcased all of
her best assets, including her long blond hair and pouty
lips, and the new breasts Taylor had talked her into getting.
Using the nom de bunny Kerissa Fare, she told readers she
liked to take risks and try new things. She enjoyed roller
skating and Jet Skiing. Her professional ambition was a
career in the entertainment industry, and her personal ambition was "to be in the moment." It was a philosophy Harmony would certainly endorse, and she credited the
program with changing her life. "I became a woman after
that course," she told *Playboy*. "I got in touch with myself
and my femininity."[4]

She also told the magazine she had grown up having to do things for herself and now valued her independence. Taylor had already figured that one out and was not in the mood to congratulate his ex-girlfriend on her newfound self-reliance and career achievement. He was busy, but he wouldn't tell her what he was doing. The conversation descended into a fight. He told her not to call him again unless she was hurt or dying and then hung up the phone.

———

He was running late, as usual. Selina sat at a table at the Bison Brewing Company and waited. The Berkeley brew pub was one of her and Taylor's favorite meeting spots, in between her Woodacre apartment and his house in Concord. They would typically find some quiet corner to cuddle and have a few beers. But tonight, Selina kept waiting and waiting. She was certainly used to his tardiness, but this was pushing it. She walked up to the bar and asked for change. Bartender Matthew King smiled knowingly.

"Why am I waiting for him so long?" she said, rolling her eyes. "I don't know why I go out with him."

She walked over to the pay phone and made a call, then sat back down. Finally, about 7 p.m., Taylor appeared. He sat down and chilled with Selina for about a half hour before saying it was time to go. Follow me back to my house, he said. Selina readily agreed.

Dawn greeted Taylor's girlfriend when she arrived. Selina was happy to be there, and the trio wanted to keep it that way for now. In the last few days, the brothers and their friend had come up with a better killing technique. After unsuccessfully pounding the Stinemans' heads against the bathroom floor, they decided that far more forceful blows were necessary to successfully bludgeon someone to death. This time Justin would use a hammer. And he would attack Selina from behind, an important point for him. He had been shaken by having to look Ivan in the eye as he was killing him. He decided he wanted a bit more distance between himself and his next victim. It would be easier for him if he could sneak up on her.[5]

Dawn made small talk, mentioning to Selina that they were thinking about remodeling the bathroom. Would she take a look and tell them what she thought? The two women went into the now-clean bathroom. It was still stripped down, with nothing on the walls or counters. Dawn pointed to various things as Justin loitered just outside with the hammer, but Selina never turned her back.

Eventually the remodeling conversation ran its course, and Dawn was forced to show Selina back into the living room. They sat down and started smoking some pot with Taylor. Out of Selina's earshot, they revised their plan. Taylor would suggest that he and Selina take a shower and then a nap. Once she was asleep, Dawn and Justin would creep into the bedroom. Dawn would throw a towel over Selina's head and Justin would hit her with the hammer.

Taylor made his suggestion, and the two headed back to the bathroom. Even though Taylor had his own shower next to the master bedroom, he wanted to use the hall bathroom, the same one in which they had killed the Stinemans. It didn't have a shower curtain, but that was okay, he reassured Selina. They showered and went to bed. A half hour later, Taylor came out. Selina wasn't tired and wouldn't go to sleep, he said, sighing. So all four of them went back to the living room and smoked some more pot. They broke open the Risk board game and a bottle of wine. Taylor and Dawn slipped back to Dawn's room, where she had crushed up several Rohypnol pills. They added them to Selina's wine in the hope that if they gave her enough, she would just go to sleep and never wake up.

Selina took the glass, but quickly noticed the powder floating in it. Taylor snatched it away.

"Oh, there's something dirty in it," he said. "I'll get you a clean glass."

They kicked back for a while longer, but without the Rohypnol-laced wine, everyone knew it was back to the hammer plan. Taylor said he was going to give Selina a back rub. He told Dawn to go to bed. She obeyed, but got up a half hour later, saying she couldn't sleep. Essentially, however, she was declining the opportunity to miss this killing. She'd already witnessed two murders. What was one more? She went into the family room, where Justin and Taylor were spreading blankets on the floor. Selina lay down, and Taylor began rubbing her back. Justin took hold of the hammer and came up behind her. He made sure he had a firm grip and brought it down on the back of her head.

Taylor watched, thinking that this was not at all like the movies[6]—Selina had survived the blow and was still conscious. She cried out and brought her left hand up to shield herself. But Justin didn't stop. He struck again and again, breaking her hand and shattering her skull.[7] She didn't speak again.

Justin and Taylor used the blanket to carry Selina into the kitchen, a trail of blood left in their wake. Taylor told Dawn to start cleaning it up. He and Justin had work to do. They took a sawhorse, an extension cord, and the saw into the bathroom.

Dawn got down on her hands and knees and tried to clean the blood out of the carpet. She heard noises coming from the kitchen—from Selina. Still on her knees, Dawn started praying. "Just let her die, so she won't suffer anymore," she thought. Then Taylor returned to the kitchen and saw his girlfriend's leg twitching. That was too much movement to be just residual nerve reactions, he thought. He picked up the hammer and hit her again.[8]

But Selina's leg would not stop moving. He called

Justin out of the bathroom to help roll her up in the blanket.
They carried her into the bathroom. Dawn stayed rooted to
the carpet. Taylor had seen her look of fear. He needed to
impress upon her once again the importance of their mission. He'd had enough of this I-can't-believe-this-is-really-
happening crap. He called her into the bathroom.

Selina was in the bathtub, which was full of water. He
stood over her in his underwear. He reached down, pulled
her hair back, and looked pointedly at Dawn.

"Spirit says you get to know this isn't a dream," he said.
And then he slit Selina's throat.[9] The only sound in the
bathroom was the air hissing out of her windpipe. He
pushed her under the water.[10] Her dark hair rose in a wa-
tery cloud around her face as the hissing slowly stopped.

THIRTEEN

No One Will Tell

━━━━━━◆━━━━━━

It was reality, all right. Taylor turned to the task at hand, hoisting Selina's body onto the sawhorse. Justin helped as Dawn fled back to the family room to finish cleaning the carpet. The saw revved to life. But its roar could not mask the sound of limbs hitting the bottom of the bathtub. The loud, hollow thunks reverberated through the house.

When they were done, they put the bags in the hallway recently vacated by the bags containing the Stinemans' bodies, which had been moved into Justin's room. Justin dropped Selina's car off at a store parking lot and took a cab back to Saddlewood Court. Then for the second time that week, he cleaned the blood-drenched bathroom and went to bed.

Taylor and Dawn stayed up to burn evidence. The fire was the only light in the room as he pulled Selina's clothes out of a bag and fed them to the flames. Then he fished out a piece of flesh and dangled it from the tip of his finger. He had been interested for some time in what exactly his dogs would eat. Now was the perfect opportunity to find out. He

called Jake the rottweiler over and showed him the tattoo
he had cut from Selina's shoulder. He coaxed the dog to eat
the piece of skin as Dawn watched.[1]

As he reviewed his plan and how close he was to getting
away with it, Taylor realized that there were still people out
there who could identify him, who could link him with the
woman he had just cut into pieces. Selina's mom knew
what he looked like, he told Dawn. The nosy woman had
stopped by unannounced at Selina's apartment a couple
weeks before and seen him. And there was some friend of
Selina's whom she worked with at the café who had seen
him, too. The friend would have to wait, but he knew
where Jenny Villarin was that night.

She was staying at Selina's apartment while her daughter was supposedly off camping at Yosemite. Taylor could
take care of her now. They would drive over to Marin and
kill her. He jumped up and ran in to wake his brother. He
said Justin needed to go back to Selina's car and get her
address book, just in case Jenny Villarin was not at Selina's
apartment and they needed to know where she lived. Taylor did not want to travel all the way across the bay and not
be able to kill his witness. He ordered Justin to call him
and Dawn with the information.

Taylor dressed all in black; after all, it was a nighttime
raid. He tossed a change of clothes in the back of his Saturn as part of his alibi. If he and Dawn got stopped by police, he planned to say they were headed to the beach. Then
he grabbed his key to Selina's apartment, a .22 he had gotten from former roommate Brandon Davids, and Justin's
Beretta and climbed in the car. Dawn slid into the passenger seat.

She carefully wiped the bullets free of fingerprints and
loaded the guns as Taylor steered toward Marin County. It
was after 4 a.m., and there was no traffic as they sped across
San Francisco Bay. Few streetlights bothered them as they

made their way into the rural San Geronimo Valley and the
tiny town of Woodacre. Taylor wound the car through a
maze of residential streets and found the house with the
little basement studio apartment. He pulled over, tires
crunching on the gravel turnout. He took the freshly loaded
guns from Dawn and walked up the hill.

———

Earlier that day, Jim Gamble had been unable to make up
his mind. He had spent Wednesday morning choosing
which day trips he wanted to take during his upcoming Eu-
ropean cruise. He and his mother were leaving exactly one
month from tomorrow, and they had needed to get their
itinerary set. Now that was done and a free afternoon
stretched in front of him. Should he go see Jenny? There
were other things he could be doing—should be doing—
but it would be fun to go hang out at the Paper Mill, maybe
see Gloria, too.

He waffled for a bit, then finally decided. What the
heck, he'd go down to Marin. He told his mother good-bye
and headed out the door.[2] When he got there, he met up
with Gloria for dinner at Rancho Nicasio, a cozy restaurant
and bar with a high beamed ceiling, big brick fireplace, and
hunting trophies adorning the walls. They sat at the bar and
talked about the other cruise Jim was planning. He, Gloria,
and Jenny wanted to go to Mexico, and they had almost decided what reservations they needed to make. They called
Jenny—who was working her usual shift at the Paper Mill
Creek Saloon—and asked if she wanted dinner. She did, so
Jim got her a meal and headed down to the valley to see
her.[3]

He enjoyed himself at the Paper Mill while Jenny ate
and served drinks. A couple of friends talked about going
over to Selina's place with her and Jim, just to hang out for
a bit. As the conversation wound down around her, Jenny

jotted a note to the bar's owner, Thomasina Wilson. She
left such messages on the nights she worked so her boss
would find them in the morning and know how everything
had gone the night before. She wrote that she would be a
little late on Thursday because of the canning class she was
teaching the kids at the nearby summer camp. Then she
served a last drink to one of her regulars and closed the
bar.[4]

Her friends decided they would go home instead of
coming over to Selina's, so Jenny and Jim headed up the
hill to the apartment alone.

————

Taylor crept through the quiet garage with Justin's Beretta
ready in his hand and pushed open the apartment door.
Shit. There was a guy there. There wasn't supposed to be a
guy there. He started firing. The guy leaped out of bed and
put up his arm. Taylor kept shooting, hitting him in the
neck, the leg, the arm, the chest. Then he turned to Jenny.
Two bullets in the face and she fell back in the bed. Taylor
backed up as the man collapsed on the floor, gasping for
breath through a windpipe just torn apart by a bullet.[5]

Taylor sprinted down the hill and jumped into the car,
excited and out of breath. Dawn had already started the engine and took off as soon as he was inside. As they headed
east, Taylor began to calm down. It occurred to him that
Justin had never called with the address of Selina's mom's
house. Turned out they had not needed it, but that was not
the point. Justin was not following orders. They tried calling the house, but Justin did not answer.

When they got home, Taylor woke up Justin.

"Why didn't you go to the car like I told you?" he yelled.
"Why didn't you do what I asked you to do? Why didn't
you call us?"

He had been asleep, Justin said wearily. Taylor fumed.

But the sun was coming up. It was a new day, and they had plenty to do. Taylor sent his lazy brother and Dawn to Denny's for food. They came back with three breakfasts, and Children of Thunder sat down to eat.

FOURTEEN

The Cleanup

—————◆—————

After breakfast, Taylor took stock of the situation. Everyone who needed to be dead—at this point in the plan at least—had been taken care of. Things were moving along nicely. But they did have more work to do. They needed to make it more difficult to identify who was in the duffel bags in Justin's room before dumping them in the Delta.

Taylor told Dawn and Justin to remove the victims' teeth so police could not trace their dental records. He left Justin digging through the bags in search of the three heads and went out to the backyard. It was a clear day, still early enough to be pleasant before the midday sun baked everything to one hundred degrees. He sat down in a rocking chair in the middle of the dirt and weeds and stared off into space.

Justin found the heads and took them into the bathroom. Dawn did not think about what she was doing as she wedged herself into the tiny space and tried to keep each head steady so Justin could successfully knock out the teeth. Justin used a chisel—and the same hammer he had used to kill Selina.

It took about half an hour to dismantle all three jaws. Justin took the heads to his room and shoved them back in the duffel bags. Then he and Dawn put all the pieces of teeth and fractured jawbones into a separate plastic bag and put the bag into the duffel bag that held Annette's legs and left arm. They zipped it up and left it with the others.

Dawn, still not dwelling on what she had done to the bodies, walked out front and backed the truck into the driveway. Taylor and Justin tossed all nine bags into the back and attached the trailer. Then all three piled into the cab and pulled out.

They drove through the rolling, bleached grass hills of eastern Contra Costa County and crossed the Antioch Bridge. They were in Sacramento Delta country, and although the area was widely used for recreation, not many people lived on the isolated little islands and inlets. Children of Thunder felt sure they could find a nice, secluded spot to dump their cargo.

One of the brothers had been out this way before and remembered a boat launch that would suit their purposes. They pulled into Korth's Pirates Lair, a quiet marina lined with palms and shade trees that sat where the San Joaquin and Mokelumne rivers met, and paid owner Kip Korth five bucks to launch the WaveRunner. The ramp was so steep, Dawn couldn't get the truck's manual transmission in gear to drive out. Taylor, who had been about to get on the watercraft, had to stop and take the wheel. Even he couldn't get the Nissan up the hill without smoking the clutch. Finally, he turned the truck back over to Dawn, and he and Justin chugged away on the WaveRunner.

The acrid odor of burning clutch filled Dawn's nose as she pulled away from the marina, but it was better than the

smell coming from the bags still in back. Taylor had told
her to meet them at the first open spot down the road. She
drove for several minutes looking for the most accessible
place to get the gym bags down to the water. Once she
found a spot, she parked and walked down the bank so they
could see her from the river.

Justin got off the WaveRunner and climbed up the bank.
He reached for two bags. Dawn stopped him. She remembered a few things from her time as a nurse's assistant, and
one of them was that dead bodies release gas, which tends
to make them float. They needed holes in the bags to let the
gases escape, she told Justin. He obliged, pulling out a
knife and sinking it into each bag several times. He carried
the bags down to the water and loaded them onto the Wave-
Runner. Taylor turned and headed with Justin toward open
water. Dawn watched them go as the sun glinted off the
craft's bright blue-and-yellow paint and caught the cheery
"Rent Me" slogan on the side. They just looked like a couple of guys out for some midweek water fun. She settled
herself on the bank and opened up her copy of *The Four
Agreements*.

The brothers came back and repeated the process twice
more. As they were loading bags five and six, someone
from the marina came by and told Dawn she could not sit
there. Taylor told her to drive down the road, and they
would find her after they got rid of their current load. It
took them about forty-five minutes to drop the bags and
then find Dawn, who had parked farther away from the Pirates Lair.

After dumping eight of the nine bags, Taylor said he
was tired and needed a break. He told them he would take
the truck and meet them at the marina, so Dawn climbed
on with the last bag, and she and Justin motored off down
the river. She drove for about half an hour before stopping
to let Justin drop the bag over the side. It floated for several

minutes. Dawn calmly drove in circles around the bag until it disappeared, then she steered the WaveRunner back to the marina, and to Taylor.

The three loaded the WaveRunner on the trailer and hit the road, stopping briefly so Dawn could use the bathroom at a nearby bar. And since they were there anyway, she and Taylor decided to each do a quick shot of tequila. Justin, as usual, declined. He did want to eat, though, so a little later, they stopped again and had an early dinner. By the time they got back to Saddlewood, the sun was beginning to set.

———————

David Villarin answered the phone. It was his kid sister's best friend.

"What's the matter, honey?" David asked her.

"You don't know?" Gloria said, shocked that police had not called him.

"Know what, honey?" he said.

"Jenny's dead."[1]

David stared at the phone. He would not believe the news until he talked to someone official. He found the number for the Marin County Sheriff's Office and dialed. The people at the other end of the line wanted to know who he was, where he lived, what he wanted. He explained, again and again. After a half hour of being transferred around the department, he finally got someone to confirm that his little sister was officially a homicide victim.[2]

He put down the phone and then picked it up again. Everyone else needed to know. He sighed, then began trying to reach his sprawling family with the news.

He called his sister Lydia, the one closest in age to Jenny.

"Are you sitting down?" he asked. Lydia thought this was ridiculous. She was up and about, fixing dinner, but then she had a feeling. She sat down.

"Jenny got shot."

"No, she didn't. Come on, what's going on?" she said.

"Jenny got shot, Jenny was shot," he repeated.

"Why?"

"I don't know," David said, frustrated that he did not have more information.

Lydia stood up, ready to drive immediately from her Lake Tahoe home to Marin County. But then she broke down. Dinner forgotten, her roommates talked her into waiting until morning before making the trip.[3]

Across California in the Santa Cruz Mountains near the Pacific Ocean, Olga's loved ones convinced her of the same thing. Too distraught to drive after David's call, she took a friend's sedative and advice not to go to Marin County until the next morning.

David kept dialing. He reached his sister Yolanda in Texas. He got in touch with his brother Robert, and called his nieces Melissa and Lusha, two of the family's other dark-haired beauties, who were close in age to Selina.

Melissa started crying and screamed to her sister that Aunt Jenny was dead, murdered.

"What happened? Where's she at?" Lusha demanded of her uncle. "And where's Selina? Because Selina's going to freak."

The girls knew Selina was supposed to be camping with her boyfriend in Yosemite. David passed on this piece of information when sheriff's officials called him back to ask if he knew where Selina was. Lusha and Melissa immediately started paging Selina, calling the number over and over. She did not call back.

————

It had been such a busy week, Taylor had not had a chance to prepare for a commitment he had made months before. He was supposed to leave within hours for Reggae on the

River, a popular annual music festival five hours away in far Northern California. He called his friends Alex and Jessyka Chompff and told them he was going to be late, but not to leave without him. They were not surprised. They had known Taylor for five years and were well aware of how flaky and unreliable he could be. That was why they had planned for him to come to their house hours before they wanted to leave so they would not be stuck tracking him down as they drove out of town at the crack of dawn Friday.

Taylor arrived at the Chompffs' about 12:30 a.m. with a kind of uncomfortable, almost jangly energy Jessyka thought was unusual. She sent him upstairs to take a nap in the guest bedroom while they finished packing the camping gear they would need. They roused him a little before 5 a.m. and started the drive.

It was midnight, and Fran Nelson was in bed. The seventy-five-year-old hadn't locked her doors—she never did—and she was awakened by a light coming on.

"Jim?" she called.

"No, it's Larry," said her other son.

Fran had been expecting Jim. He had not shown up for a scheduled bridge game earlier Thursday, which was not like him. Now her other son was standing in her bedroom. He had driven through the night, more than two hours from his home in a small mountain town to tell her something that needed to be said in person.

Jim was dead. He had been shot, along with Jenny, over in Marin County. Fran was stunned. Then, to postpone the pain, her mind focused on the practical. What on earth was she going to do with the out-of-town guests she was expecting tomorrow? she thought, before succumbing to the grief.

———

Prior to leaving for his party weekend, Taylor gave Justin and Dawn a list of things to do: clean the house, dump the Stinemans' van and Selina's car, and get rid of all the evidence still in their possession. The two set to work. Justin wiped down the van for prints and then followed Dawn in the truck as she drove it to a bad neighborhood in Oakland. She left the keys in the ignition, hoping someone would steal it and sell it for parts. Then she got into Justin's truck, and they headed back to Saddlewood, tossing the Stinemans' credit cards out the window as they drove.

Early the next morning, Justin called and canceled the chiropractic appointments all three had that afternoon at a local clinic. They were going to be busy with other things that day. Dawn started loading the truck with everything they needed to trash. There was the bag of ashes from the fireplace, and the two suitcases Taylor had made the Stinemans pack with changes of clothes they had not needed. There was also the reciprocating saw Justin and Taylor used on the bodies and a Skil saw Taylor used to cut up the sawhorses, which were soaked in blood as well. Dawn cruised around Concord, stopping at random trash bins hidden away behind businesses, tossing the evidence as she went along.

Justin took the truck and returned the WaveRunner. They were getting a lot accomplished, but they still had one major errand to run. Selina's car was sitting in the parking lot of a nearby shopping center, way too close for comfort. They picked it up, and Dawn drove it back to the house, with Justin following in the truck. She parked it in the garage, and he wiped it down for fingerprints. Then they headed for Petaluma, where Taylor had decided they should plant the car. He also had given Dawn a rather peculiar instruction. He wanted her to leave Ivan Stineman's wedding ring in Selina's Honda. It would throw the cops off their trail by making them think the old man had run off with Selina. That didn't make a lot of sense to Dawn, but she shrugged off her doubts and took it with her anyway. She parked in a spot downtown, near the bus station, and left the keys in the car—and Ivan's simple gold ring in plain view on the passenger-side floorboard.

———

Both Olga and Lydia left their homes in such a hurry that when they got to Marin County, they realized they had not packed properly. Olga had tossed pants, shoes, and socks into a bag, but had not brought a single shirt. She had floss and toothpaste, but no toothbrush. The sisters headed to Target, where they roamed the aisles without really thinking about their shopping.

Lydia noticed some children staring at her. They would look, then run off down the aisle, only to return and stare some more. Finally, they got their mother, who gasped at Lydia's high cheekbones and sheet of long, dark hair and said, "You look just like somebody we know."

Lydia had heard that all her life. "You must mean Jenny," she said. All three women burst into tears.

The sisters headed back to Gloria's house, and other relatives started to arrive. Selina had missed her waitressing shift that morning at the Two Bird and everyone was extremely worried. They began searching everywhere they could think of, but there was no sign of her.

———

Taylor and the Chompffs got to Eel River around noon. Jessyka and Alex drove their Nissan 4×4 up close to the rocky banks of the river to find a good spot. Taylor and Jamie, another friend, parked Taylor's Saturn and hiked in to join them. They all began to set up camp.

Jessyka and Alex were looking forward to a fun weekend

of listening to thirty different reggae bands, splashing around in the river, and kicking back with good pot and like-minded people. But things did not start out that way. Taylor, still full of twitchy energy, was not satisfied with their eight-foot-square campsite and started to get picky about which way the tent should face. He and Alex kept moving it from spot to spot, while Jessyka and Jamie sat and watched. The two started rolling their eyes at each other.

"This is stupid," Jessyka said. "It doesn't matter which way the tent is facing."

Taylor turned around angrily. "This is not about you," he spat. "This is not about you. This doesn't concern you. Stay out of it."

"Yeah, it does matter," Jessyka shot back. "We're sick of it. We want to unpack. We want to have fun."

"Nobody else cares," Taylor said.

"Everyone else cares, but no one else is saying anything," said Jessyka, who was getting tired of sitting in the hot sun. She told Taylor that Alex would stop the silly tent moving whenever she told him to, so they needed to get on with it. Taylor was quiet for a bit. But then he turned and started yelling at her. She told him to shut up. There were people pitching their own tents close by, and she was getting a little embarrassed by his angry behavior.

"Stop being a tweaker, and let's just get this over with," she said.

Taylor took exception and asked Alex if he really was acting like a tweaker, just coming down off a meth high. "Yeah, you are," Alex said, backing his wife. He hauled his friend back to the car in an effort just to get away from the tent setup, but Taylor would not relax.

"I don't appreciate your attempt to control what's acceptable for me in my camping area," Taylor said.

This was ridiculous, Alex thought. Taylor was blowing

this whole thing way out of proportion, which wasn't like him. The guy was seriously agitated, unwilling to listen to anybody, and bizarrely confrontational. He also was rail thin and obviously had not had a good meal or a good night's sleep in days. What was his problem?

———

Dawn finally finished her tasks for the day and wanted to relax. She went to Debra's place in the early evening as the heat of the day was just starting to subside. They sat in Debra's messy living room and played canasta until Dawn announced that she had a craving for an Applebee's Mudslide. Debra said sure, as long as Dawn was buying, so they grabbed Debra's daughter, drove a couple of miles down the road, and found seats among the Friday-night crowd.

They got back to Debra's apartment after 10 p.m., and an exhausted Dawn headed straight home. She was coming down off the meth high that had kept her awake for days. Now the plan was mostly complete, and she fell into a deep sleep. She had done what she was supposed to do for Taylor. No dreams tickled her conscience as she slept.

———

When Justin and Dawn woke up Saturday morning, they tackled the carpets. They had borrowed a carpet-cleaning machine from Debra that they thought would get rid of the bloodstains. But the stupid machine only soaked everything with water, which created a stink and didn't do anything to get Selina's blood off the living-room rug.

By that evening, Dawn had had enough. She had wrestled with the awful carpet cleaner and bloody water all day. And despite still firmly believing that she was carrying out God's wishes, she was feeling more and more uncomfortable in the house as the realization of what occurred there slowly sank in. She could not get thoughts of the bodies out of her head, or the smell out of her nose. She tried to take her mind off it—puttering around and attempting to color her hair. Her efforts didn't work, and she decided she had to get out of there. She headed over to Debra's.

When she got there, Debra laughed at her friend's bad pink hair. Dawn colored her hair all the time, but this shade had not worked, and Dawn knew it. She had rethought the dye job and arrived at Debra's house armed with two new boxes of hair color, scissors, a brush, and a comb. She also hauled a suitcase, a cardboard box, and the wheelchair up to the apartment. She asked if she could store the wheelchair there. Sure, Debra said, not once bothering to question why her perfectly mobile friend was carting around a wheelchair.

"I'll be back in a minute," Dawn said, and disappeared into Debra's room with the suitcase and the box. She locked the door behind her and pulled the safe off the closet shelf where they had stashed it months earlier. She unloaded the suitcase and started methodically stuffing its contents into the safe. It would be secure there, she thought, conveniently housed in one place away from Saddlewood.

Dawn came out of the bedroom to find Debra waiting for her. If the authorities ever show up, get rid of the safe, she ordered. Dawn then added the cardboard box and the suitcase to Debra's own extensive collection of clutter, and the two women returned to the living room.

While Dawn unwound at Debra's, Justin tried his best to relax as well. He headed down to the local Blockbuster. Wandering the aisles, he came upon *Boondock Saints*. "Brothers. Killers. Saints." Hmm. He flipped the video over to read the back. It was about two brothers who felt they had been ordained by God to rid the world of evil. They did it by offing members of the Russian mob, murders that even the cop chasing them felt okay about.

Well, this looked interesting. Not exactly on the money,

but darn close. And everyone agreed with what they were doing? Nice. A conscience balm in a videocassette tape. He rented it and headed home.

————

The next morning, Dawn asked Debra to go out and buy the Sunday *Contra Costa Times*; there were a couple of articles she was interested in reading. She had already recorded television news reports of a murder in Marin County that had police searching for the missing daughter of blues guitarist Elvin Bishop. Now she was curious whether they knew about the disappearance of an elderly Concord couple.

Justin was at the Saddlewood house, where he stood in the living room and surveyed the still-stained and stinky carpet. Their attempts at cleaning it had only made it worse. As the smell of death filled his nose, he decided it was time to bring in a professional. He started calling around, trying not to sound too desperate.

"I'm looking to get several carpets cleaned, today if possible," he told the clerk at Prestige Cleaning.

"Is this an emergency cleaning?" she asked.

"Well, nah . . . but it needs to get done," he said. "My roommate tried to clean the carpets and she never—it went from bad to worse. She couldn't get all the water up and we were trying to air it out and let it dry, but now it's starting to mildew."

Justin gave his name and number, and the clerk said she would call right back to say whether her company could do the job. When she didn't return his call, Justin called back, then went through the phone book, calling other businesses until he found one that would come out on a Sunday. When the man got there, he told Justin the water had soaked through to the padding and it would cost $570 to clean everything. Justin phoned Dawn and told her to get home.

She had his credit card, and he would need it to pay the hefty bill.

On her way home, Dawn stopped at a drugstore and bought two packages of carpet deodorizer and four bottles of air freshener. Still unhappy with her hair, she also got a bottle of hair-color correction conditioner and two new boxes of hair color. She tossed in a box of donuts, two Snickers bars, and a pack of gum for good measure. She got back to the house, and she and Justin started eating in the kitchen as the carpet cleaner worked on a red stain nearby.

"Maybe it's Kool-Aid," he said.

"Yeah, it's Kool-Aid," said Justin. "We spilled some drinks."[4]

The carpet cleaner finally left. By the time Taylor got home that night, the stain situation was better than before, but big fans were still blowing in an effort to dry the carpet, and certain spots still had a reddish tinge. He decided they would just have to deal with that in the morning.

FIFTEEN

Monday, August 7, 2000

Steve Nash had been up for almost twenty-four hours, but the adrenaline surging through the Marin County detective more than made up for the lack of sleep. He was close to finding Selina. He sped across the San Rafael Bridge over San Francisco Bay, heading east toward the rising sun and what he hoped would be a happy outcome to the case that had consumed him for days.

He had finally figured out who "Jordan" was—the mysterious boyfriend with big plans. He was a thirty-year-old man named Glenn Taylor Helzer who lived on the outskirts of Concord. Nash was looking forward to paying him a visit. And he had quite the introduction ready: a dozen fellow deputies decked out in tactical raid gear and a search warrant that authorized him to look for a gun, clothes and anything else related to the murders of James Gamble and Jenny Villarin and Selina's disappearance.

But first, Nash needed to let Concord police know what he had planned. It was considered a breach of police etiquette to bust into a house in another agency's jurisdiction without letting them know beforehand. Plus, he wanted to borrow their SWAT team. So the Marin contingent sailed into Concord and headed for the police station.

The first thing they saw when they pulled up was a television news truck parked out front. Nash looked at it in horror. How had the press found out about their raid? This can't be happening, he told himself. If they know, it could blow the surprise element and make the whole operation much more complicated.

He and his team managed to get into the building without attracting untoward attention from the reporters outside, who were actually waiting to interview a Concord police lieutenant about the mysterious disappearance of a local elderly couple. Nash heaved a sigh of relief. This might work out after all. He briefed the Concord SWAT team, and everyone headed for Saddlewood Court. They pulled up just before 6 a.m. and silently surrounded the house. Nash and colleague Alisia Lellis went around to guard the back fence, which bordered an access road and an empty field choked with brush and trees parched from the summer heat.

They heard Detective Erin Inskip knock on the front door and then the battering ram crash into the heavy wood. One of the windows in the back of the house flew open and a lanky man with long dark hair, wearing only boxers, scrambled out. He looked a lot like the driver's-license photo that detectives had been showing around Marin County.

Taylor jumped the fence and landed with Nash and Lellis's guns in his face. They threw him to the ground and handcuffed him. There was not much to search on his body, so they hauled him to his bare feet and started toward the front of the house. It was slow going; Taylor had run through weeds during his short flight from the law and was now complaining about the stickers and burrs. Nash and Lellis were not sympathetic.

Taylor admitted he was the man known as Jordan. He said he should have called about his girlfriend when he got back in town. They nodded, marched him around to the front of the house, and handed him off to Inskip. She had his handcuffs removed and sat him in the front passenger seat of her unmarked police car, rolling down the window about eight inches for ventilation on the rapidly warming morning. She explained that he was not under arrest; would he talk to her? He said yes.

Inskip decided to move her car farther away from the commotion at the house. She pulled around the corner, parked and started with the questions. Did he have any nicknames? Jordan, he replied. Did he know Selina? Yes, he said, they met at a rave. He helped her move into her apartment, and he had a key. They last spoke August 1 and had a fight, although he was not thinking fast enough to come up with a reason for the argument.

Inskip asked if he and Selina had plans. Yes, they were going to go to Yosemite, but Selina never showed up to meet him August 2. So then he went to Reggae on the River for the weekend and just got back late Sunday, he said. Thinking he had probably said enough by now, Taylor flatly denied knowing anything about the murders of Jenny Villarin and James Gamble.

Inskip was about to continue the questioning when her cell phone rang. Her sergeant needed something out of the trunk of their car. She hung up and told Taylor that her commanding officer needed them to return to the house, but then they could come back and finish talking. He watched her put the car in gear and look away from him over her left shoulder as she checked for traffic. If he had any chance at all, this was it. He hit the rolled-down window, popped it out of its frame with the force of his body and took off running. He quickly disappeared into the early-morning quiet of the neighborhood.

Inskip whipped back around at the sound of the horrible thud. She stared in astonishment at Taylor's rapidly retreating form and then grabbed her phone. She told her sergeant what happened, and he quickly had Concord police begin to cordon off the area.

———————

As soon as Nash stepped through the heavy wooden door and into the tiled entryway, he knew. Selina was killed in the house, he thought. The carpet had a reddish cast to it, and fans had been set underneath to help the drying process. He visually took in the messy living room, then turned and walked down the hall. The first bedroom he came to made him even more sure his pessimistic conclusion was right. The bloody outlines of bodies were still visible in the carpet. This was one nasty scene, he thought.

It got even worse in very short order. They found duct tape, along with clothing that did not fit any of the three taken into custody. And then they saw leg irons and handcuffs in Justin's truck. Nash had seen enough. He knew he needed another search warrant, one that would give him permission to search this place from top to bottom—not just for a gun related to Jennifer and James's murders but for everything these guys might have done. Completely deflated that he could probably never have saved Selina, an exhausted Nash headed back across the bay to ask his county judge for another warrant.

———————

Taylor ripped through the sliding screen door and stumbled into a nearby house. A startled man with a coffee cup halfway to his lips gawked at him. Taylor pointed his hand like a gun.

"Give me your car keys or I'll shoot you," Taylor said.

"You can have all the keys you want, my cars don't work," said William Sharpe.

Taylor was sweating heavily, and Sharpe could smell the fear. So could his two dogs, who burst out of another section of the house, barking wildly and lunging toward Taylor. He took one look at the pair and fled.

Taylor kept running until he found himself on a street two blocks west of where he had busted out of the police car. He needed some clothes, and he needed them fast. He spotted a fairly open backyard, skirted the pool and the comfortable scatter of deck chairs, and approached the back sliding-glass door. A woman was walking across the kitchen toward him. She opened the door.

Mary Mozzochi thought the young man was one of her son's friends and let him in. But when he grabbed her and pulled her farther back into the room, she realized she was in trouble. He would kill her if she called the police, he said. He grabbed a knife off the kitchen counter and raised it.

"Give me the keys to the car," he said.

The stunned woman told him her car wasn't working. "You're lying. Give me the keys," he said.

Mozzochi repeated that her car had broken down and pointed to the phone book on the table, which was open to a page of listings for rental-car companies. Still holding the knife, Taylor noticed a display of guns by the fireplace and said he needed bullets. She told him they were replicas and did not work. So he asked for another knife. She pulled one out of the butcher block in the kitchen and handed it to him.

Then she ventured to ask the now doubly armed man a question. "Have you killed someone?"

"Not yet," he said.

Taylor looked around the kitchen

"Just give me a fucking change of clothes," he said.

Mozzochi went through a pile of nearby laundry and

handed him an orange polo shirt, some pants, and a pair of
her husband's white socks. She had no ponytail holder, so
he demanded scissors. She sat and watched him cut several
inches off his long dark hair and dump it on the telephone
book sitting on her kitchen table.

He stripped off his boxers and put on the clothes she
gave him. The pants were too big, so he asked for a belt. She
told him there was one in the bedroom and offered to get it.
He followed her closely down the hallway, telling her she
needed to be quiet so as not to wake up anyone else.

When they got to the master bedroom, Mozzochi—
desperate to get him out of her house before her son
awoke—offered him sweatpants that would fit better than
the pants he had on. Taylor took them, and she begged him
to leave through the room's outside door and not go back
down the hallway. She didn't want her twenty-six-year-old
son to walk out and confront this crazy bastard who had
spent the past several minutes waving her own kitchen
knives in her face. After he dressed, Taylor ran outside, and
Mozzochi slammed the door behind him and locked it.

Taylor took off to the west again, jumping fences and
sprinting through backyards. He made it to the main thor-
oughfare of Concord Boulevard before officers managed to
surround him and take him into custody.[1]

Marin deputies arrested Justin and Dawn without incident
and then began to search the Saddlewood house for the
handgun and other clues to Selina's likely demise. A Concord officer was called in and asked to log a little bit of pot
and some "psilocybin mushrooms" that had been found in
a paper photo envelope stashed in a suitcase in the living
room. He also took a glass smoking pipe found in a leather
pouch tucked inside Dawn's organizer, which had been left
on the kitchen counter.

Later that day, the officer was called back to the house to collect more drugs. Lellis had discovered an even bigger stash in the living-room suitcase—a baggie stuffed with twenty-six tablets of ecstasy. The pills and another smoking pipe were logged into Concord police evidence. That would be enough to keep Justin and Dawn in jail for at least a couple of days while investigators tried to figure out what else they had done.

––––––––

The three residents of 5370 Saddlewood Court were bundled into police cars for the quick five-mile trip through Concord to the police department. It was still morning, but the day was beginning to heat up as the cars pulled up to the station and the suspects were led in through the back and booked. The requisite mug shots were taken, none of them pretty.

All three had the slightly vacant look around the eyes that comes with getting roused from bed too early. Taylor looked worn out. His eyes were unfocused, and he had an almost petulant look on his face. His dark hair was uneven and disheveled, and he still wore the orange shirt taken from Mary Mozzochi. Dawn, her hair dyed back to a fairly ordinary shade of blond, looked hungover and a little angry as she glowered at the camera. Justin was the only one who looked like someone you would not mind running into on the street. His long straight hair was tucked behind his right ear and appeared combed. His eyes were fairly clear, and the ghost of a smile tugged at his lips.

––––––––

Vicki Sexton tuned in to the Monday-morning news, only to hear the typical roundup of everything bad that had happened over the weekend. Then something caught the bank manager's attention. A Concord police lieutenant was on the screen, talking about the disappearance of an elderly couple. If anyone had information regarding the whereabouts of Ivan and Annette Stineman, the authorities would like to know.

"Oh my God," Sexton said to her husband. "Those are my customers." She stared at the TV as her brain went into overdrive. That Jackie woman had come into the bank last week, talking about the Stinemans. They needed their brokerage money deposited into an account at her bank. The whole transaction had smelled funny to Sexton, which was why she put a hold on the deposit into the account of somebody named Bishop.

Selina Bishop.

Wasn't she missing, too? Sexton's head started to spin. She suddenly remembered hearing news reports about police searching for Selina Bishop. It was in a different county, across the bay, and in no way connected to what was going on here, right? But that Jackie lady had sat across from her last week and gone on and on about Selina Bishop and her grandparents, the Stinemans. Now all three people were missing. Sexton ran for the phone.

———

Concord police Lieutenant Paul Crain had already been at work for several hours that Monday morning. He had done a live shot for the very early news about the missing Stinemans and was waiting for his detectives to get in to work when his phone rang about 7:30 a.m.

"I saw your broadcast this morning," Vicki Sexton said. "I just wanted to let you know that some days ago, a woman came in and tried to negotiate two checks for one hundred thousand dollars on the Stinemans' account."

Oh, shit, Crain thought. There was no way the disappearance was just a missing-persons case anymore. It was at least a kidnapping and ransom, or some kind of extortion situation. Maybe even a homicide.

Sexton kept talking, and Crain tried to focus on what she was saying. Something about a woman named Selina Bishop. He dutifully took down the name, which he had not heard before. Sexton mentioned something about her being missing, too. He told her he would send someone over to the bank to get her full statement and thanked her for calling. Then he sat back for a moment. What a Monday. Not only had one of his cases just gone from serious to probably deadly, he also had some Marin cops busting into a local house on an out-of-town homicide. His guys on the scene were already telling him the place looked like a crime scene itself. Hmm.

"Hey, in this Marin County case, is there a woman by the name of Selina Bishop?" He finally found someone who could answer the question. Yeah, Bishop was the homicide victim's daughter, and she was missing. Crain sighed. His Monday, and everyone else's, had just gone from bad to worse.[2]

The Marin detectives continued to search the Saddlewood house for clues to Selina's whereabouts. As they went through the house, they began to see documents pertaining to other people, especially checks and other records with the name Stineman on them. Concord officers were still at the scene, just to assist. Hey, one of them said, we have a missing couple named Stineman.

Concord detectives Steve Chiabotti and Judy Elo had had the day off until their missing retirees began to figure into the Saddlewood investigation. They were told to head to Saddlewood Court immediately. Once there, however, they had to cool their heels a bit. Marin had a confirmed double homicide; Concord just had two people reported missing, people who theoretically could be partying in Vegas, Chiabotti thought in his typically wry fashion. While he knew in his bones that this was not the case with the predictable Stinemans, the detective still had to stand back and let the Marin investigation take precedence.

Then he heard about Vicki Sexton's report to police and her statement that the checks were drawn on the Stinemans' Dean Witter accounts. That dovetailed nicely with the old Dean Witter business cards investigators just found in the Saddlewood house with Taylor's name on them.

"We're into this, too. This is our case, too. We got a piece of this, and it's not going to turn out good," Chiabotti said.

He quickly sent his Concord colleagues scrambling for information. One went to the Stinemans' bank, where employees told her that $10,000 had been deposited in their checking account on July 31, the day after they were last seen by neighbors.

Investigators might not know where the Stinemans were, but they had learned more about the three people they were starting to think had something to do with the couple's disappearance. One detective took a photo lineup of booking mug shots back to Vicki Sexton, who positively identified Dawn Godman as the woman in the wheelchair whom she had dealt with face-to-face a week earlier. And Concord crime scene technicians quickly matched a palm print they had already lifted from the Stinemans' Chevy van to the one just taken from Justin Helzer.

After getting a positive identification on Dawn at the bank, Detective Russ Norris headed to the Concord offices of Dean Witter. Taylor Helzer had worked there for about five years, the manager told him. He went out on disability about a year and a half ago and left the company permanently in November 1999. Before that, he had been the

Stinemans' financial adviser—and they had been very happy with his work. The links between the Helzer household and the Stinemans—which just twelve hours earlier had seemed unimaginable—were starting to form quite a chain.

———————

The dark shadow bobbed along in the still waters of the Mokelumne River, just off the shore of Brannan Island. Steven Sibert thought it was a life jacket at first. He often found such things floating in the water, lost by boaters during busy weekends on the delta. He steered his Jet Ski over and saw that it was actually a duffel bag. Still nothing more than idly curious, Sibert grabbed at it as he chugged by. It was so heavy it almost yanked him off his Jet Ski. He fought to hang on, swinging his whole body to the opposite side of the watercraft to balance out the weight. He carefully made his way to shore.

Once on dry land, he unzipped the bag and saw a stepping-stone inside. And then the smell hit him. He had had enough to do with this, he thought. He ran to get his cousin, who worked at a nearby marina, and told him he found what he thought was a dead body.

The two men made their way back to where Sibert left the bag. Inside, they found six river rocks, one concrete stepping stone, black plastic trash bags, some yellow wire ties—and a human torso. They called the police.

SIXTEEN

Making the Connection

———◆———

Taylor sat alone, staring at the walls of his Concord Police Department holding cell. He had not talked to anyone in quite a while, but he had something to say. He had to talk with somebody. After hours with no one, he would settle for anybody, even a cop. He knocked for the jailer and asked to speak to someone.

Chiabotti heard that Suspect Number One, Glenn Taylor Helzer, wanted to talk and hustled down to the holding area. He stuffed a tape recorder in his pocket on the way.

"Glenn. Glenn? Hey, man. I'm Detective Chiabotti. Somebody said you wanted to talk to one of us?"

"At this point, yeah," Taylor said. He looked at Chiabotti standing on the other side of the door and reconsidered. He was feeling freaky and paranoid, he said.

"They took my fingerprints and that freaked me out," he said.

"Okay," Chiabotti said. He tried to sound understanding, but his dry wit and gathering disdain for this guy seeped through a bit. "Well, that happens down here a lot—they take fingerprints and stuff."

Taylor decided he wanted to relax a little more and let his stomach settle after dinner before he talked. Chiabotti agreed. Sure, he would come back. An hour later, the jailer called again to say Taylor had asked for him. Chiabotti headed back down and peered through the door at Taylor.

"Glenn. You knocked again?"

"Yeah," Taylor said.

"Did you want to talk to me?" Chiabotti asked.

"I did. I do," Taylor said.

"You want to go someplace to sit down, or do you want to talk in here?"

Taylor seized the chance to get out of his cell, at least for a few minutes. Chiabotti swung open the door. The two walked down the row of cells toward a series of interview rooms around the corner—Taylor, long and lean with his badly chopped black hair all askew, and Chiabotti shorter, with a bit of a paunch, sandy hair, and a mustache contributing to a hangdog look that hid a sharp mind.

Chiabotti planned to get Taylor in an interview room, read him his rights, and then start the interrogation. The detective had no plans to pound him with questions. That was not his style. He liked to establish a rapport, slowly build a conversation, develop a familiarity. Then he would mine the results, picking out information suspects often did not intend to give him as they chatted away.

Taylor paused in the corridor. He was getting nervous. Boy, did he want to talk at someone, but telling this cop what he had been up to for the past week was not a good idea. He backtracked.

"I just wanna go back to my cell, 'cause I gotta—I can't help you. Just want to go back to my cell," he said quickly.

"That's fine," Chiabotti soothed. "You can go back to your cell."

Taylor's thoughts started to scatter. "I'm telling you right now that there are things I'm remembering regarding Selina and regarding Ivan and Annette, uh, that Selina and I did that . . ."

Well, well, Chiabotti thought. He hadn't even told Taylor he was a Concord officer. The guy knew he had been arrested by Marin authorities who had questioned him about Selina. But no one had said anything about the Stinemans. This has got to be our guy, he thought.

Taylor was still talking, spilling out words in a way that was both fast and halting at the same time.

"And I didn't at the time, but I am starting to think those weren't dreams, that I need to—because, see, that means that those two shouldn't be here. And I knew that already, but these two shouldn't be here," he said.

Taylor looked around the corridor at the cells. Justin was in one of them. He craned his neck around to look for him and started speaking very distinctly and more and more loudly, his voice rising in the metal space.

"As soon as I get to hug my brother and tell him I'm sorry in person—in front of his lawyer and to his lawyer—I've got a lot to tell you regarding Selina, and Ivan and Annette and myself, and—so I want to be able to talk to them and tell them that I am sorry if I did anything, and for the betrayal of their trust because my actions have obviously made it look like they did something."

He fixated on the lawyer thing. "But I need to make sure that they each have a lawyer before I say anything. And I need to be able to say my good-byes to both of them. Better get me in the same room at the same time, whatever. So I just wanted to say that, I guess."

Suddenly Taylor had to see them. He hadn't had a chance to talk to either Dawn or Justin before they all got arrested. He hoped the cop would go along with his request.

The cop, however, had no intention of doing that. He was busy gritting his teeth at his legal limitations.

"I guess you asked for an attorney, so there's really nothing that we can talk about without you saying it's okay to talk to me," he told Taylor. "They've asked for their own attorneys, so they'll be provided with attorneys."

Taylor would not be reassured so easily.

"I need to see that they happen to have an attorney and see—because I am not very good at things like this. I sort of—I—right now I'm having a hard time," Taylor said.

No kidding, Chiabotti thought. Nothing was going to happen that day, he thought as they walked down the corridor. There was no sense going to an interview room at all. "Okay, you want to go back in that cell, then?"

"Yeah, I'll do whatever you say," Taylor responded. Then he saw Justin in a cell right where the corridor turned toward the interview rooms. He wanted the door opened. No way. Say something through it, Chiabotti suggested, interested to hear what that would be.

"I just want to say I love you, man, and I'm sorry," Taylor said loudly. "That's all. I don't want to say anything." Chiabotti started to lead him back to his cell. "I love you, man. I love you," Taylor called down the corridor toward Justin.

Chiabotti got Taylor back in his cell and then tried one last time to focus his attention.

"Okay, Glenn. Just so I understand this right, once they have an attorney and you're sure of that, then you're interested in talking with me?"

"Right now that's what the Spirit says. Spirit says that I should not let them be in here. So that's what I feel right now. Yeah, I got things to say right now."

Yeah, right, Chiabotti thought. "We'll be back in touch, then, okay? Just holler if you need anything else." I'll come

back down and we'll play this charade again, he thought as
he walked away.[1]

————

Judy Nemec and Nancy Hall settled in to watch some television. They were finally off their feet. They had spent the
day reluctantly talking with reporters in an attempt to
spread the word about their missing parents. Then they had
done some searching, but did not know where to look. Ivan
and Annette Stineman were creatures of habit, and all of
their normal haunts had already been searched, their everyday steps retraced by the police. As far as they knew, nothing had been found.

Judy and Nancy felt moderately better, however, because that morning they had met Concord police lieutenant
Paul Crain. He had taken on the care of them, and it was a
duty he would never relinquish. He came over to Nancy's
house. The day was already hot, and the sisters hurried
around opening windows and airing the house of its stuffy
kitty smell. They set a chair for him in front of the fireplace,
and then everyone—Nancy, Judy, Fred, Aunt Marcia, and
Uncle Al—gathered around and listened. Crain laid out
what was going on. He didn't offer many investigative details, but he did tell the group that he would brief them on
any developments before he told the press anything.

But the sisters turned on the local evening news
anyway—just in case somebody knew something they did
not. The story about Mama and Daddy came on, with no
new information. Then there came a report of arrests in another missing-person case. Two men had been taken into
custody in connection with the disappearance of Selina
Bishop. One was thought to be her mysterious boyfriend,
"Jordan." They both had ponytails.

Judy was sitting on her knees on the floor. She kept

scooting forward as the news segment played. "I think this is related," she said. She knew their parents' neighbor had seen men with ponytails at the house. She scooted closer and closer to the television screen, like a child hoping that getting nearer would bring everything into focus. "I think this is related," she repeated.[2]

Fifty miles away in Marin County, Oggie Land finished watching another news story on her missing niece. The newscast then switched to a report about an elderly couple from Concord who had disappeared the week before. Their poor daughter came on camera, explaining that her parents were set in their ways and would never have gone anywhere without letting the family know.

Oggie looked at her brother David. "They're from Concord," she said. Jordan was also from Concord. "It's the same case."

"Oh, Oggie," he said. "Quit making it bigger than it is."[3]

———

Nash walked into the Concord police station with his lawyer. He had thought it best to call in his own representative from his county's district attorney office. Ed Berberian was there to safeguard Marin's interests during a hastily called hearing, during which Concord police planned to ask for their own search warrant. The two sat down with Chiabotti, Judy Elo, and other detectives and turned to Bob Hole, who would be running the show. Hole was technically a deputy district attorney for Contra Costa County, but he did not do trial work. He preferred the field. He was the county's authority on search warrants and would happily meet officers out at the scene to discuss things. Instead of writing down all the evidence and suspicions and having a judge review it—the typical route—Hole decided that, with the rapidly increasing evidence from many different sources, it would be best to hold a hearing and have the officers testify in front of a judge. It would go more quickly and any questions could be addressed immediately.

Nash sat in Concord's major-case room, a windowless box on the station's second floor with a big conference table and plenty of white dry-erase boards on the walls. His wife had brought him a fresh set of clothes, but he had not had time to change. The stuff he had been wearing for days could probably stand up on its own at this point, but he was having trouble staying upright. He'd gone forty hours without sleep. He tried to focus for the judge. He listed the evidence he had found so far and detailed his still paramount concern for Selina's safety. Then he sank back in his chair and listened to what everyone else had. The investigators outlined the evidence for Judge Peter Spinetta. Chiabotti played him the tape of his conversation with Taylor Helzer only an hour before. He pointed out that the suspect had mentioned the Stinemans without even knowing that Chiabotti was a Concord police detective. Spinetta listened to the tape, Taylor's voice sounding slightly tinny through the recorder as it reverberated through the conference room.

The officers then went through their "wish list," what they wanted Spinetta to grant them permission to look for. It included financial records, various receipts, and one lime-green pantsuit that Vicki Sexton vividly remembered "Jackie" wearing. The list did not include the kitchen sink, but it would eventually grow to include the bathtub.

Hole had one final request. He wanted to make the affidavit—the document laying out all the evidence in support of the search warrant, which was basically the transcript of the two-hour hearing—unavailable to the public. Letting the media know what law enforcement knew would make screening potential witnesses—who could have just learned of evidence on television instead of seeing it themselves—much more difficult.[4]

Spinetta, an experienced criminal trial judge, agreed. He signed the warrant and then sealed both it and the affidavit transcript of the hearing. Everyone looked around the table at one another. They would start up again in the morning, with Concord now able to work right alongside Marin.

By now it was almost midnight. Word was percolating through the building that there had been a find in the delta. Duffel bags full of body parts were popping up. If it wasn't near Concord, it wasn't their problem. But the way this case was snowballing, the detectives working it considered the very real possibility, as they headed out the door for a few hours' sleep, that Selina and the Stinemans were in the process of being found.

————

Tuesday morning dawned way too early for the exhausted Nash. He attended a short briefing at the Concord Police Department and then headed back out to the Saddlewood house, where a moving truck now sat in the driveway ready to cart away what everyone knew would be an enormous amount of evidence. Nash and his Marin colleagues got to work, sifting through things alongside Concord's Judy Elo and others. And then a guy in a suit showed up. He had to have a badge, otherwise he could not have gotten past the barricade at the end of the street, Nash thought. And he did. Hal Jewett had been a county prosecutor for almost two decades and had just been handed the Stineman case.

He walked into the little tiled entryway and took a look around. He told Nash he had been assigned the case. Nash hesitated. Prosecutors in his county did not typically come waltzing into crime scenes and introduce themselves like they were attending some law conference.

Jewett saw that the Concord officers were logging evidence in under their own system, which was different from what Marin was already doing with what it had collected.

That was not going to be good at all once the whole thing ended up in court, he thought.

"Time out," said Jewett, a tall man with reddish-brown hair, pale blue eyes, and a notorious affinity for ill-fitting suits. "It's becoming very clear these homicides are related; this is one investigation. It's a multijurisdictional investigation, but it's one investigation, and we need to stop and reflect and meet."[5]

A meeting? He had a house full of evidence, two homicide victims, and a still-missing twenty-two-year-old, Nash thought. A touchy-feely sit-down was not on his agenda. "Wait a minute," Nash said. "These are Marin County murders and a Marin County search warrant. That's how it's going to be at this point."

Jewett got on the phone. He had to stop all this evidence from getting trucked all over creation. He did not want to have to explain to a jury why it was stored in different places and cataloged with different numbers if it was all supposed to be part of the same case. Plus, he didn't see the Marin County crime lab there. He called the director of his own county's lab and told him he needed people out there and fast.

Jewett did not know that Nash, in addition to being a detective, was also a trained crime scene technician. The Marin man knew what he was doing, even if he was running on empty after a weekend of frantic police work. Fine, you have your meetings, Nash said. He would let people higher up in both agencies argue about jurisdiction. He had work to do.[6]

————

Oggie Land sat curled up in the passenger seat of her pickup truck as her husband drove them back home. They had been in Marin County searching for Selina the entire weekend with no luck, and now they needed to make a quick trip home before continuing the hunt. Her husband, Mark, took the back way, up north of the San Francisco Bay through the rural fields and marshes of Sonoma County. It is there that the waters of the Sacramento Delta finally meet the bay. As they crossed the bridge over the sun-sparkled waves, Oggie stared out the window.

"She's in the water," she said.

"What?" Mark asked.

"They killed her, and she's in the water," Oggie said, still staring out. Selina's in the water; that's why they can't find her, she thought. And if her boyfriend was supposed to live in Concord, this was the in-between, where the delta met the bay. After hoping—insisting—all weekend that her niece would return, Oggie threw her optimism into the waves below, where she now believed Selina was.

SEVENTEEN

The Duffel-Bag Murders

Lieutenant Paul Crain wanted to meet again with the Stinemans' family. He came over to Nancy's house and took his seat by the fireplace while everyone else settled themselves in the same spots they had chosen the last time. He said that his office wanted to take a blood sample from either Nancy or Judy to use for DNA identification if they found their parents.

"I'll do that," Nancy said with a deep breath. "Firstborn should be doing it." When they got up to leave for the police station, Judy pulled Crain aside. "We're going to have to leave at some point, and if they are found, I don't want Nancy to have to identify them," she said. That's why they wanted the DNA, Crain said, to ensure no one would have to visually identify a body. Judy nodded, and they left the house.

The sisters were shown into a small conference room with a couch, chairs, and a table. They were waiting for the nurse to come draw Nancy's blood when Crain walked in. Remains had been found in the delta, he said.

Judy, the Southern California girl, said, "What's the delta?" Crain exhaled and relaxed a tiny bit. That was an easy question, and he leaped to answer it. He picked up a dry-erase board and started drawing the delta region, explaining that it was a mixture of salt water from the bay and freshwater from the rivers flowing down from the Sierra Nevada. But soon the lesson was done, and he had to put down his board and get back to the task at hand. A torso had been found in a duffel bag in the delta, but it appeared to be a young woman, he said.

"Selina," Nancy whispered.

They knew Crain was about to brief the press on the investigation, but Nancy asked if he would first go tell Fred and their aunt and uncle the news about the remains. Crain agreed and left the two women sitting in the little room, with nothing left to do but stare at a freehand drawing of the delta and wonder about their parents.

Judy had come to the realization that she just wanted them to be found. They had to be dead, and she just wanted them back, wanted to know what had happened to them. Nancy kept thinking that the whole experience couldn't get any worse. Then Crain came back through the door. He pulled up a chair, twisted it around, and straddled it. There had been another development, he said. They had found a man's arm in one of the bags. He looked at the sisters, sitting at right angles to each other with their knees so close they were almost touching. They stared back.

"You girls had better prepare yourselves," he said.

"We are," said Judy. "If they were okay, they'd be home by now."

———

A jail deputy ushered Dawn into the court holding cell already crowded with women. Everyone was waiting for their turn in court, but their more immediate interest was the news story about to come on television in the cell. They were all talking about the sensational duffel-bag murders as Dawn made her way into the small room and settled herself on a seat as the newscast began. She looked around and threw out a nonchalant question. What was going to happen to her? She was slightly curious about the legal aspects, but remained completely firm in her belief that Taylor would take care of everything.

A woman sitting across from her looked up from her Bible. "What are you here for?" she asked.

"Drug charges for the house in Concord," Dawn replied.

The woman asked if it was Dawn's first arrest. Yes, she answered. The woman, who had experience in such matters, made sure. "Are you on probation?" Dawn said no. "You'll be out in seventy-two hours," the woman told her.

"Not if they charge me with the house in Marin," Dawn said. What house? the lady asked, now curious enough to put down her Bible for a minute. The house where the Bishop people were killed, Dawn explained. She fell quiet as more women were brought into the holding cell. Then the newscaster started talking about Dawn Godman being the girlfriend of one of the male suspects. Dawn started laughing.

"That's not my boyfriend," she said. "Why do they keep saying that?"

Dawn continued watching the television, laughing to herself with a large smile on her face. As the woman Dawn had spoken to was led out of the holding cell toward the courtroom, other inmates started to rustle with anger at this fat girl chuckling about old people getting killed. She must have had something to do with it. "If you don't get her out of here, we're gonna kick her butt," they told the deputies, who quickly hustled her out and stuck her in a tiny room reserved for attorney visits.[1] She sat there until her court case was called.

———————

The courtroom was packed. It was Wednesday morning, and this was the first chance for the press to see the three people whom police were now linking to two different cases. The morning's headlines reported the connection in boldface type. "Bizarre Twist in Probe of 2 Slayings; Body Parts Found in Bags; Case Tied to Missing Pair," cried the *San Francisco Chronicle*. "Two Cases Could Be Linked: Police Cite New Evidence in the Disappearance of a Guitarist's Daughter to That of an Elderly Concord Couple," proclaimed the *Contra Costa Times*. Veteran KRON-TV reporter Mark Jones, reporting from the delta as authorities fished yet more bags out of the water, called the whole thing a "Stephen King nightmare."

The case made national news, and the public's desire for details fed the frenzy. The case touched communities from the Pacific Ocean, across San Francisco Bay, and almost a hundred miles inland to the state capital of Sacramento. People everywhere were talking about it and reporters, of course, were only too happy to satisfy their curiosity. They camped out at the entrance to Saddlewood Court for days on end. They tried to peer over the fence into the house's backyard, only to be none too politely shooed away by officers. News helicopters circled the neighborhood before heading out to the delta, where they took footage of boats searching the waters for more duffel bags. New aspects to the story popped up constantly as journalists talked to anyone who had ever known the trio, learning little tidbits that might or might not pertain to the case.

So it was standing room only when court bailiffs quietly ushered Taylor, Justin, and Dawn into a glass holding cell along one wall of the courtroom. There had not been time to assign them specific attorneys, so random lawyers stood in, advising nothing more than that the suspects keep quiet.

The accusations—at this point nothing more than drug charges for Dawn and Justin and the escape-and-burglary case against Taylor—were read as Jewett stood and stared at them with his arms folded across his chest. There would be more charges to come, Jewett told the judge, and he asked that all three be held without bail. The judge agreed, and Jewett strode out of the courtroom and into a crush of cameras and microphones.

It was the kind of onslaught Jewett had faced before—he had come to the public's attention four years prior, when, as the head of the office's juvenile division, he charged a six-year-old with attempted murder for attacking a one-month-old baby after he broke into a house to steal a tricycle. The case drew national debate about whether a boy so young could possess that level of intent. Jewett thought he did—calling the beating an "outrage"—and reduced the charge to assault only after psychiatric evaluators decided the child knew the difference between right and wrong but did not understand the permanence of death. His decisions infuriated many in the heavily African-American city of Richmond—where the crime took place—who thought the boy should have been placed in the care of social services. One group of protesters even assembled in front of the courthouse, chanting, "Harold Jewett, you can't hide. We charge you with genocide."[2]

The reaction did not daunt Jewett at all. Two years later, he slapped murder charges against an eleven-year-old, calling the boy a sniper who deliberately shot and killed a thirteen-year-old friend. He said at trial that the boy was motivated by revenge and envy—the older child had accidentally shot him with a BB gun earlier and seemed to have the idyllic family life the eleven-year-old did not. The defense attorney in that case scoffed at Jewett's attempted foray into his client's heart, saying the prosecutor considered himself a "human polygraph."[3]

Now, the forty-four-year-old Jewett was in charge of the district attorney's homicide division, where the killers were adults. The assignment fit him much better. His tendency to go for the throat with puritanical flair, no matter what the defendant's background, was better suited for grown-up murderers. He had tried several other capital cases earlier in his career. And now he was ready to take on the Helzers.

"I don't think I have words to describe what I'm beginning to see develop in this case," he told the assembled media horde. "There is something truly horrible and perhaps evil in the commission of these crimes."[4]

He could not talk much about the ongoing investigation, he told reporters. It seemed that Glenn Taylor Helzer's relationship as the Stinemans' stockbroker played into why the couple had been targeted for their retirement account, but Selina's involvement was more of a mystery, he said.

Carma and Gerry Helzer attended the hearing. Afterward, Carma made the first of many announcements that would sound peculiar unless one knew Carma. "I want everyone to start praying . . . so that innocent ones all over can be free,"[5] she said before heading back to the parking lot. The reporters dispersed. There was a rumor that Concord police were putting together a press conference for later in the day. They wondered what new bombshell awaited.

———

The phone kept ringing. Nancy's machine would fill and then it would just ring and ring until the people at the other end finally gave up and hung up. "We have got to get out of this house," Judy said. Her aunt had never been to a Starbucks, so they thought it would be a nice treat to go out, get some fresh air and a latte, and maybe distract themselves from the awfulness for a while.

The five of them went one town over, to Walnut Creek's tony outdoor mall. They ordered Aunt Marcia a café mocha and wandered around. Nancy went into a store for a battery pack she needed and saw a little remote-control car based on the recent *Stuart Little* movie. The little mouse was one of Nancy's favorites; she had bought the movie and watched it with her parents only two months before. It was the last film they had seen together. She stared at the toy and started screaming. She just could not hold it together anymore.

She tried to compose herself before heading back to her family. She did not want Judy to know she had lost it. It seemed like every time she looked at her little sister, Judy burst into tears. Nancy losing control would not help at all.

They all window-shopped some more and settled down at the fountain in the center of the mall when Judy's cell phone rang. Paul Crain needed to meet with them. They looked at one another and immediately headed back, gulping their coffee on the way. He was waiting in his car when they arrived back at Nancy's house. They filed inside and took their time opening the windows and starting the fans. Somehow, there was no hurry to hear what they suspected Crain had come to say. Finally, they settled into their assigned seats.

Crain told them that forensics had matched a fingerprint from the man's arm in the duffel bag with one from Ivan Stineman's driver's license. It was Daddy. The sisters looked at each other and said, but where's Mama? There was no news of her—yet.

"You know, if you never find her, we know where she is," Judy said. "She's with my dad. Obviously they would not have been separated. They never went anywhere alone." Nancy didn't want to think that quite yet. She wanted actual evidence that Mama was there, too, before she extinguished that last little glimmer of hope.

Crain stayed for about forty-five minutes, telling them what he could about the investigation. Then he headed back to the police station—he had a press conference to hold. Reporters packed the ground-floor briefing room and spilled out onto the sidewalk, where camera cables snaked along the ground and cameramen readied their live shots. The air buzzed with speculation and then fell silent as Crain and Marin County sheriff's spokesman Doug Pittman entered the room.

Crain announced that authorities had identified Ivan Stineman's arm. They had not yet confirmed the identities of the other body parts, but they believed they belonged to Annette Stineman and Selina Bishop. Police knew they had not yet found all the pieces, but they were working on it. In fact, just as Crain's update was broadcast live on the local noon newscasts, a Sacramento County sheriff's deputy was pulling a black Athletech bag out of the water of the south fork of the delta's Mokelumne River. It contained Ivan's left arm and lower torso and Annette's head.

———

The Villarin family was not as lucky as Nancy and Judy. Authorities were not updating them on developments because they were not considered Selina's next of kin—Elvin Bishop was, and he was not communicating with them. He said sheriff's officials had asked him not to because it could jeopardize the case,[6] but the Villarins—who felt they were the ones who had raised Selina, supported her and taken active roles in her life—were frustrated beyond words.

Their frustration turned to anguish when they learned through the media that bags containing remains likely to be Selina's had been discovered in the delta. Oggie Land heard the news from a television reporter while standing outside the Paper Mill bar. She broke down, and her husband, Mark, picked her up and carried her into the bar, where the owner locked the doors to outsiders and gave her space to breathe.

Other family members had just gone into San Francisco when they got a call from Gloria. "They found her," she said. Lusha, Selina's cousin, was ecstatic. She raced back across the Golden Gate Bridge to Marin County and rushed to Gloria's house. "Where is she? Where is she?" she asked, thinking Selina was alive. "Baby, you have to look at the news," said Gloria, gesturing at the television. Lusha looked, and saw uniformed officers pulling duffel bags out of a river. Her cousin was not coming home after all.[7]

Later that day, Gloria took a nap on the couch. It was the first good sleep she had been able to get since Selina had disappeared. And she had a dream. Jenny was tugging on her arm. "Come on, get up. I've got to find you a best friend," Jenny said. "Come on, get up. I've got to find you some friends." Gloria woke up. Jenny was still trying to take care of her. What was Gloria going to do without her?

Taylor still felt an overwhelming urge to talk. And it was now apparent that there were plenty of people who would love to listen. The crowd in court had been amazing. Everyone straining to get a look at him, riveted by the whole saga. Maybe he could turn that into more than just a conversation. If everyone was so interested, they would be willing to pay to hear what he had to say. His story should be worth at least $400,000. But whom should he approach? He did not want an ordinary reporter. He needed someone with broader reach, more of a following.

Playboy. That would be perfect. After all, he knew a Playmate, right? The magazine would have to be interested. He sat down and addressed a letter to the company's CEO.

I hesitate to say any more than this until I am talking

with someone on the phone or in person. I have details regarding the Selina Bishop/Stineman case that would serve their families and public in general to know . . . details that the press, police, and my own lawyers don't know yet.

Taylor then offered the goods.

I'm writing to find out if you would like to have an exclusive interview with me. I have talked to no one yet, and will wait until the 24th August for a response from you before contacting someone else.

I plan on sharing, in detail, EVERYTHING that happened and putting myself in God's hands. This would be a big scoop for you guys. Their families would benefit and I would be at peace know [sic] I'm doing the Lord's will.

Unfortunately, his means of communication were limited. He would have to have his mother's help. He had been talking to her over the phone about selling his story, and there was no way for *Playboy* to get in touch with him other than through her. He would have to hope she could get any message the magazine CEO left with her right.

He signed the letter "Glenn Helzer." Only then did he finally think about the possibility that *Playboy* might turn him down. He added a postscript: "Call Quickly Please—people need to know and I need to talk so even if you're not interested it would be nice if you'd leave a message saying so on Mom's machine. You're [sic] 5 minutes would save me days. Thank you."

———

While her colleagues fanned out throughout the Bay Area looking for witnesses and information, Concord detective

Judy Elo moved only from room to room at the Saddlewood house. After the hearing with the judge Monday
night, her partner, Chiabotti, was itching to get another
crack at Taylor Helzer, so she volunteered to serve the
search warrant and work with Nash and the others from
Marin County. It was an offer that would keep her occupied for more than a week as she combed through the
minutiae of the three suspects' existence.

A lot of the work was boring, but even the ordinariness
of it gave Elo pause. Their kitchen looked similar to hers.
The food in their refrigerator was the same type she ate.
The toothpaste in the bathroom was the same brand she
used. It all looked so normal.

But then there was the drop of blood they found on the
fireplace. And when they took up the carpet in the family
room, there were bloody outlines underneath, lined up on
the floor like the three little bears. And one scrap of paper
they found with numbers and times scribbled on it also had
a notation that gave detectives a start: "head & teeth, 2 hrs."

The sloppy housekeeping in the rest of the place ended
at the bathroom door. The room was spotless. Nash
doubted it was because someone had a fetish for clean tile.
He was fairly certain that this was where the killings had
occurred. And he was going to prove it. He ripped out the
bathtub and took the subfloor, too, just for good measure.
Along the way he bagged up all sorts of random things that
might or might not be important, including a hammer one
of the suspects had left lying around.

The sheer scope of the investigation—where in the
house had the three suspects not left evidence?—had
Nash's resources stretched to the limit. Usually, it was his
well-stocked agency lending forensic supplies to others,
but now he was the one borrowing. And billing. He ran out
of everything, including the special—and expensive—

vacuum filters he needed early on. He had to pay double for overnight shipping to replace them in time.

Then there were personal logistics. Elo at least got to go home and collapse in her own bed at night. Nash was an hour and a half away from home and too exhausted to trust himself to commute. He crashed at hotels and had his wife bring him fresh clothes. One night, he could not find a room and finally talked the staff at one hotel into letting him have one without a working shower or sink. He just needed a place to sleep, he begged.

The day after their worst fears had been confirmed, the Stinemans' daughters left town. It had only been a week since Nancy first reported them missing, but it felt like forever. They did not need to stay, with the constantly ringing phone and the incessant news coverage. They could easily return if the police needed them, Judy told Crain, and they would certainly be available by phone. But they had to get away. They headed back down to Judy's house in Southern California, where they could at least grieve in quiet.

EIGHTEEN

Charging Ahead

◆

The residents of the San Geronimo Valley were still trying to make sense of the killings. The arrests of those people across the bay had only added to the questions. Everyone now knew who "Jordan" was, but why on earth had he killed Selina? And then to shoot Jenny and James as well? It was just too much.

On Saturday, the community began trying to heal. Organizers blocked off the streets around the Paper Mill Creek Saloon and held a memorial for the three victims: Jenny, Selina, and Jim. More than two hundred people—Jenny's former students, their parents, Selina's old playmates, bar regulars, Jim's old buddies—turned out to honor the victims. They milled around the ever-increasing display of flowers and notes attached to the fence across the street from the Paper Mill and listened to the tributes.

Mark Land talked about Selina's patience with his children and her knack for getting them to read when no one else could. Others spoke about Jenny's sense of humor and

Jim's friendship. They tried to eclipse their horrible deaths with the goodness of their lives.

"The things in the paper and on the news, we've got to forget about it," Jenny's friend Shelley Mehrtens told the crowd. "We've got to think of the things that these people brought us."[1]

Elvin Bishop's brother-in-law attended the service in his stead, saying that the family was overwhelmed with grief and touched by the gathering.[2] Elvin had decided to perform in Mississippi and Oklahoma that weekend, just to give himself something to do. Selina's death took the joy out of everything for him and he turned to his music—to the blues—to keep from going crazy.[3]

And the latest news did not help. The day before, authorities had positively identified both Selina and Annette. Police also were raising new concerns by showing Selina's friends a photo of someone new, a man no one had ever seen before whom they wanted to talk to in connection with the case. Another suspect, or another victim?

Investigators went public with a photo several days later. They released a grainy picture of a white man, thirty-five to forty-five years old, of average build, with short dark hair. He was wearing jeans and a light-colored T-shirt on July 31, when he visited a bank in Petaluma. "He's not a suspect, but he is someone we'd like to locate, identify, and interview," said Paul Crain.

That man—photographed at the same time and place $10,000 was deposited in the Stinemans' bank account—certainly was not the only person investigators wanted to speak with. They contacted friends, neighbors, coworkers, anyone who had even rubbed shoulders with the Helzer brothers or Godman. The interviews generated an enormous number of tips, all of which had to be cataloged and prioritized for follow-up investigation. That job fell to

Concord's Steve Chiabotti, Bob Hole, and Ted Spyrow
from the district attorney's office. The three moved into the
Concord Police Department's major case room and began
organizing.

A detective would come back from an interview, tell the
three men what transpired, and write a report. Each report
could mean several new leads, which Chiabotti or the
others would identify, write out on a lead sheet, and then
assign to someone for follow-up. What looked like the best
leads were assigned to the best detectives, who tracked
them down, came back, and wrote another report. Then the
process began again.

Chiabotti had been working twenty-hour days to start
with, and knew others were, too. If he got a lead that involved a Marin angle, he would try to give it to a Marin detective early in the afternoon, sending the poor guy back
across the bay so he could stay at home that night and not
have to come back over to Concord for another tip.

But with the sheer scope of the places where the suspects had been and the things that they had done, he could
not avoid sending some people all over creation. Heidi
Stephenson, the other primary Concord detective on the
case, went to Sacramento to interview people who might
have attended raves with Taylor. She visited hotels in
Berkeley to see if Selina and Taylor had possibly checked
in somewhere on the date she disappeared. And, a definite
low point, she followed up on a tip about someone who had
seen a suspicious delta map in a Dumpster at the Oakland
airport. After digging through the pile of trash, Stephenson
found an ordinary map of the delta region that had no apparent link to the investigation. She wrote a report anyway.

And then there were the phone tips. Concord police had
established a hotline with voice mail to take the public's
tips. Chiabotti would brace himself and check it a couple
times a day. He was used to people with no connection to a

case wanting to help. With all the publicity this one was re-
ceiving, the usual handful of kooks grew tenfold. "I knew a
guy who was a Mormon once, and I want to talk to you
about this." Chiabotti would dutifully write it up, but then
stick it in the bottom of the pile.[4]

––––––––

Both Contra Costa and Marin counties had jurisdiction
over portions of the crime, since killings had taken place in
each area. But because they all resulted from the same conspiracy and appeared to have been committed by the same
suspects, it made sense to everyone that the cases be prosecuted together. The only question was which county
would take on the task.

Two main demographic issues came into play. The first
were the murder rates; a lot more people were killed in
Contra Costa County than in Marin. The year before the
Stinemans, Selina, Jenny, and Jim died, there were fifty-
seven homicides in Contra Costa County. There was one in
Marin.[5] A large source of the disparity was Contra Costa's
city of Richmond and county areas directly adjacent,
which were home to violent gangs and depressingly in-
tractable cycles of violence. As far as Contra Costa district
attorney Gary Yancey was concerned, that gave his deputies
considerably more experience with homicide trials and his
office plenty of justification to take the Helzer case. A tall
man with a down-home demeanor who had held the
county's top law enforcement job for fifteen years, Yancey
had never shied away from going after cases with unsettled
jurisdiction. This one was no different.

But the notion that her office was not as qualified to
prosecute a homicide was ridiculous to Paula Kamena, the
Marin County district attorney. She had been elected only
two years before, but she was a career prosecutor who did
not like being condescended to. Instead of arguing about

prosecutorial skills, however, she analyzed the case. The conspiracy originated in Contra Costa County, and most of the financial crimes relating to the Stinemans happened there as well. She also considered the ultimate outcome. Getting a jury to recommend the death penalty in the liberal bastion of Marin County would be difficult. The conservative suburbanites in Contra Costa would be more likely to vote for execution, the verdict Kamena felt appropriate for these horrendous crimes.

She decided it would work best if the prosecution was handled by Contra Costa, but she did want one of her deputies to work with Jewett on the case. But Yancey was not interested in that proposal. If his office was going to do it, it was going to do it alone. Kamena ceded the point, and Jewett began to ready charges against the suspects.

————————

Carma Helzer had looked into hiring attorneys for her sons. One San Francisco lawyer told her he would need a $100,000 retainer and the total fee would be at least double that. And that was just for one son. The Helzers certainly did not have that kind of money, even if they mortgaged the house. So the boys' cases were sent over to the county public defender's office, where Dawn's also awaited assignment.

Standard procedure in criminal cases dictates that attorneys from the same office cannot represent clients involved in the same case. In Contra Costa County, the effort to avoid such conflicts of interest for indigent defendants led to the creation of a spin-off office of sorts. The Alternate Defender Office was technically under the umbrella of the main public defender, but it operated as an independent office. Cases with two defendants could have one each assigned to the different offices, thereby circumventing any problems.

The small-time drug and burglary charges the Helzer brothers were currently facing would normally have warranted public defenders of moderate experience. But even though neither Helzer brother had yet been charged with murder, everyone knew it was only a matter of time. They were going to need seasoned defense attorneys.

The main office kept Taylor's case and assigned it to chief assistant public defender Suzanne Chapot. A petite woman with curly gray hair, Chapot had been a criminal defense attorney since the mid-1970s, and had worked for the county public defender's office since 1981. She met with her client and very quickly began formulating a defense. "He's severely mentally disturbed," she told reporters after one court hearing. "He's very distraught, sad. And he's horrified about what he hears, what people tell him has happened."

Justin's case was sent to the Alternate Defender Office, where the lead attorney took it on himself. With brown hair, a neatly trimmed beard, and a lilting gait, Bill Veale was a certified specialist in criminal law. He also was the polar opposite of his seemingly meek new client. Ferocious and confrontational, he went for the jugular in court, oftentimes without bothering to put a sheen of politeness on it.

He, too, was forced to comment for the cameras about his client. "He's never killed anybody, he's never hurt anybody, he's never had any interest in extorting money out of anybody or stealing from anybody," Veale said confidently.

The brothers now had representation, but Dawn still needed an attorney. Unless the office wanted to go to a panel of private attorneys who would sometimes take indigent conflict cases, there was only one option left. It was called the Special Defense Project. It was, in essence, a couple of deputy public defenders who did nothing other than capital murder cases. Dawn's file landed on the desk of David Headley, who had been with the public defender's office as long as Chapot had. A pragmatic attorney with longish gray hair, he had taken his cool and unflappable courtroom demeanor to the Special Defense Project a few years before. He also had a knack for ducking away without getting cornered by the press.

All three attorneys prepared for the murder charges that Jewett would soon file. From what they knew about the horrific nature of the case, they were also fairly certain that the district attorney's office would take things one step further and announce it was seeking the death penalty.

As Jewett reviewed the evidence against Taylor, Justin, and Dawn, he knew the case was eligible for the death penalty. In California, certain "special circumstances" must be met before a case can even qualify for death penalty status. They include circumstances like killing more than one person, killing someone while lying in wait, or killing someone in the commission of certain felonies such as robbery or rape. If a jury finds a special circumstance to be true, the minimum punishment a defendant can hope for is life in prison without the possibility of parole. And if the district attorney decides to ask for it, the jury can decide between that outcome and death.

Jewett found several on the long list of special circumstances that fit his case. He alleged that Ivan and Annette were killed in the commission of a robbery and that Selina was killed because she was a witness to a crime. He also attached the special circumstance for multiple murder. He also charged the trio with robbery, burglary, false imprisonment, extortion, conspiracy, and obstruction of justice. He would wait until September to charge them with the murders of Jenny and Jim, again accusing them of killing the pair because they were witnesses to a crime.

The decision to ask a jury to consider the death penalty now rested solely with Yancey. He had been in office since 1985, when the county board of supervisors appointed him to fill a vacancy left when the then-DA accepted a judge-ship. He had won reelection four times since and took that string of victories as a mandate for his philosophy, which was to pursue the death penalty with zeal on cases where he judged it appropriate.

It was a stance that sent shudders through the local defense bar, whose members usually thought there were many more shades of gray to cases than Yancey's stark black-and-white, life-and-death. But in fairness, the old guy had mellowed—a little. When he first took office, he pursued the death penalty on any case that qualified for special circumstances and left it to a jury to decide whether that punishment fit. That stance gradually evolved to the point where each case was considered individually. Often, he also waited to decide until after a preliminary hearing, where a judge weighed whether there was enough evidence for a case to go to trial, because new information might come out during the proceeding that could affect his decision. That delay also postponed a defendant's right to an additional lawyer. California law mandates that defendants in capital cases have two attorneys. By waiting until after a preliminary hearing to officially seek the death penalty, a district attorney can keep suspects with only one defense counsel for a longer period of time.

But just as Marin's Kamena had decided capital punishment was appropriate early on, as soon as Yancey learned the details of the Helzer case—the elderly victims, the desecration of the bodies—he made his choice. Two lawyers or not, he was going all the way on this one from the beginning, he thought. There was no question in his mind.[6]

As the evidence against her sons slowly mounted, Carma Helzer continued to wade into the mix despite their attorneys' pleas for her to keep quiet. She insisted on making

kooky pronouncements whenever someone stuck a microphone in her face. After attending a police press conference, she asked the victims' families to join her prayers
that the truth come out and called upon everyone involved
to use "every fiber in your soul and heaven and earth to dis-
cover the impeccable truth; I know what that truth is, but I
won't tell you."[7] Her husband was more circumspect, saying only what any parent would in such a situation: "We
think the truth is that our boys are innocent."[8] He and
Carma had reconciled earlier that summer after her affair
with Don ended—despite the counseling she and Don received from Taylor, who fancied himself a relationship
coach as well as a prophet.

Carma's assertions of innocence caught Jewett's ear.
She was going far beyond what a mother would normally
say in such circumstances, he thought. It sounded like she
actually knew something about the crimes, and he intended
to find out what. There was already a grand jury in session
in the little War Memorial building across from the courthouse. He would put it on the case, using its powers to
compel witnesses to testify under oath. And he planned to
start with Carma. He was investigating the murders of five
people, and if he had to question a mother to get pertinent
information, so be it.

But Jewett did not go about his task quietly. He had both
Carma and Gerry served with subpoenas just before their
sons appeared in court August 17, right in front of a courtroom full of reporters. When the journalistic contingent
proceeded to camp out on the steps of the War Memorial
building for the rest of the day, he politely refused to tell
them anything during his occasional outdoor smoke breaks.

Inside, he was going over everything he could think of
with Carma. She spent hours in front of the grand jury,
courteously trying to answer everyone's questions. She sat
in a chair, her small frame dwarfed by the sturdy wooden

desk before her. Jewett stood at a podium off to one side and the grand jurors sat directly in front of her. Eventually, she grew more accustomed to her surroundings and decided to get more comfortable. She climbed up on the desk and sat there cross-legged as she fielded questions. Everyone stared at her in surprise. Well, Jewett thought, as long as she answers questions, whatever made her feel at ease was fine with him.

He asked her about her family's history, whether her elder son acted as if he was mentally ill (the answer was no), and the very interesting proposal Taylor had recently made to *Playboy* magazine. Carma explained that Taylor had told her he wanted an interview with Hugh Hefner himself and thought it would be worth some money. Ever the businessman, he thought that publishing his story would benefit *Playboy* by increasing their circulation. "And then he said he thought perhaps when Keri's issue came out, that it would benefit her," Carma said. "And he said in the long run everybody would be blessed."

She maintained that he wanted the money to be used for five different purposes: his children's education, scholarships for people to attend Harmony, a victims' assistance fund, the Martinez jail where he was currently incarcerated, and a fund in memory of Selina. This last one had grand jurors ruminating on why he would care about a Selina fund if he was still insisting he did not know her.

"Do you know why he would think that his everyday life story, without any criminal element in it, would be of value or of interest to the public?" one grand juror asked her.

The ironic thing was that had the juror known Taylor, he would have easily believed that Taylor thought his everyday, Spirit-speaking life was worthy of such interest. Carma, however, was focused on her belief in her son's innocence. Her son just wanted the truth to be heard, she said.

"Do you know what the truth is?" Jewett asked.

"Yes, the truth is my son did not murder anyone," Carma said.

"What did he do?" Jewett asked.

And finally, Carma began sounding like a mother—one with faith, but no knowledge.

"Now, I can only tell you what I know. And it comes from in here," she said, pointing to her heart. "I know he did not murder anybody. I know that. I know it."

————

One of the issues the DA offices in Marin and Contra Costa agreed on when settling the jurisdictional question was that everyone would be circumspect when it came to dealing with the press, which was still intensely interested in the case. So when Kamena opened up her *Marin Independent Journal* one morning and saw Hal Jewett liberally quoted, saying things she thought should not be divulged, she felt that agreement had been violated.

She had always been cautious about saying too much, not wanting to trigger a change of venue that would force her deputies to go to trial in a county halfway across the state just because there was too much publicity at home. Yancey, on the other hand, usually had individual prosecutors handle media inquiries for whatever cases they were assigned, even though that often resulted in wildly divergent ways of information getting released.

Jewett had always talked to the press. He often would not comment on many case details, but he at the very least gave statements to the media after court appearances. His attitude had been formed in childhood. Although he chose a career in law, for years the family business had been journalism. His grandfather was William F. Knowland, a former U.S. senator and the editor and publisher of the *Oakland Tribune,* a daily newspaper the family owned until the late 1970s. That background, coupled with his experience dealing with the media in other high-profile cases, meant he had no reservations about what he should and should not say to reporters.

After reading her paper, Kamena called Jewett up. It was not a pleasant conversation. The two disagreed on what information he had released. He knew what he was doing, he said. She felt he was being rude and quit the conversation. Her next call was to Yancey, with whom she arranged a meeting the next day. When she arrived at the Contra Costa office, accompanied by Marin sheriff Bob Doyle, she flatly told Yancey and his chief deputy, Dale Miller, that Jewett had violated their media agreement.[9] She wanted him taken off the case.[10]

Miller tried to reassure her. Good trial lawyers were like racehorses—high-strung animals that needed to be allowed to run. And Jewett was a Thoroughbred, he said. "He is under control," he told her. "He'll be handling this case."

———

Word of his parents' grand-jury testimony filtered back to Taylor in jail. He was not pleased, especially with his mother's take on the whole experience. He couldn't believe she thought it was a good thing that she had had to testify. She told him they planned to call Debra. He quickly fired off a letter to her.

"Just remember, the less you say, is always the best you can say. Try and create that if you can. Dad talked for 45 minutes and Mother talked for 7 hours or so. BAD BAD MOMMA!"

He reminded her that he dealt ecstasy and that he was on SSI for mental disability. She did not need to lie about either of those things. "I AM NOT ASHAMED THAT I AM IN CONSTANT COMMUNICATION WITH THE LORD AND HIS ANGELS AND I DO NOT NEED YOU

TO TRY TO HELP ME BY BEING DISHONEST ABOUT THESE THINGS," he wrote.

After addressing various mundane matters, like offering her his video collection, Taylor closed the letter: "And thank you for not writing me back. I've been shown to only focus on the Lord's will and not get caught up in the dramas of the 3rd dimension."

Taylor knew his letter would be read by jail officials before being put in the mail. Justin, who was housed in a different section of the jail, had warned his big brother and Dawn of this in his own letters to them soon after their arrests. So Taylor invoked his connection to God whenever he could, writing again to Debra that he wanted to tell his story but had to remain silent unless Spirit commanded otherwise.

While Taylor clung to the ethereal, Justin set about addressing more practical matters. He learned how to negotiate the maze of jail regulations, finding out how to get things from the canteen and how to request additional supplies from the sometimes reluctant guards. And he decided that if he was going to stay healthy, he had to start taking advantage of the jail's exercise equipment. The food they served in this place certainly was not going to help his constitution. Most of it had questionable nutritional content, but he soon found that if he stuck to things like instant oatmeal, sunflower seeds, peanuts, and trail mix, he could stay reasonably fit. He eagerly bought the vitamin packets they offered, but found that they were of such a low-grade quality, they were a complete rip-off.[11]

He was upbeat and cheerful, convinced that everything would work out in the end. As the days wore on, his positive outlook began to fade somewhat. By the end of the month, he was starting to realize that he would not be going anywhere for a long time. And it could be Taylor's fault. He kept reading the newspapers and tried not to jump to conclusions about what had gone on. But despite his doubts, Taylor's hold over him was still strong. Even though he had participated in all of the plans and knew exactly what had happened, Justin stopped just short of blaming his brother for getting him into this mess.

Dawn's belief in her prophet appeared to remain rock solid. She continued to believe he was protecting her and would engineer her release from jail when the time was right. So there really was no need for the two lawyers who kept trying to talk to her. She told Headley and his colleague Kim Kruglick all of this. Dawn said she did not need the legal system and she did not need them. Spirit would decide what happened next. Anything she had done, she did after consultation with Taylor the prophet and with the approval of Jesus Christ. She was surrounded at that very moment by a band of angels.

The two men sat in the little jail visiting room and stared at her. Holy shit, they thought. They had never seen a client like this before. She could not help them with her defense at all until they undid Taylor's brainwashing. As they left the jail, Headley turned to Kruglick. "I've got just the woman to help us," he said.

It just so happened that one of Headley's Berkeley neighbors was a woman named Margaret Thaler Singer, one of the world's foremost experts on cults and brainwashing. She started her research in the 1950s with soldiers who had been held captive in North Korea, then gained national recognition when she testified at the trial of Patty Hearst, the kidnapped newspaper heiress who eventually helped her captors rob a bank. Singer thought that Hearst had been brainwashed into committing the crime by her kidnappers.

Most importantly for Headley and Kruglick's purposes, Singer knew how to deprogram cult members. Ideally, former cult members would participate in "exit counseling,"

showing current adherents that life is possible outside a
cult. Since Dawn's cult had only ever consisted of three
true members, there was no one available to offer that kind
of help. Instead, her lawyers began to slowly take her
through the process, which is not unlike an intervention for
a drug or alcohol abuser. Advised by Singer, they and a psychologist described the coercive techniques and thought
manipulation they thought Taylor had used to bend her to
his will. They prodded her to ask questions and think critically about her time with Taylor. But the deprogramming
did not have a profound effect on Dawn. Even as she sat in
jail far removed from his twenty-four-hour-a-day manipulation, Dawn still insisted that Taylor was a prophet.

NINETEEN

Safecracking
◆

As detectives worked furiously to piece together the lives of the Helzer brothers and Dawn Godman, they kept coming across a particular name: Debra McClanahan. She was an odd woman who lived in a little apartment in Concord with her daughter and their ferret, and she seemed to be quite close to all three suspects.

She told the first detective who spoke with her that she went to the movies and dinner with her three friends the night of July 30. She had even saved the receipts. Heidi Stephenson, who was assigned the follow-up, didn't buy the alibi for a second. No one just saved receipts like that and then tucked them into a cigarette case for safekeeping, ready to pull out the minute someone asked about them, which was exactly what Debra did. She eagerly showed them to Stephenson and Chiabotti, who began probing her for information about what actually occurred. Finally, after hours of talking, Debra admitted that Taylor had her manufacture the alibi. She had not actually seen him, Justin, or Dawn that night. She told the detectives she thought they needed help covering for a drug deal, and she insisted she knew nothing about the murders.

Stephenson was certain, however, that Debra knew more than she was saying. The detective kept coming back, trying to establish a rapport that would put Debra at ease. It was exhausting. This woman was all over the map. She told Stephenson about her interest in witchcraft, about the massages she gave, about all kinds of things that made Stephenson's head spin. But Debra still said nothing of any value to the case—until the pressure finally got to be too much. She called Stephenson crying in the middle of the day and asked the detective to come to where she worked. Stephenson grabbed Chiabotti and headed out the door. This is it, she thought. She's finally going to give it up.

The three of them sat down at a little table at her office. Debra was obviously scared. She started talking about Taylor and his emphasis on loyalty. If people broke his trust, they would pay. He had told her so, told her he would "fix the car" of anyone who betrayed him, she said. She's afraid he's going to kill her, Stephenson thought. Look, she told Debra, Taylor's in jail right now. He can't hurt you.

The detective had started to feel a little sorry for Debra. She believed the poor woman did not know about the murders and that the trio had basically just taken advantage of her gullible nature. But that did not mean Stephenson was going to let up on her until she figured out what Debra knew.

And then it happened. "Well, I've got some stuff back at my apartment," Debra said.

"What kind of stuff?" Stephenson asked nonchalantly as Chiabotti put on his best poker face and stayed silent.

A wheelchair. A safe. The detectives looked at each other. Everything they had been trying to find for weeks could be mere minutes away. When they got to the apartment, Stephenson and Chiabotti quickly identified the safe and the wheelchair, which they were positive was the one Dawn used when she visited Vicki Sexton at the bank. They called in more officers to do a thorough search of the place. Since they had permission from Debra to be there, they did not need a search warrant. But she had made it clear that the safe was not hers, so she did not have the legal authority to grant access. It stayed locked as everyone wondered what was inside.

After the exhausting interviews with Debra as well as weeks of nonstop investigation, Chiabotti, Stephenson, and Elo finally got a rest. It was August 25, and it was their first day off that month. After twenty-hour days that gradually dwindled to a more manageable twelve, the three gratefully took the small respite offered.

Others involved in the case kept working. David Chilimidos, the Concord sergeant in charge of investigations, thought the safe too important a piece of evidence to sit unopened. He set about getting a search warrant that would allow him to open it without jeopardizing the admissibility of any evidence it might contain once the case came to trial. He drew together the threads of the investigation into a forty-nine-page document outlining the probable cause that authorities had to suspect that there was evidence in the safe. He asked for permission to serve the warrant at night. The safe was stored at the police station, and unlike searching a house where people slept, no one would be inconvenienced by authorities cracking it open late at night. "We have an important investigative need to search the safe as it may yield very significant evidence," Chilimidos wrote. He did not state in the affidavit why the search could not wait until morning, but thought that in this case—even though the suspects were safely in jail—anything was possible.

He took his warrant request to Peter Spinetta, the same judge who had presided over the night hearing for Concord's initial Saddlewood search warrant. The judge signed it at 10:07 p.m. Within an hour, Chilimidos, Bob Hole, and Ted Spyrow were peering inside the mysterious safe.

On top was an eyeglass case, a metal cookie tin, and the thin edge of a binder. A pair of water-sport gloves was neatly wedged against the side. They took out the binder and the gloves, and—would you look at that . . . A gun and two boxes of ammunition. It was a 9-mm, the same caliber used to shoot Jenny Villarin and Jim Gamble. The investigators were thrilled at their discovery. They forced themselves to go slowly, photographing everything as they emptied this treasure chest so thoughtfully packed up by Dawn three weeks before.

Chilimidos got a lump in his throat when he saw Annette Stineman's wallet, complete with her driver's license. They pulled out prescription insulin with Ivan's name still on the label. Then came the couple's checkbooks and their retirement account statements, as well as a copy of Selina's driver's license and Social Security card. They found a bank-deposit hold document with Vicki Sexton's business card neatly stapled to it. And then there was the typed script explaining why the Stinemans needed money for their granddaughter's operation.

How could these suspects have been such idiots? To keep all this evidence and then store it in one spot was the height of stupidity. But the cops were not complaining. Their job had just gotten a whole lot easier.

When the lead detectives on the case returned to work the next day, they were stunned to learn that the safe had already been opened. It was not as if their presence was necessary, but after putting in countless hours for weeks on end and being the ones to locate it at Debra's, the psychological boost of being there when the evidence was un-

veiled would have been nice. As it was, they did not understand the rush to open it in the middle of the night. It felt
like someone had given them a Christmas present and then
opened it early without them.

———————

The cache of evidence found in the safe verified the link
between the Marin shootings and the victims found in the
duffel bags, a connection investigators had previously been
able only to speculate about. But, although the new proof
vaulted the case forward, there were still holes that needed
to be filled. Chief among them was Selina's missing car. Its
description and license-plate number had been broadcast
throughout the state for weeks, and still no one had seen it.
Police divers searched the delta and found nothing. Selina's
friends searched the valley and found nothing. Meanwhile,
the car was sitting in the nearby city of Petaluma where a
parking enforcement officer ticketed it—and did nothing to
check on its owner.

The city, which normally had two parking enforcement
officers, was down to one during the month of August.
There had been complaints about one of the downtown patrol beats, so he concentrated on that area and not the one
where a blue-gray 1984 Honda Accord was parked. When
he finally did work the second downtown beat on August
24, he marked the Honda at 9 a.m. Two hours later, he
wrote a citation and slapped it on the windshield, then was
called away from the area. He next noticed the car on August 31 and was about to write a ticket when he saw one already on the car. He ran the license plate.

Marin and Concord investigators descended on downtown Petaluma, cordoning off the corner of Fourth and A
streets. They were astonished. The car had been parked on
a busy downtown street patrolled not only by parking enforcement but by actual cops. Yet no one had bothered to

run the plates. Their suspects had been in custody since
August 7. Had it been parked there before that, or did the
trio have someone else move it after their arrest? There
was no way to tell how long it had been there, the parking
officer told them feebly. Detectives shook their heads and
prepared to tow the car away. Marin County was closer and
had a secure facility, but after some back-and-forth, Contra
Costa County won, and Selina's little car was taken to
Concord, where it sat until it could be properly processed
for evidence.

Could the mystery man from the Petaluma bank have
parked the car there? Authorities still did not know why he
had deposited $10,000 in the Stinemans' account or the ex-
tent of his involvement. They reviewed the surveillance
tape of him making a deposit on July 31, after the Stinemans disappeared. And then they rewound it. Seven minutes before the man approached the teller's window, a fat
woman in a wheelchair and wearing a cowboy hat had conducted a transaction. Knowing from Vicki Sexton what
Dawn wore during her August 1 trip to the Walnut Creek
bank, they were suddenly certain that the mysterious man
had had nothing to do with that $10,000 deposit. Instead,
the clock on the video surveillance system was not in sync
with the one that recorded the time of the deposits. Once
the discrepancy was fixed, it became apparent that the
wheelchair-bound woman was the one who put $10,000 of
the Stinemans' own money into their account that day. The
man had merely been at the bank to cash his paycheck.

Police cleared the man on September 6, the same day
Jewett finally filed murder charges against Taylor, Justin,
and Dawn for the shooting deaths of Jenny Villarin and Jim
Gamble. The next day, everyone appeared in court again,
this time to actually enter pleas to the charges. All three
pleaded not guilty, but not before Taylor once again took
center stage.

"Personally, I don't know why we can't say what happened and get it over with," he told the court when asked if he agreed to waive his right to a speedy trial. Chapot frantically tried to shush him, reaching up toward her much taller client, who was peering out through an opening in the glass wall of the courtroom's holding cell. "Your honor," Taylor continued, "I've wanted to talk about this for so long."

Jewett stared at Taylor. He slowly asked if the defendant understood his right to a speedy trial.

"I'm not sure what you're doing here. I'm not sure," Taylor replied.[1]

"Listen to me closely," Jewett said.

"I am," said Taylor.[2] It was the first time Taylor spoke directly to the man who would become—more than any other participant in his long, twisted tale—his nemesis. No one would fight him harder, or believe his story less, than the prosecutor standing across the room. Every time he went to court, he would see Jewett. Every time they let him out of his cell block, every time he got the smallest change of scenery, Jewett would be there—a constant, glowering reminder that he was no longer free.

———

The coroner finally released Ivan and Annette's bodies in early September. Judy and Fred flew up from Southern California and wanted to stay at their parents' house instead of another hotel, but it was still in the possession of the police, who had gone over every inch of it for evidence. The plumbing was not even working, since they had taken the drains and things apart in their search for clues. Before the couple arrived, Paul Crain—stretching far outside his job description—took over a few tools and managed to get most of the faucets working so they would at least have running water.

Ivan and Annette had been so organized, they had already purchased spaces at a local cemetery and planned for
their services. Judy and Nancy were forced to make a few
changes, however. There would be no open caskets for obvious reasons. The mortician recommended cremation, but
the sisters declined. Mama had always hated fire. She also
had been scared of the water, which was why she and
Daddy had reserved spots in a vault instead of plots in the
cold, wet ground. Nancy and Judy hated that—after all of
their parents' careful preparations, Mama had been dumped
in the water anyway. Now she deserved to rest somewhere
clean and quiet and dry.

The first Saturday that everything would be ready for
the service was September 16, what would have been Ivan
and Annette's fifty-fifth wedding anniversary. The mortician looked at the sisters with trepidation.

"Oh, you don't want to do that," he said.

"Why?" Nancy and Judy both said. "That was their date."

The sisters had always commemorated the day their
parents got married. One year when they were young, they
went to a store near Ivan and Annette's cabin in the mountains and used their pocket money to buy two little fuzzy
toy squirrels, one for each parent. On the way home, one
fell out of the bag and got lost in the snow. Nancy spent all
winter looking for it, and when the snow finally melted she
found it, missing a bit of fur but otherwise unharmed. And
Mama and Daddy at last had their matching set.

As they sat at their parents' funeral, the sisters knew
that no spring thaw would make things right this time
around. But they thought their parents would have liked the
matching light blue caskets that sat angled toward each
other in the shape of a V. There were flowers and candles
and not very many people. They would have a memorial
service later for all the friends and neighbors, but they

wanted to do this first and give themselves a little bit more time before they had to mourn in public.

———————

Jenny Villarin, who had always worked so hard to accommodate her family and friends, continued to do so in death. Her big brother David wanted her buried in Salinas, next to their father and brother. Oggie thought she belonged in Marin County, where she had lived for so long and been such a part of the community. David told her that their sister was gone; the burial was for them and their peace of mind. Oggie relented and they decided to split the ashes.

On a beautiful fall day, many Marin denizens gathered at Heart's Desire Beach for a Native American blessing in honor of Jenny, who had so loved her Indian heritage. They sent the ashes into the wind over Tamales Bay and had a picnic. Later, they gathered again at a funeral parlor in Salinas. Elvin Bishop sent some of his daughter's ashes and Jenny and Selina's remains were later buried together.

Their good friend Jim was laid to rest in Fort Bragg, a coastal town several hours north of Marin County and close to where his son, Erin, lived.

———————

After all the whirlwind publicity, public appearances, and other pressing Playmate obligations abated, Keri Furman found time to sit down with detectives investigating her exboyfriend's case at the end of September. The September Playmate of the Month was cooperative, telling them very interesting stories about Taylor's drug use, some strange business venture called In To Me See, and his efforts to pretend he was mentally ill in order to collect disability payments. Two months later, she worked out a deal giving her immunity from prosecution for crimes, such as drug use, she might have committed while with Taylor in exchange for her truthful testimony.

The massive investigation into the Helzer brothers and Dawn Godman's activities began to slowly wind down as winter passed. It was a good thing, too, because the departments involved could not keep that level of intensity going. The controlled chaos that the case had created was enormous. For the Concord Police Department alone, overtime and forensic costs would eventually top $250,000[3]—more than double the amount the suspects had hoped to gain from the murder spree that started the whole thing in the first place.

But gradually, the pace began to slow. People started taking vacations again. Detectives had the resources to devote to other cases. Officers resumed their patrol shifts. In 2001, Chiabotti, Elo, and Stephenson all transferred out of investigations. Each had decided it was time for a change. And that April, Bob Hole and Ted Spyrow finally moved out of the Concord Police Department's major-case room. As they packed up their files and gave the cops back their conference room, the investigation effectively came to a close.

TWENTY

Freedom at Any Price

———————————◆———————————

Margaret Singer continued to advise Dawn Godman's attorneys, who now were convinced that their client had been subjected to cultish brainwashing. The expert made one recommendation that would help them understand their client better than they thought possible. She introduced them to a private investigator out of San Francisco named David Sullivan.

An engaging man with a compact frame and sympathetic blue eyes, he had investigated cults before—infiltrating them, debriefing former members, sampling large group awareness programs. He tracked one guru so closely that he had managed to get the man's prized Cadillac towed, which forced him to take the bus, putting a severe dent in his all-powerful guru aura. Sullivan was able to get his clients' family members out of the cult when the man eventually could not maintain his guru credibility and fled the country to avoid his outstanding warrants.

But his new client no longer needed to be rescued from the clutches of a guru. Dawn Godman's behavior needed to be explained. Her defense team needed to show how Taylor and her involvement with group trainings had broken her moral underpinnings and caused her to commit the crimes. And the most effective way to do that was for Sullivan to take the course himself. He enrolled in Harmony in March 2001. He took the course in Salt Lake City from the same trainer who had instructed Dawn in Sacramento two years before. He needed his experience to be as similar to Dawn's as possible.

The trainer was brutal. He tore people down, berated them, called them names. He upset one woman so much she vomited down the front of her clothing as she was forced to stand in front of the group while participants shouted abuse at her. After two days of the program, Sullivan was exhausted. He had to act like he was breaking down his walls and finding his inner child, yet at the same time keep that from actually happening. Since there were no unsupervised breaks, or even any solitary bathroom trips, Sullivan could only write notes of his experiences when he was released late each night. As the days progressed, he began to realize just how effective this training was. The participants came into the training as ordinary, upstanding citizens. After two days, their moral compasses had been totally destroyed and they headed easily toward a sort of mob mentality. They laughed at fellow participants who had been molested. They made fun of those with physical handicaps. Sullivan had never seen this happen with such speed.

This is really effective stuff, he told Kruglick during one of their late-night phone conversations, when Sullivan would check in so the attorneys would know he was doing all right. The trainers used behavioral psychology to open people up and then they slipped in ideas that made you believe what they wanted you to believe, Sullivan said.

Kruglick, a veteran criminal-defense attorney and long-

time, cheerfully unrepentant smoker, was unfailingly polite and formal in court. But out of it, he did not mince
words. "I don't want to hear this shit," he rumbled over the
phone line to Sullivan. "It sounds like you're getting brainwashed yourself. What's going on with you?"

In subsequent phone calls, Sullivan reassured him that
he would be able to finish the training, although he really
did want out. The whole program was emotionally drain-
ing, physically exhausting, and nauseating to watch. But
now he understood what had broken through Dawn's defenses and allowed Taylor to take hold of her so firmly.

Later, he was able to sit down with Dawn and take her
through the training, reminding her of the humiliation she
had endured and explaining that the sleep deprivation,
guided imagery, verbal assaults, and then the final days of
"love-bombing" were all designed to break down her defenses. While she might have recovered from this if left
alone afterward, Taylor had been there ready to lead her
astray—and she had followed.

———

Justin was also having difficulties adjusting to his new life.
He started reading *The Book of Mormon* again, but that did
not stop his spiritual quest from heading in other directions. He had always wanted to go to Tibet and try living as
a monk. Now he decided that the Contra Costa County jail
would be his monastery.[1] By May 2001, he'd lost thirty
pounds, helped along by a fasting regimen he told people
he was undertaking to cleanse himself. He also slowly began to think, as he stared at the walls of his little cell day
after day, that his big brother had been inspired not by
God, but by the devil.

The realization did not come easily, and Justin occasionally lashed out under the force of his weighty concerns. While lining up for lunch one day in late May, he

jumped ahead and took a sandwich out of the bin without permission. A deputy told him to move to the other side of the cart.

"I was already in the front of the line!" he shouted. "Why don't you just chill out!"

"Excuse me?" said the deputy, who was not about to be addressed in such manner in front of forty other inmates.

"You heard me," Justin yelled.

The deputy grabbed Justin's left arm and turned him toward a holding room. Justin spun toward the guard just as another rushed in, grabbing his right arm. The two men propelled him into the holding room and away from the line of hungry prisoners. Justin sat in the little room, took some deep breaths, and caught his temper. Twenty minutes passed before the deputy came in to check on him. Justin knew he had crossed the line and needed to get back in authority's good graces. He apologized. That might have soothed an irked deputy, but it did not impress the discipline committee; he received three days in lockdown for his actions.[2]

———

The monotony of jail time was broken by periodic court dates, at which the case was continually delayed. Finally, in December 2001, everyone gathered for the preliminary hearing, where Judge Douglas Cunningham would decide whether enough evidence existed against the suspects for the case to go to trial. Such hearings were designed to move quickly. Evidence could be entered through police officers, who were allowed to testify about interviews they had conducted instead of having the witnesses themselves take the stand, as was required at trial. Most preliminary hearings could be finished in an afternoon. One concerning a homicide might go a full day. The Helzer preliminary hearing would take two weeks.

Jewett planned to lay it all out. For the victims' families and the public, it would be a revelation. Until now, only investigators—and of course Taylor, Justin, and Dawn—knew what the motivation had been: murder in the name of spreading peace, joy, and love throughout the world. As they sat in court day after day, listening to police officers testify about the plans Taylor had expounded about to friends, the Villarins, Jim Gamble's mother and aunt, and the Stinemans' daughters grew more and more incredulous that their relatives had been caught in such a crazy scheme.

They heard that Taylor had asked his cousin Chi Hoffmann how to fake mental illness. They learned that he had passed out questionnaires at raves in an attempt to recruit women to work as prostitutes. They listened as officers recited a long list of purchases—including the duffel bags and the water-ski equipment—that were made long before the crimes and were proof the trio had long planned the killings, Jewett said. And they saw the poster with Taylor's Twelve Principles of Magic. As Jewett read the list, Taylor followed along, mouthing the words to all the dozen items.

Jewett did not find it necessary to bring in many actual witnesses, instead letting the detectives testify about their interviews. But there was one key player he wanted the judge to hear, and the defendants to see. Debra McClanahan walked into court wearing a long, flowing black skirt, white shirt with a sheer collar, and a black blazer. Her long brown hair was pulled back into a ponytail. It was a look that coordinated with what Jewett spent a lot of time questioning her about—her Wicca beliefs. Because of the looser standards at preliminary hearings, a lot of testimony not relevant at trial is allowed. Jewett took full advantage, having Debra explain all about white, gray, and black magic; different rituals; and Druids, fairies, leprechauns, and "the hellish creatures from the bowels."

More pertinent to the prosecution were Debra's accounts

of her talks with Taylor, which included details about In To Me See and Transform America. She also outlined her attempt to provide her three friends with an alibi by purchasing movie tickets and dinners. But she insisted under oath that she had known nothing about their plans for killing.

Debra did not often look at her three former friends, who sat in their jail-issued clothes behind a table across the courtroom from her. She was still scared of Taylor and had actually been in a witness relocation program for the last year and a half. She spent part of two days on the stand before being excused.

The trio's attorneys, who were under no obligation to produce witnesses of their own in this hearing, instead spent their time laying the groundwork for the defenses that were to come. Chapot asked questions of prosecution witnesses that stressed how crazy and foolish Taylor's plans sounded to those who heard them. Veale took shots at the identification process used by police and the obsessive media coverage that could have tainted both the IDs and the investigation as a whole. Headley highlighted Taylor's manipulative abilities and Dawn's lack of self-esteem.

After thirty-one witnesses who testified to evidence from more than ninety people involved in the investigation, Jewett rested his case. There was no doubt that Cunningham would rule that the trio had to stand trial, and on December 20, 2001, he did exactly that. The judge did not, however, agree with Jewett that the conspiracy the trio had formed stretched far back in time. He ruled that it began March 1, 2000, and ended with their arrest that August. He also declined defense attorneys' requests to strike the special circumstance attached to Selina's murder, which alleged that the killing was committed to silence a witness. The lawyers had been successful earlier in persuading the judge that the same allegations in the Jenny Villarin and Jim Gamble killings should not apply. All three suspects remained eligible for the death penalty.

———————

After hearing all of the evidence that Jewett had amassed against them, the three Children of Thunder and their attorneys began to seriously strategize their defenses. Headley and Kruglick were in by far the best position. Dawn was the most sympathetic of the suspects; her wretched background coupled with Taylor's manipulation gave the two attorneys a good shot at convincing a jury that she should not die for her actions. They also had an extremely influential expert who was prepared to testify that she was insane at the time she committed the crimes.

Park Dietz was a forensic psychiatrist nationally known for his work on such cases as those of Jeffrey Dahmer, John Hinckley, and Ted Kaczynski. He advised television shows and ran a consulting business. And he almost never testified for the defense.[3] He spent twenty-four hours interviewing Dawn over the course of several months and came to several conclusions that would be enormously helpful at trial. He concluded that Dawn was not a sociopath or psychopath predisposed to commit crimes of this nature, but had been subjected to psychological manipulation. And, most important for her defense, he thought she had been insane while committing the crimes.[4]

But even with Dietz in their corner, Headley and Kruglick did not want to take their case to trial, where the best outcome would be a sentence of life in prison without the possibility of parole. Headley started talking to Jewett. Think about what she could offer your case, he said. The prosecutor likely had enough evidence to convict the brothers, but what about the penalty? Jurors usually like to know exactly who did the killing before they condemn someone to death. And so far, investigators still had no real idea what had happened in the Saddlewood house or who had really pulled the trigger in Woodacre.

Headley offered to have Dawn take a polygraph test. What would Jewett like to know? "Personally, did she kill anybody? And if she did, we aren't going to make any deals with her. If she didn't, then we can talk," Jewett told Headley.

Dawn passed the test. She had not personally delivered any lethal blows. Jewett laid down more conditions. She had to tell the truth. If she did not, he could take back the deal and prosecute her using her own statement against her. Dawn agreed, and then the haggling over her punishment began. Jewett would not pursue the death penalty, a sentence even he thought it was doubtful that a jury would impose. The next most severe punishment, life in prison without the possibility of parole, was too much for her attorneys. They argued for a fixed sentence that would at least ensure her freedom as an old woman. Jewett would not bend that far, however. The final agreement fell in between: it called for more than thirty-seven years to life in prison, meaning that Dawn would have to convince a parole board to free her before she ever saw the outside world again. Although he needed only his boss's permission to strike the deal with Dawn, Jewett thoughtfully ran his decision by some of the victims' families anyway.

The time came to finally hear what Dawn had to say. Jewett called Steve Chiabotti and asked him to do the interview. Chiabotti agreed immediately and pulled out the reams of paperwork on the case to refresh his memory. On July 24, 2003, he sat down in an interview room in the fourth-floor office of the district attorney. Dawn sat across from him. She wanted veggie sandwiches, so two were brought in with the fresh vegetables she did not get across the street in jail. Finally, she was ready. The interview began.

During the next seven hours, Chiabotti discovered that the trio called themselves Children of Thunder and that they had strategized for months about how to kill and then dispose of the bodies. He found out that another man had been Taylor's original target before the Stinemans. And he, along with everyone watching on the closed circuit television, learned what happened at Saddlewood, and that Taylor had been the one to gun down Jenny Villarin and Jim Gamble.

Dawn told her story matter-of-factly. She showed little emotion until she started talking about knocking the teeth out of her victims' heads. Then she told Chiabotti she needed to take a break and was escorted to the bathroom, where she threw up. Good, thought Chiabotti, who did not believe she was showing enough remorse for her part in all of this. At least some of her actions finally sickened her, he thought.

Headley and Kruglick watched the interview with Jewett on the remote video feed. They were there to make sure that what Dawn said was what they knew to be true. And it was. They had been through the deprogramming with her and then the resulting period of suicidal thoughts as she realized what she had done, and now they were close to getting her the best outcome they could.

The next day they sealed the deal. All three defendants were in court that Friday for a previously scheduled hearing regarding a motion to suppress evidence. At the end of the day they were escorted out by deputies, and Justin and Taylor's attorneys left the courtroom without knowing what was about to occur. At 5 p.m., Dawn was quietly brought back in and pleaded guilty to thirteen felonies: conspiracy to commit a crime; five counts of murder; two counts of kidnapping; extortion; two counts of first-degree residential robbery; first-degree residential burglary; and possessing a controlled substance for sale. Judge Mary

Ann O'Malley sentenced her to twenty-five years to life in prison for the conspiracy charge, with the same sentence for each murder to run at the same time. She then added twelve years and eight months for the robbery and kidnapping counts. The sentences for the other crimes would run at the same time.

Jewett sternly told Dawn that she would have to serve 85 percent of the twelve years and eight months—more than ten years—and then do the entire twenty-five years for the conspiracy before she would become eligible for parole. But he also made it perfectly clear that killing five people meant she would probably never be released. She said she understood.

————————

Suzanne Chapot did not find out about Dawn's plea until the following week. She was not pleased. She had also tried to negotiate a deal with Jewett that would have saved Taylor from the death penalty, but the prosecutor was most definitely not interested. And now, with Dawn ready to take the stand, he had no need to offer Taylor anything at all.

The account Dawn gave of Children of Thunder's actions forced both Justin and Taylor into a corner. With her detailing exactly who struck which blows, neither could now blame the other for the actual killings. Their attorneys would need to rethink things, which was going to take a lot more time than they currently had. The trial was scheduled to start on October 20, 2003. Both Chapot and Justin's new lawyer, Dan Cook, asked for a delay. O'Malley, a former prosecutor who would preside over the trial, agreed and set a new date of March 1, 2004.

On October 2, Cook officially announced that Justin would soon enter a plea of not guilty by reason of insanity to all the charges. The lawyer had been laying the groundwork for the plea since taking over from Bill Veale the previous November, after the lead attorney resigned from the case. Cook, a slender, soft-spoken deputy alternate defender with gray hair and an unassuming manner, had been Veale's second chair since the beginning and knew the case. He had psychologists spend several months evaluating his client; they decided Justin had done what he believed was right when he committed the murders. They also had an unusual diagnosis—not just that Justin was delusional at the time of the crimes, but that he had acquired those delusions from his older brother. It was called shared psychotic disorder, or folie à deux. Now they would see whether neutral doctors appointed by the court came to the same conclusion.

All the waiting was taking its toll on Justin. He remained at the Martinez Detention Facility, stuck in a cell with a guy who was getting on his nerves. Two days after Cook filed the insanity plea, an argument erupted between the cellmates over who had more drawer space. They started throwing punches and crashing around the cell. A deputy rushed in and ordered them to stop. He pulled Justin out of the cell, threw him on the ground, and handcuffed him. He ordered Justin's cellmate to the ground and handcuffed him as well.

As things calmed down, everyone assessed the damage. Justin would need three stitches for a gash in his head. He also had a bloody nose. His now former roommate had scrapes on his face and complained that his head hurt. Both inmates received seven days in lockdown for the fight.[5]

———

As 2003 came to a close, Taylor was getting anxious. He was quickly coming to the realization that the trial might not go his way. But he thought himself a man of action and was not about to sit idly by while a jury convicted him of five murders and possibly sent him to death row. At the beginning of February 2004, he was allowed to leave the Martinez jail for a medical appointment. The trip, chaperoned by jail deputies, gave him the opportunity to see a little bit of blue sky and also brainstorm a few ideas that could get him out of his current situation. But he needed help.

Back in jail the next day, Taylor went to talk to a known gang member during a time when inmates were allowed out of their cells. The man gave Taylor a tutorial on the California Department of Corrections prison system, where Taylor would be sent after a conviction. He explained that Taylor would need to be in a lower-security facility in order to successfully escape. To get into such a prison, he would have to apply for a family-visit "hardship" when he entered the system. He needed to tell officials that his relatives did not live nearby and were not medically able to make the trip to see him. This could mean officials would place him at a closer, and less secure, prison.

The gang member outlined the security measures taken in such places, which he maintained were scant enough to allow his buddies to fly a helicopter into the exercise yard and break Taylor out. The idea was ludicrous, but the increasingly desperate Taylor fell for it completely. He didn't know, however, if he could get the $100,000 that the thug was demanding. It was possible, he told the gang member, but who exactly would be busting him out?

"It would be four of my dudes at twenty-five apiece," the man said. "It would be me doing it, and me telling my motherfuckers what to do. They'd do it because I told them to. They'd have no choice. And these dudes don't mess around."

Taylor then laid out a couple of different scenarios. What about trying to escape when he was getting transported from the Martinez jail to prison? The gangbanger quashed that idea quickly. The transport bus always had multiple armed guards, and the vehicle itself had bullet-proof glass, he said.

"How about during transport to or from court while I'm here, or if I'm brought to an appointment outside of this place?" Taylor asked, his previous day's doctor visit fresh in his mind. That would be easy to do, the man replied.

Taylor left the man's cell and wandered off, thoughts of escape bouncing around his brain. He searched for another receptive inmate he knew and found him down the hall. The inmate told Taylor that he had heard about what Taylor wanted to do and that he could help.

"Don't worry, dude," the inmate said. "What I've got planned is foolproof."

The two discussed the different routes jail deputies had taken to get Taylor to his medical appointments. It would be easy to lie in wait for the guards at the doctor's office and for a sniper to take out the driver while three other dudes blasted the other deputy, he told Taylor. They also could take out the van before it arrived at its destination.

"Would it be possible for me to drive while in waist re-straints after the deputies were taken care of?" Taylor asked. They debated this for a few minutes before Taylor decided that it would be feasible but not easy. What other options did his new friend have?

"[I'll have] my people waiting on the corner and blast the dudes while you jumped into the getaway car," the in-mate said. The guy was getting into this. What other ridicu-lous, straight-out-of-a-movie scenarios could he feed this idiot? He talked about using a local general aviation airport to fly to freedom, but Taylor was not very interested in that. He said that they could use a motorcycle to get Taylor away initially, and then rendezvous with a truck pulling a horse trailer. They would hide the motorcycle in the trailer, switch to another vehicle, and be home free.

This inmate's plan would cost the same as the first

man's helicopter proposal—$25,000 for each person. The money would naturally have to be paid beforehand, he said. Taylor was excited. This would work. "We definitely need to talk some more," he said.[6]

The day after Taylor's getaway conversations, the Martinez Detention Facility was quiet. It was early morning, and the inmates had not yet been let out of their cells for free time. A deputy inspecting the area stopped in surprise when he got to the exercise courtyard. A security netting high above him had a hole in it. It was only two or three inches wide, but it had definitely been created by someone since the last inspection twenty-four hours earlier. The deputy looked around. An inmate could have stood on the nearby exercise pull-up bars and used an easily available broom to poke at the netting. But that person would still have had to be extremely tall to reach that high off the ground.

The deputy and his colleagues did not have to ponder the situation long to decide on a suspect. Who was tall, stupid enough to try something like that, and had just yesterday been overheard plotting escape? The deputy immediately wrote up a report about the tampered netting, specifically naming Taylor Helzer as the inmate who was most likely responsible.

The guards wanted to see what else Taylor was plotting, so they decided not to stop a visit later that day with his mother. Carma waited in the little visiting room, separated by glass from her son as he sat down across from her. He leaned forward intently; he had important business to discuss. He needed her to raise $100,000 for him. He also made clear that he was cutting Justin loose. He wanted nothing to do with his little brother's trial. Justin would soon be on death row, which would hamper any escape attempts, Taylor said. But what was really important was the money, he told his mother. Start working on it immediately.

At Taylor's direction, Carma later placed $10,000 in some unknown person's mailbox. Whether she knew what the money was for is debatable. Gerry found out and told her not to give their son—or anybody—any more money. The cash was never seen again.

———

The inmate who had offered to help Taylor escape by car and motorcycle was out on free time. It was a dreary day at the end of February and he needed a chuckle. He sidled up to the cell door of the gang member and brought up their mutual friend. He had tried to get $100,000 out of Taylor, he told the gang member. The gang member called Taylor retarded and laughed about how he had fed the gullible bastard an even bigger escape fantasy involving "some helicopters and Navy SEAL–type shit." Taylor had believed in the plan enough to convince his mother to take money out of the bank until his father put a stop to it, the gang member said.

Both men knew what Taylor had done in order to land in jail in the first place. No model citizens themselves, they nevertheless agreed that he did not need to be set loose on society. "Yeah, I'm going to get you out," the first inmate said in a sarcastic hypothetical. "Why? So you can chop more people up?"

———

With no escape artists falling from the skies to help him make his getaway, Taylor glumly attended his court hearings the first week in March. On Tuesday, he watched Chapot argue that his trial should be separated from Justin's. Good riddance to that guy. But on Wednesday, Judge O'Malley denied the request. It looked like he was stuck with little brother once again. He had to do something about it. On Friday, he strode into court clad in the usual orange jail scrubs. The attorneys were scheduled to discuss nothing more important than some housekeeping details before jury selection started Monday, but Taylor knew better. He was going to take charge of this thing one way or the other. So he once again did the unthinkable. He pleaded guilty. To every charge against him.

TWENTY-ONE

Separated at Last

———◆———

Suzanne Chapot stood and clasped her hands in front of her. Taylor sat on her right. "I have been representing Taylor Helzer now for three and a half years," she said, putting her hand on his shoulder. Cook, sitting on Taylor's other side, braced himself. Chapot had told him a few days before what would happen. No one else in the courtroom knew.

"Almost from the beginning of the time that I began representing him," she continued, "he has wanted to enter pleas of guilty to the charges that he was accused of."

The already quiet, almost empty courtroom fell completely silent. Judge O'Malley's jaw dropped. Jewett leaned back in his chair and looked over at Taylor. That son of a bitch is fucking with the system again, he thought. He kept staring as Chapot continued.

"I have kept him from doing that," she said. Taylor had wanted to plead guilty last summer, but then Dawn struck her deal with the state, she said. He planned to do it in the fall, but then Justin entered his insanity plea. Now the time was right. She took a breath and continued. "He understands this does nothing in terms of sentencing . . . and that he still is facing a possible death sentence, but that is what he would like to do."

O'Malley leaned forward but could muster no words as Chapot finished speaking. She sat for a moment. Along with providing a stunning surprise, Taylor's guilty plea to capital murder raised some very thorny procedural issues for the judge. She ordered a recess until after lunch. Taylor calmly strode across the courtroom and out to his holding cell. Jewett watched him go. He knew there was now no way the brothers would stand trial together. Taylor had gotten his severance motion after all. Jewett went outside for a cigarette.

Even if Taylor went through with his guilty plea that afternoon, he still needed to have the penalty phase of his trial, where a jury would decide whether to sentence him to life in prison without the possibility of parole or to recommend death. Such trials usually come after the same jury finds a defendant guilty of capital murder. In those cases, jurors have already heard all of the prosecution's evidence and most of the aggravating circumstances (such as chopping up bodies) that they can consider when deciding the penalty. The penalty phase typically consists of victims' relatives testifying about their grief and the defense offering details of their client's background that might persuade a jury to pick life over death. But Taylor's penalty trial would have to include a mini–guilt phase as well. The jurors would need to hear exactly what he did in order to decide his fate.

When court resumed that afternoon, Chapot denied Jewett's accusation that the guilty plea was a tactical decision to somehow benefit his brother. Taylor simply had no defense to the charges, she said. He was prepared to plead. But when it came down to it, Taylor balked at the very first count against him. The conspiracy charge listed thirty-nine "overt acts" that the three accomplices had allegedly committed while planning Children of Thunder. Taylor refused to admit that some of these charges, like Justin's purchase of the Beretta, were true. "I am not willing to admit that I got this semiautomatic pistol in the overt act from any specific person, even though I'm totally willing to admit that I got [it]," he said in a slow, deliberate manner very unlike the torrents of speech he once employed. He had two reasons for arguing the point. The first was concern that he was harming Justin's defense case. The second was a very pragmatic and quite probably greater worry: concern for his own safety. If he had to spend the rest of his life in prison, he did not want to do it as a snitch, viewed as someone who helped convict an accomplice. After almost four years in the county jail, he knew what other inmates thought of snitches, and he had no desire to make things more difficult for himself than necessary.

Jewett refused to remove a single allegation. If Taylor did not admit them all, he would go to trial. O'Malley took a break and Chapot privately convinced Taylor that acknowledging all of the overt acts was the best thing to do. The judge returned and Taylor officially pleaded guilty to the conspiracy, five counts of capital murder, and a dozen other felonies.

When court reconvened the following Tuesday, everyone went back to bickering about separate trials. Cook argued that the notion of keeping the brothers together, when jurors knew one had already pleaded guilty, would cast such a shadow over Justin's legally entitled state of presumed innocence that there was no way he could receive a fair trial. And the attorney's position became almost frantic as Taylor dangled the hope of help in front of him—with, of course, a caveat. Taylor would assist Justin's lawyers, but only if his penalty-phase trial went first.

O'Malley granted Cook and Chapot's request for separate trials, but days later dashed Cook's dream of seeing Taylor on the stand by ruling that his client would go to trial first. She agreed with Jewett that if Taylor's trial were held first, the publicity could prejudice the jury pool against Justin. Little brother would, for the first time in his life, take center stage first.

———————

On the last day of April 2004, twelve jurors and four alternates filed into the jury box of Department 4 of the Superior Court of California in and for the County of Contra Costa. They were greeted by Judge Mary Ann O'Malley, who was thoughtful and measured in court but also exhibited just enough maternal concern for little human details—encouraging everyone to stretch after long bouts of testimony, allowing breaks after particularly emotional questioning. Past juries had, in a nod to her initials, dubbed her Judge Mom.

She welcomed her new jurors and turned to Jewett, who rose, hitched up his badly tailored pants, and strode to the middle of the courtroom to present his opening statement. It would be long, it would be thorough, and it would be fierce. It was how he always did it. He stood at the podium not unlike a Puritan preacher ready for Sunday sermon. He began, quickly reaching a rapid rhythm of words that went on for more than three hours, and painted Justin as a depraved killer. He raised his voice and threw his arm up, pointing to the defendant and reciting fact after fact about the trio's crimes, outrage and disdain dripping from every word. In his fire-and-brimstone oratory, Justin—and his two accomplices—were indeed sinners in the hands of an angry God.

When Jewett finished after the lunch break, Cook stood and faced the jury. He had been defending the indigent for almost twenty years and knew that the pressure that came with a capital case was enormous. His client's life was in his hands, and it was a responsibility he took to heart. He was the kind of public defender who genuinely believed there was something redeemable about all of his clients, even those accused of unspeakably horrific crimes.

He did not have as much to say to the jury as Jewett did; he spoke for less than half an hour. He did not deny Justin's involvement in the crimes, but told jurors that the real criminal was the man Justin believed to be a prophet of God. Even though he no longer sat next to his brother in court, this trial would still be all about Taylor.

Jewett knew that as well. To explain Children of Thunder required presenting all of Taylor's actions, and he did just that, calling old girlfriends and protégés to testify about his plans and beliefs. Then he called the cops, who spent hours on the stand detailing the evidence against Justin. And in a small bit of irony, after initially questioning Steve Nash's ability to run the Saddlewood crime scene, Jewett chose to use Marin detectives' method of organizing evidence throughout the trial. He thought Nash's clear labeling and logical categorizing made it much easier for the jury to understand the tremendous number of items involved.

It helped that Jewett knew the case better than anyone. He was well known for the ability to recall even the most minute detail on cases he prosecuted. He could usually offer up a fact or contradict an opponent without even having to look at his notepad. It was a talent that made even perfectly competent defense attorneys look woefully unprepared for trial. And that was exactly what it did to Cook and second chair Charlie Hoehn in the eyes of the jurors. Neither looked confident in their case or seemed to have a very firm grasp of things, some thought.

Jurors had listened to a month of testimony when they

walked into court one afternoon to see a large blond woman in jail clothes sitting in the witness chair. They knew immediately who it was. "Is she shackled down?" one juror whispered to another who could better see the witness stand. "No," the other juror replied.[1]

Dawn Godman spent days on the stand testifying about Children of Thunder. She talked about her belief that Taylor was a prophet. She detailed his bizarre schemes. All of it corroborated Cook's contention that Justin was merely a follower who thought his brother was a prophet. And then she told the jury about the killings. She said Justin was the one who beat Ivan and the one who struck Selina with the hammer. Of all the information she had, that was the most important to Jewett. Justin had personally delivered lethal blows; when it came time to decide his penalty, it would be easier to argue to the jury that he deserved to die.

Just because Dawn was his witness did not mean Jewett was kind to her. After she talked about soaking the carpets and creating a stink in an attempt to clean out Selina's blood, Jewett stared at her.

"Did you ever get that smell out of your nose, Ms. Godman?" he asked.

"No," she said.

"You carried that smell around in your nose even when you weren't in that house?"

"Yes."

"For how long?" he asked.

"Weeks," she replied.

When Cook finally got a chance to cross-examine Dawn, he was able to accomplish a rare thing—surprise Jewett with something he did not already know about the case. He asked the witness about a plan of Taylor's called "Brazil." Dawn explained that it involved assassinating the leaders of the Church of Jesus Christ of Latter-day Saints and having Taylor named its prophet. People shook their heads in amazement. He wanted to kill the leader of a major world religion? Just when they thought they had heard all the outlandish plans that Taylor had concocted, here was one more to put the icing on the crazy cake.

The Villarin family and the Stinemans' daughters sat through Dawn's testimony, often clutching one another's hands or wiping away tears with fistfuls of tissues. They had not heard any of it before, and the details hurt. But many of them needed to know—*had* to know—what happened and why. It was, someone said, better to know than to fill the void with imagined scenarios that were even worse.

There were lighter moments during the six-week trial. Debra McClanahan walked into court barefoot. Keri Furman missed her flight from Southern California the morning she was scheduled to testify. When she finally showed up, her appearance generated a large crowd of courthouse staff, sheriff's deputies, and lawyers, all of whom had not shown much interest in the proceedings until a *Playboy* centerfold came to town.

Keri was not a helpful witness. She obfuscated, pouted, and cried during most of Jewett's questioning. She had not done anything to deserve this. She wasn't involved in the plans, even if Taylor had talked to her about them. She could not recall the things Jewett was asking. During one five-minute span, she said "I don't remember" sixteen times.[2] The testimony started late and took so long that O'Malley had to order her to return the next morning. She had not expected to have to spend the night in a hotel. That prompted a bright-and-early outburst as Jewett resumed questioning the next day.

"I don't like you, Hal. You're not my friend," she lashed out. "You're fake with me, and I don't appreciate how you're treating me. You harassed me to get up here. And I don't like you. I have on the same clothes."

Finally, she was excused. She stomped out, just wanting to get home to her family and now sedate life. Jewett followed. Whatever he said in parting she did not stop to hear; she paused just long enough to flip him off before boarding the elevator.

Many of the witnesses allowed Cook to make a few points about Taylor's influence. Kelly Lord, a friend of both brothers, told Jewett that she had fallen under Taylor's spell as well.

"Well, I just have one more thing that I want to ask you about, Ms. Lord," Cook said during his cross-examination. "You said yesterday that—a couple of times at least—that you came to the realization, there but for the grace of God go I. Did you have somebody in mind when you made that statement yesterday?"

"Dawn Godman," she answered.

"Why was that?" Cook said.

"Dawn Godman or Selina, to be honest with you. Either one of them."

"Thank you," Cook said. "Those are all the questions I have, your honor."

Statements like Kelly's would have to be enough around which to rally a defense. Cook decided he was not going to present any of his own witnesses. He informed Justin of that decision just before announcing it in court.[3] It was a decision that would hurt him. Jurors thought he did not deliver what he had promised at the beginning of the trial. The jury forewoman felt let down; she thought any defense would have been better than nothing at all.[4]

On June 16, after deliberating less than seven hours, the jury found Justin guilty. Now the real fight began. Because Justin had pleaded not guilty by reason of insanity, the next phase of the trial needed to settle that question. Doctors who interviewed him would testify as to whether they thought he was mentally ill and insane at the time of the crimes. For this part of the trial, the burden of proof fell on Justin's lawyers, who had to convince the jury of their case. If they did, Justin would be sent to a mental hospital and the possibility of a death sentence would vanish.

Judging whether belief in a prophet is a delusion or simply religious faith can be a tricky thing. The mental-health field has made obvious allowances for major world religions; doctors cannot go around finding every Christian, Muslim, or Jew crazy simply because they believe that God has spoken through a chosen few. So when does faith cross the line to insanity? The doctors who interviewed Justin could not agree on an answer.

Two psychiatrists retained by the defense believed Justin was indeed deluded to believe his brother a prophet, and they diagnosed him with a very uncommon ailment—shared psychotic disorder. He became delusional and thought that the murders were divinely sanctioned because his brother was also delusional. Taylor's mental illness had infected Justin and caused him not to know the difference between right and wrong, the doctors testified.

Stephen Raffle, the first psychiatrist to take the stand, said Justin still suffered from the disorder. He thoroughly explained it for the jury and said he believed it began in 1998, when Taylor had gone on mental disability. Justin was insane during the crimes because his psychosis interfered with his ability to know right from wrong on a moral level, he said.

It was an opinion that Jewett, naturally, did not share. In more than a full day of cross-examination, he pounded the doctor with questions, returning again and again to the topic of right and wrong.

"Are you saying . . . that Justin Helzer knew that according to the moral standards of society, what he was doing was wrong," Jewett said, "but he believed it was morally right?"

"Yes," Raffle replied.

Jewett injected an extra measure of incredulity into his tone. "But it's your understanding . . . in that situation, he's legally insane?"

"Correct," Raffle said. "You just have to come to the heart of the matter."

"Yes, I have, Doctor," Jewett said. "Thank you very much."

The next defense psychiatrist, Robert Dolgoff, offered variations on the same theme. He told jurors that when Justin finally decided Taylor was a prophet, he felt great because after lacking direction for so long, he finally had a mission in life. It was a completely insane solution to his feelings of worthlessness, the doctor said.

Jewett hammered at this doctor as well. Justin knew society would condemn his actions, but he did not believe that the killings he was committing qualified as murder, Dolgoff said again and again.

"At that time, he also knew that murder was morally wrong?" Jewett asked.

"Yes, he did. Sure he knew murder was morally wrong at that point," said the doctor.

"Thank you, Doctor," Jewett said.

Dolgoff hastened to qualify his answer.

"But what he was doing was not, in his opinion, murder," he said quickly. But the damage had been done. Jurors noted his response, and Raffle's as well, and remembered them later on in the jury room.[5]

Two court-appointed psychologists both testified that Justin was sane at the time he committed the crimes. One doctor, Paul Good, agreed that Justin had lost his way and was vulnerable to Taylor's influence. But Justin's actions were the result of religious belief influenced by his Mormon upbringing, not delusion, he told jurors. Justin also knew right from wrong at the time, he said.

After two days of deliberation, jurors chose faith, not

insanity. They decided Justin had not been delusional when he committed the crimes; some were even skeptical that he honestly believed his brother to be a prophet at all.[6]

Now, after more than three months of trial, the only question left was Justin's punishment. The jury filed into the courtroom to begin the last phase of the trial. As they settled themselves, Justin decided it was his turn to speak.

"I want this life to be over," he said calmly as he sat ramrod straight in his chair next to Cook. "I want to die."

O'Malley immediately ordered the jury outside. She tried to talk over Justin, who kept speaking as Carma burst into tears in the audience.

"I'm just being truthful," he said. "I'm sorry, I'm not trying to be rude—I just want to be free. I want freedom or death."

As the door closed behind the bewildered jury, O'Malley glared at Justin.

"Mr. Helzer, I don't know what possessed you," she said, as Carma's sobs grew louder in the otherwise stunned silence.

When the jurors returned—several looking tearful and shaken—O'Malley instructed them to disregard anything they might have heard Justin say. Then it was finally the families' turn. Jenny Villarin's siblings took the stand, telling jurors about their loss of both a sister and a niece. The Stinemans' daughters testified, too, as did Fran Nelson, Jim Gamble's mother.

Then it was the defense's turn. They called Justin's sister, other relatives, former teachers. They talked about what a wonderful person he was, peaceful and loving, and that they felt he could still do good while in prison if he was allowed to live. Jurors took note. But they also noticed who did not take the stand. Neither Justin's mother nor father testified. Jurors had expected to at least hear from Carma and were very disappointed when they did not.[7]

Once in the jury room, the panel began weighing the aggravating factors—the dismemberment of the bodies, the betrayal of trust—against the mitigating factors, such as Justin's lack of any other criminal record and his previous contributions to society. They agreed that he knew Jenny was going to be killed, but several jurors disagreed with the majority that those murders warranted death. So eventually, the panel settled on life in prison without parole for those crimes. Then they turned to Selina and the Stinemans. After much thought—and looking again at the pictures of all three victims—they voted for death.

The ten women and two men walked into the courtroom on the fourth anniversary of Jenny and Jim's deaths and listened to clerk Tom Moyer read the verdicts. "Yes!" someone cried from the audience as other relatives sobbed. Jurors also could not hold back tears, and neither could O'Malley, who thanked them for their service.

"You will never have an experience like this one, I hope," she said.

The judge had her bailiffs take the jurors out through the special inmate elevator in order to avoid the press. The move meant that after months of being forbidden to speak to the victims' families, they were now unable to offer their condolences. Several of the female jurors had been meeting regularly after court at the upscale outdoor shopping mall in Walnut Creek. "Shopping therapy" would help them decompress after long, emotional days of testimony. So after the verdicts, they gathered at the central fountain—the same one Judy and Nancy had sat at so many years before as they waited for news of their parents—and decided that they had to do something more. They decided to buy flowers and go visit the Stinemans' graves.

When they got to the cemetery, employees would not tell them where the Stinemans were buried because the family had asked long ago that the location not be divulged. The women explained that they were the jury who had just finished the case against one of the couple's killers. The cemetery director looked at the group of sobbing women and said he would take them to the vault himself. The afternoon heat had burned the sky a brilliant blue as the jurors laid their flowers down and told the resting Stinemans how sorry they were.

The visit gave them a sense of closure. They added to it several weeks later when the same group traveled to Woodacre and had Sunday breakfast at the Two Bird Café. They then drove down the road to the Paper Mill Creek Saloon. A bunch of suburban women, they knew they were out of place in the working-class bar, but they did not care. They ordered beers and shot a game of pool. It made them feel better.

TWENTY-TWO

Sons of Perdition

———————●———————

What Taylor had tried his best to avoid had now come to pass. His trial began two months after his little brother's ended. And no one cared. Sure, all the victims' relatives were still in the audience. But the breathless attention that surrounded every revelation had evaporated. The television cameras were not lined up outside the courthouse. The newspapers would not write stories every day. He was now old news.

Jewett talked for hours again, outlining Taylor's plans. Although he did not have to prove the conspiracy or other crimes because Taylor had pleaded guilty, Jewett did need witnesses to explain for jurors what the accused had done so they could factor it into their decision on a death sentence.

Chapot spoke for less than half an hour. She told the jury that Taylor's family had a history of mental illness and that he heard voices and had bipolar disorder. That, combined with his drug use and obsession with Scripture, caused him to spiral out of control, she said. To support her contention, Chapot called an expert in substance abuse. Douglas Tucker was a psychiatrist who had diagnosed Taylor as suffering from schizoaffective disorder, which was in essence schizophrenia coupled with bipolar disorder. He told jurors that Taylor's rampant drug and alcohol use had exacerbated his mental illness. His methamphetamine consumption had been especially harmful because the drug can heighten delusions and other symptoms of mental illness.

Taylor claimed that he faked his mental illness in order to get disability, Jewett said. How do you know he is telling the truth now? Tucker explained that mania—part of Taylor's mood disorder, and described as a state of rapid, pressured speech and constantly shifting focus—was extremely difficult to fake. People pretending to be manic could not sustain the energy levels needed for very long. Only truly manic individuals could go on as long as Taylor did.

Taylor was also still wrestling with whether or not he was a prophet, said John Chamberlain, the other psychiatrist retained by Chapot. Taylor had told the doctor he was incredibly intelligent and on a divine mission. He gave Chamberlain a list of scriptural references that he said proved his points about sacrifice. In reality, like so much else about Taylor's life, the texts were taken out of context and molded to fit his own thinking. He made it clear to the doctor that he had considered the possibility that he was mentally ill and decided that he was not. Chamberlain disagreed and also diagnosed him with schizoaffective disorder.

Since this jury did not need to reach a verdict regarding Taylor's sanity when he committed the killings, Jewett went easier on these doctors than he'd done with those he'd questioned during Justin's trial. His case for the death penalty was built on the circumstances of the crimes, which he felt were aggravating enough to carry the day.

Chapot and her cocounsel, Gordon Scott, played to the

contradiction her client presented. They illustrated it with a poster board with two photos of Taylor: a close-up of him clean-shaven, clad in a suit and tie and smiling, and then, separated by a jagged red line, a picture of his strung-out, disheveled arrest mug shot. She called witnesses who knew him as a caring, charismatic young man and devout Mormon who slowly turned his back on what society believed was moral and right. She maintained that this change was the result of his mental illness and drug use.

Jewett, on the other hand, saw the situation as nothing more than a man choosing to use his charm and guile to amass money and power. In his eyes, Taylor was just plain greedy. And during his daylong closing argument, he unloaded on the man he called a conscienceless killer.

"He cut those people up, and he cut those families up," Jewett said. And then in a bit of courtroom theater, he drove home the point by starting a saw and letting its roar fill the courtroom as he pointed to the smiling faces of the Stinemans, Jenny, Jim, and Selina projected on the wall.

The next day, in a much quieter and shorter closing argument, Chapot acknowledged that her client's actions were inexcusable. However, he had never hurt anyone before and was mentally ill, she said during her hour-long speech. She asked the jury to show mercy and sentence Taylor to life.

The jury declined. After slightly more than a day of deliberation, the nine men and three women decided he bore full responsibility for all of the deaths, and that he should pay with his own life. They recommended death sentences for all five murders. As the first verdict was read, Taylor turned toward his mother. "It's okay," he mouthed. Carma left the courtroom crying. Oggie Land did not. She was happy with the verdicts and relieved that her four-year quest for justice was almost over. Now the brothers just needed to be formally sentenced.

Justin entered the courtroom in a blue blazer over a white shirt and brown patterned tie. His head was shaved and he had a light, straggly beard. Cook sat on his left and Hoehn on his right.

"All rise."

It was a formality O'Malley usually dispensed with, but today the audience rose as one until she took her seat. She took a breath and launched into her ruling. In California, when a jury recommends death, there is an automatic appeal to the trial judge to reduce the penalty to life without parole. To no one's surprise, O'Malley did not do this. She did take the opportunity, though, to rehash the graphic details of the Stinemans' and Selina's deaths. Her voice shook slightly.

Villarin and Stineman family members wept in the audience. Steve Nash put his arm around Jim Gamble's aunt as O'Malley continued her recitation. She then called a recess so she could read Justin's probation report. People spent the forty-five minutes in the stuffy hallway chatting or making trips downstairs for coffee. And Cook delivered a few letters on behalf of his client. He had not wanted to just drop them in the mail, so he asked Jewett what he thought would be appropriate. Jewett suggested he give them to the families personally, so Cook approached them in the hall.

Words are so inadequate. Yet they are all I have to give. I'm so sorry I didn't see how to handle my pain, fear & confusion responsibly. I thought I was. I now see I wasn't. I thought I was helping humanity's spiritual evolution. I didn't. I thought I was right. I was wrong. I thought I was doing good. It was bad.

I'm so very, very sorry. I don't expect forgiveness, although I hope some day you will. Whether you forgive

*me or not, what I hope most for you is somehow you're
able to obtain peace of mind. I hope the best for you.*

He signed it simply, *Justin.* The Villarins were not impressed, but it did make Fran Nelson feel better. She appreciated the apology. Nancy thought it was more about how
he felt instead of how he had made the victims feel. He's
just sorry he got caught, she thought.

Everyone was back in their seats at 10 a.m., when O'Malley returned and sentencing truly got under way. Jewett stood,
hitched up his pants, and asked that Justin's death sentences
be served concurrently, not one after the other. That way,
when he was executed, it would be for the murders of all
three of his victims. It was another symbolic point from the
guy who regularly wore a scales-of-justice tie tack to court.

Before the hearing, Fran told Jewett she did not need to
say anything. That left a representative from the Villarins
and from the Stinemans. Robert Asuncion rose first, standing in the audience among his many relatives.

"It's been a long time for us," he said. "As a family,
we'd like to not only express our thanks but our love for
each other during this time.

"What happened should never happen," he continued.
Justin did not meet his gaze.

"We understand that there is a benefit from this tragedy.
That we as a people pull together and say this can't happen." Love and nourish your children, he said. Hold your
families close. "We hope that everyone here finds peace.
That's what we're looking for."

Then Judy stood, papers clutched in her hands. For more
than three pages, she calmly theorized how frightened her
parents must have been and what they went through.

"Mama and Daddy should have died with dignity. Instead, we laid our murdered and dismembered parents to
rest on their fifty-fifth wedding anniversary.

"Throughout the Helzer trials, I heard repeatedly they had a plan to bring unconditional love to the world," she said. "I found it ironic that the first comment I made when my parents' remains were recovered from the delta was that my unconditional love was gone. I didn't appreciate it for what it was until it was taken away."

Judy sat down in the hushed courtroom. Jewett stood up.

"There's nothing the people can add to that, your honor."

Then it was Justin's turn. He read quickly and quietly from a sheet of paper.

"Briefly, I hope to see the day when globally all spiritual truths are fully and voluntarily embraced in our collective spiritual beings, the awareness in every mind great and small, and violence is never necessary. That love, joy, and peace are the only eternal constants so that confusion, fear, and suffering no longer exist among us. That day's birth is in process, and though, at times, the process is painful, when that day arrives, all will rejoice together." He paused. "Thank you. That's all."

His sermon was met with silence. Cook, who had been tasked with explaining his client's actions for more than four years, did not have to do so today. He just stood and signed off the case with grace.

"It has been a great honor for me to represent Justin," he said. "Although I have never been able to reconcile in my own mind how a person capable of love . . . also [could] be capable of such great evil."

O'Malley then got to the nuts and bolts of the sentencing, assigning years-long prison terms for Justin's lesser convictions. As she was speaking, Carma hesitated, then got up from her seat and whispered in a deputy's ear. When O'Malley finished the lesser counts, Cook interrupted. Mrs. Helzer, he said, would like to speak.

"I want to acknowledge the tremendous amount of suffering that has been experienced because of all of this," she said, her slight form beginning to shake as she stood in the audience. Gerry rested his hand protectively on her chair. She started to cry. Her son turned his head slightly back and watched her out of the corner of his eye.

"I also acknowledge the natural tendency to blame families and mothers and parents," she said, her breath coming in gasps now and her voice anguished and rising. "Everybody who does blame me, I don't blame you for blaming me."

She paused.

"And those who blame Justin, I don't blame you for blaming him. And I understand all the reasons for it."

She thanked the judge, Jewett, and the juries. She thanked Justin's attorneys. And she thanked her little boy.

"I want to thank my son for being my son and for all the blessings he's brought into my life and to many other people in his life before these events and even in the jail after these events occurred. I know, Justin, that you are not the sum of what you've been convicted of, but that you are far more than that. And all of us are far more than one event in our life—and one stupid mistake." She paused and took a breath. "Thank you for letting me speak."

She sat. O'Malley, who looked stricken and near tears during her speech, recovered and handed down her first death sentence.

"It is the judgment and sentence of this court . . . you shall suffer the death penalty, said penalty to be inflicted within the walls of the prison of San Quentin."

Jewett stared at Justin. Justin didn't look at anyone. The scratch of O'Malley's pen as she signed the death sentence was the only sound in the room. Justin shook Cook's hand, stood up, got cuffed, and walked out.

———

After lunch, everyone packed back into the courtroom as the sun from an unseasonably warm March day poured through the windows. Taylor walked into the courtroom also dressed in civilian clothes—a blue cardigan he had worn during the trial, a light blue collared shirt, and dark pants. His black hair was long, almost down to his collar, but neatly brushed back from his face. Just as she had done with his brother, O'Malley denied Taylor's motion to reduce the death sentence.

Oggie sat in the audience. She had not planned to speak today, but could not help herself. She stood.

"He believes in God, or what he said," she said of Taylor, who sat looking at her with a trembling chin.

The Book of Deuteronomy says he is to be sent home so he can face the people he murdered, she said. "I just beg that that is what you follow through with," she told O'Malley.

Robert Asuncion spoke again, saying much the same thing he had earlier that day. Taylor looked at him too, and appeared to fight back tears.

Then it was Suzanne Chapot's turn to bow out. She stood and acknowledged the horrors suffered by the victims and their families. But . . .

"Taylor is not all evil," she said, then added with regret, "I was not able to show that sufficiently to the court."

This is a man with incredible potential who did horrendous things, she said, then turned to face the packed audience. "There is more to this man than the acts he committed," she said forcefully.

But there really was no more to Taylor than himself, his views, his opinions. And the courtroom was treated to those thoughts as he picked up a sheet of paper and began to read.

"The position in which I find myself today seems like one where I risk giving offense by keeping silent and saying nothing or to risk giving offense by responding, either by the things I don't say in my response or by the things I do say, by the way I say it.

"If the content, the lack of content, or even the manner of my speaking adds further offense to anyone here, I'd like you to know it was not my intention nor my purpose to do so because I think the sound of my voice itself is offensive to most here. And in its absence, the sound of my breath, equally offensive. And after that quits, the thought of me very probably forever abhorrent."

He turned as far as he was able to in his chair and faced the audience.

"I am sorry. I am so sorry. I clearly see now that my actions were unspeakably horrific," he said. "I was actually under the impression I was doing a good thing."

Dismissive sniffs came from the audience.

"If I were evil, I would enjoy your misery, and hating me, you're contributing to my satisfaction," he said through tears. And then the sermon started. "If I'm not evil, your hatred is misplaced and harmful to you."

He encouraged his victims to, if not forgive him, then forget him before he was executed. "If I were evil, then anything—every time you think on me with hatred and anticipation of vengeance prior to that date, your misery is handing me an additional victory, an additional success. Why taint your thoughts with me?"

Then the lecture shifted focus. He began to rail against the death penalty and his fate at the hands of a state executioner.

"That life or death, independent of the truth, could hang on the balance of the performance of two unequal actors with an agenda to win, in spite of the facts exposed in a case, is a shame anywhere in the twenty-first century," he went on. "But the fact is, in this country we have put an incredible effort to create a fair trial prior to sentencing a human being to death. Worldwide, governments less noble than others use the legalization of state-sanctioned murder to kill thousands of people . . ."

Jewett had stared unblinkingly at Taylor throughout his statement. As his rant continued, Jewett snapped out, asking the judge to make him turn away from the audience. O'-Malley agreed, and Taylor shifted reluctantly in his seat.

He finished, looked at his sheet of paper, and thought for a moment. "That was going to be the end, after I apologized one last time," he said. He took a breath, and then turned to the families. "You can believe it or not. This is the truth . . . I care so much about people," he almost sobbed, his voice cracking and rising. Several people in the audience actually snorted.

"Worldwide, I feel like we're a collective unit." There are people in poverty, in slavery, in pain, he said. "Murders, rape, theft, terrorism, wars, and we don't care."

People shifted in their seats, and the contempt began to roll like a wave.

"I reached the point where I was so blessed in my life that I got fixated. I couldn't sleep at night with the hypocrisy I found in myself, enjoying the absolute beauty of life while millions of people suffered." He spoke more and more quickly. "And I had a vision in my head what I could do to solve it if I cared enough, to follow God as much as Nephi, as much as Abraham, the prophets throughout the ages."

As he finished and slumped a little in his chair, Jenny's friend Rosanne Lusk Urban waved a small photo of Selina at him from the audience. Taylor nodded. Carma sobbed in the audience, but she did not rise to speak. After his five death sentences were pronounced, Taylor was led away in handcuffs.

———

Paul's First Epistle to the Corinthians speaks of Christ's resurrection. As Joseph Smith read it all those years ago, a series of verses caught his eye.

There are also celestial bodies, and bodies terrestrial:
but the glory of the celestial is one, and the glory of the
terrestrial is another. There is one glory of the sun, and
another glory of the moon, and another glory of the
stars: for one star differeth from another star in glory.
So also is the resurrection of the dead.[1]

After reading these words, Joseph Smith had a revelation.[2] He saw three kingdoms of God, where all people
would go when they faced Judgment Day. Which kingdom
they deserved to enter depended upon their actions while
on Earth. The celestial kingdom was glorious as the sun,
and reserved for the faithful members of the church, who
could be together as a family forever. They would walk
with God.

The terrestrial kingdom, akin to the moon, was for those
who rejected the word of God during their mortal lives, but
lived honorably nonetheless. There would be no family
units.

The telestial kingdom shone the most weakly, like the
stars, and was where those who had blatantly refused the
laws of God would dwell. Even liars, sorcerers, adulterers,
and whoremongers would at least receive welcome in the
telestial kingdom. They shall only be redeemed after
the last resurrection.[3] Only the worst of the worst would be
cast out, believers who once knew Jesus Christ as their
Messiah but rejected Him and doomed themselves to an afterlife of torment and darkness. They would be known,
Joseph Smith decreed, as the Sons of Perdition.

———————

Taylor was left in a solitary jail holding cell after his sentencing. The usual transport to San Quentin State Prison
usually took days, and he fully expected that someone
would escort him back to his cell upstairs until it was time

to go across the bay to his new home. But the deputies who appeared at his door led him instead to a van. Jail officials wanted nothing to do with inmates sentenced to death; they considered such men dangerous and removed them from their facility as quickly as possible. Taylor—just like Justin only hours before—was no exception. Two deputies helped him into the back of the van and climbed in front for the ride across the bay. Another two-deputy team followed in an unmarked police car. After all the self-created drama that had come before, the drive was quiet and uneventful. The van bounced and rocked on the highway, sending Taylor swaying a bit in the back.

The thirty-four-year-old had certainly fallen far from the promise of his patriarchal blessing all those years ago. There had been no ultimate service to the Lord, no using his pure heart as an example to others. Back then he had been on his way to the Celestial Kingdom, and the brilliant glory of God's presence. Now, as he sat in the windowless van, he could not see the bright spring sunshine glinting off the water as he crossed San Francisco Bay, headed toward perdition.

EPILOGUE

———◆———

It was a sunny summer day, and the breeze coming off the water cooled the air as it drifted through the main room at the yacht club in Benicia, a bedroom community a half-hour drive from San Francisco. It had been two months since the final court date in the Helzer case, and the families of their victims had decided to gather one last time. It was a "closure party" organized by Judy Nemec, and it was the perfect way to remember loved ones—not in a courtroom with killers sitting only feet away, but in a pretty place unassociated with death.

Judy, who ran a balloon party decoration business, decorated the club in a blue-and-white ocean theme. She wanted something cheerful and hopeful. The long slog through the criminal justice system was over, and it was finally time for a smile.

Several of the police officers who helped solve the case were there—including Steve Nash with fresh mud on his jeans from a new crime scene just that morning. Many jurors came, as did Judge O'Malley's courtroom staff. Hal Jewett brought his wife.

Relatives of the Stinemans and the Villarins mingled and said thank you. The two families, who came from such different circumstances, would likely never have met if not for the crimes committed against their loved ones. Now they knew one another in ways no one else possibly could. There was little talk of the crimes or the killers. People preferred to dwell on Jim, Jenny and Selina, and Ivan and Annette. David Villarin passed out little computer-printed photos of his sister and niece. Nancy Hall, whose multiple sclerosis had been severely aggravated by the stress of the trials, felt a little better and walked through the crowd talking and smiling. Fran Nelson had not been able to make it, but was asked after by many.

As everyone enjoyed the buffet and had a few drinks, Judy stood and took the microphone.

"As you know, five years ago, three separate families received very bad news about their loved ones. With time, our families met and discovered we shared a unique, common bond. With that realization, we were no longer three families, but one," she said. "As family, we look around this room and are in awe of the people here today.

"Whether you chose law enforcement as a career, witnessed something, or simply got stuck with jury duty, you have all done something amazing. We realize your jobs were difficult. No one should have to do what you do, but we are so thankful you do it," she said.

Several of the cops looked bashful as they listened to Judy talk. It was not often that they were so publicly thanked for their work. Then Jewett got up to do the same.

"I know in the practical sense there might not be any such thing as true closure, frankly, but boy, a day like today can get you about as close as you're going to get in a situation like this, I think," he said.

He thanked everyone who worked on the case but then focused his gratitude on the families.

"I can tell you as a prosecutor—and you folks know what we went through during the trials—we get inspiration from many places, but the single biggest source of inspiration for me, to get me through a very long job, was those people who were sitting behind me. Because I couldn't have got that job done without you." He paused and fought back tears.

"So you say thank you to us. Well, we the justice system say thank you to you." The crowd broke into applause. "And by the way, those shish kebabs weren't bad either," he said, pointing to the buffet table as people laughed.

"So that's all I have to say," said the often long-winded prosecutor. "Thank you all, and thank you for taking the time to listen to me—one last time."

But it was Judy's appreciation that echoed in quiet conversations as people hugged good-bye and slowly left the gathering.

"So how do we say thank you? Those two words are so overused. As children, we are taught to say 'thank you' when someone gives us something. From there it is shortened to 'thanks' and is said without much thought. There is no word in the English language that adequately expresses the gratitude we feel deep in our hearts for your caring and support," she said. "We will be forever grateful for your efforts in resolving this case and giving us an opportunity to regain some peace in our lives."

ACKNOWLEDGMENTS

———◆———

This book would not have been possible without the help of many people who graciously gave their time and expertise so that I could tell this story properly.

I was lucky enough to have the kind help and encouragement of family members, including Judy Nemec and Nancy Hall, Olga and Mark Land, David and Clara Villarin, Robert Asuncion, Lusha Villarin, Alixis Villarin, Lydia Young, Nelda Culver, and the indomitable Fran Nelson. Many of Jenny and Selina's friends also offered their assistance, especially Rosanne Lusk Urban, as well as Gloria LaFranchi, Dennis Ogilvie, Thomasina Wilson, and Tony Miceli.

This story would never have come to light if not for the work of those who investigated the crimes. Steve Nash of the Marin County Sheriff's Office, and Steve Chiabotti, Judy Elo, Heidi Stephenson, Paul Crain, and David Chilimidos of the Concord Police Department were kind enough to share their thoughts on the case, as was Hal Jewett of the Contra Costa County District Attorney's Office.

Heather Helzer graciously offered insights into her family, and David Sullivan shared years of expertise in cults and undue influence that was invaluable.

I also want to thank Judge Mary Ann O'Malley and especially her clerk, Tom Moyer, who had more patience with me than I had any right to expect. I very much appreciate the transcripts provided by court reporters Melanie Haynes, Jeanine Maltbie, Linda MacFarlane, and Raquel Sharp, and the help I received from many people at the Contra Costa County Superior Court clerk's office, including Susan King, Joycelyn Gomez, Leila Mitra, Marie Aquino, Suzi Daily, Kathy O'Melia, and the file unit staff.

From the Contra Costa County Sheriff's Office, Joe Caruso, Genoa Brown, and Diane Lynch provided assistance at different times during the case. I also want to thank several officials for talking with me about the case: Ed Berberian and Paula Kamena of the Marin County District Attorney's Office and Gary Yancey, Dale Miller, and Bob Kochly of the Contra Costa County District Attorney's Office.

Former *Times* colleagues Matt Krupnick and Bruce Gerstman kept me up-to-date on developments, Michiele Roderick contributed valuable insights, and Deb Hollinger and Ray Saint Germain helped with several photos for this book. I am lucky to have a great agent in Jim McCarthy and editor in Katie Day. I also could not have gotten through the writing without my trio of readers and wonderful friends—Kim Rutledge, Andrea Widener, and Yvonne Condes.

And finally, I would not have been able to do this without the support of my family, especially my husband, whose unwavering faith in me makes everything possible. Thank you.

NOTES

————◆————

CHAPTER 1
1. Nancy Hall, author interview.
2. Based on the recollections of Nancy Hall and Judy Nemec.

CHAPTER 2
1. Villarin relatives and friends, author interviews.
2. Fran Nelson, author interview.

CHAPTER 3
1. Olga Land, author interview.
2. Steve Nash, author interview.

CHAPTER 4
1. Carma Helzer, testimony given to the 2000 grand jury.
2. Childhood details come from Heather Helzer, who wrote a frank and
   honest assessment of her family that she kindly shared for this book.
3. From Heather Helzer's written statement. She goes on to say that if
   her mother could be persuaded to see a psychologist, she is confident
   Carma would be diagnosed as suffering from a psychosomatic illnes,
   a physical disorder caused or influenced by the patient's emotional
   state.

4. Court exhibit T, a tape recording of Doyle Sorenson describing his visit with the Savior submitted during Taylor Helzer's trial.
5. Court exhibit S, a copy of Taylor's patriarchal blessing, was entered into evidence by his attorneys for the jury to read. Its contents are so important to future events that it has been included here.
6. Heather Helzer, written statement.
7. Charney Hoffmann, testimony given at Taylor Helzer's trial.
8. Taylor Helzer missionary journal. This and all recollections from this time period in Taylor's life, unless otherwise noted, come from his journal, written while he trained in Utah and served in Brazil. Taylor Helzer did not respond to requests for an interview by the author.
9. *The Book of Mormon,* Helaman 10:4–5.

CHAPTER 5
1. Sermon taken from Taylor Helzer's missionary journal.
2. Exodus 20:12. This and all biblical citations are taken from the King James Version, the translation commonly used by the Church of Jesus Christ of Latter-day Saints.
3. 2 Thessalonians 2:2–3.
4. California National Guard service records.
5. From the trial testimony of Nenad Nikolic, who served with Justin Helzer in Germany.
6. California National Guard service records.
7. Heather Helzer, author interview.
8. Details regarding group awareness trainings were compiled from author interviews with participants and sworn testimony given during Justin Helzer and Taylor Helzer's trial.
9. Heather Helzer, author interview.
10. Charney Hoffmann, testimony given during Justin Helzer's trial.
11. Taylor Helzer ended employment with the telemarketing firm April 1, 1993, according to the National Association of Security Dealers. He began at Dean Witter on May 17, 1993.
12. Heather Helzer, author interview and testimony given during Justin Helzer's trial.

CHAPTER 6
1. Fawn M. Brodie, *No Man Knows My History: The Life of Joseph Smith* (New York: Vintage Books, 1995).

2. Doctrine and Covenants 28:2–3,7. The Doctrine and Covenants is a compilation of "divine revelations and inspired declarations" from the church's prophets—most from Joseph Smith—and is one of the religion's standard works, which also include the Bible and *The Book of Mormon*.

3. Brodie, *No Man Knows My History: The Life of Joseph Smith*.

4. Dr. Richard Foster, testimony given during Taylor Helzer's trial.

5. Dr. Douglas Tucker, testimony regarding Taylor's self-reported drug history given during Taylor Helzer's trial.

6. Heather Helzer, author interview.

7. Chi Hoffmann, testimony given at 2001 preliminary hearing for Taylor Helzer, Justin Helzer, and Dawn Godman.

8. Ibid.

9. Gerry Helzer, testimony given before 2000 grand jury.

10. Carma Helzer, testimony given before 2000 grand jury.

11. Heather Helzer, author interview.

12. Justin Helzer, interview with Dr. Stephen Raffle as related during Raffle's testimony during Justin's trial. Justin Helzer did not respond to requests for an interview by the author.

13. *The Book of Mormon*, 2 Nephi 2:23–25.

14. Kaiser Permanente medical records, submitted as court exhibit M at Taylor Helzer's trial.

CHAPTER 7

1. Dawn Godman sentencing memo, May 2005. Many details of her life prior to meeting the Helzer brothers come from this document, which her attorneys filed with the court at the time of her sentencing in an attempt to explain her background and how it factored into her subsequent criminal behavior. She did not respond to requests for an interview by the author.

2. Amador County court documents. Dawn's emancipation was granted July 23, 1991, only seven days after she requested it.

3. Amador County Sheriff's Office incident report, February 21, 1994.

4. Dawn Godman sentencing memo.

5. Taylor also referred to his plan as "Impact America," using the two interchangeably at times. For the sake of clarity, only Transform America is used in the book.

6. Dawn Kirkland, testimony given at Justin Helzer and Taylor Helzer trials.

7. Brent Halversen, testimony given at Justin Helzer and Taylor Helzer trials.

CHAPTER 8

1. Mark 3:17.
2. I Samuel 15:23–33.
3. *The Book of Mormon* 1 Nephi 4:12–13.
4. I Samuel 15:33.
5. *The Book of Mormon* I Nephi 4:11.
6. Carma Helzer, testimony given to the 2000 grand jury.
7. Debra McClanahan, testimony given to the 2000 grand jury and at the 2001 preliminary hearing. McClanahan testified extensively at both Justin Helzer and Taylor Helzer's trials as well, making her the most-called non-law-enforcement witness in the entire case.
8. Ibid.
9. Dawn Godman, testimony given at Taylor Helzer's trial.
10. Ibid.
11. Concord police report regarding interview with Bay Alarm supervisor.

CHAPTER 9

1. The explanation of Justin's thought process comes from various interviews that he gave several mental health professionals after his arrest.
2. Doctrine and Covenants 85:7.
3. Doctrine and Covenants 7:1–3. The D&C goes on to state that John, James, and Peter will be given the keys to Christ's ministry, which they will return to Joseph Smith centuries later.
4. Contra Costa Superior Court case 97994. *Catherine Ma v. Dawn Godman*.
5. Debra McClanahan, testimony given at Taylor Helzer's trial.
6. Dr. Douglas Tucker, interview with Taylor Helzer.
7. Rosanne Lusk Urban, author interview.
8. Selina journal entry.
9. Gerry Helzer, testimony given to the 2000 grand jury.

CHAPTER 10

1. Details regarding the commission of the crimes in the following chapters come from Dawn Godman's testimony during Justin Helzer and Taylor Helzer's trials, except where otherwise noted.
2. Debra McClanahan, testimony given to the 2000 grand jury.

3. Alexandra Price, testimony given to the 2000 grand jury.

4. Debra McClanahan, testimony given during various court proceedings.

5. *San Francisco Chronicle,* May 28, 2004.

6. Nancy Hall, testimony during Justin Helzer's trial and August 2000 statement to police.

7. Dr. John Chamberlain, interview with Taylor Helzer.

CHAPTER 11

1. George Calhoun, Dean Witter manager, testimony given at Justin Helzer and Taylor Helzer's trials.

2. Dr. Larry Wornian, interview with Justin Helzer.

3. Dr. John Chamberlain, interview with Taylor Helzer.

4. This detail is from the 2003 interview given by Justin Helzer to psychologist Larry Wornian. In her trial testimony, Godman admitted only to standing at the bathroom doorway during the killings. In his interview, Justin also said he stabbed Ivan before he died.

5. Sacramento County Coroner autopsy report.

6. Dr. Larry Wornian, interview with Justin Helzer.

7. Selina's journal, August 1, 2000, entry.

CHAPTER 12

1. Vicki Sexton, testimony given at Justin Helzer's trial.

2. Nenad Nikolic, testimony given at Justin Helzer's trial.

3. Selina's journal, August 1, 2000, entry.

4. *Playboy,* September 2000.

5. Dr. Larry Wornian, interview with Justin Helzer.

6. Dr. John Chamberlain, interview with Taylor Helzer.

7. Sacramento County Coroner autopsy report.

8. Dr. John Chamberlain, interview with Taylor Helzer.

9. Dawn Godman, testimony given at Justin Helzer's trial.

10. Dr. John Chamberlain, interview with Taylor Helzer.

CHAPTER 13

1. Dawn Godman, testimony given at Justin Helzer's trial. At Taylor Helzer's subsequent trial, she denied seeing whether there was a tattoo on the skin Taylor fed the dog. The autopsy of Selina Bishop confirmed that skin from the back of her left shoulder had been removed. Her tattoo was in that location, according to family members.

2. Fran Nelson, author interview.

3. Gloria LaFranchi, author interview.

4. *San Francisco Chronicle,* August 6, 2000.
5. Marin County Coroner autopsies of James Gamble and Jennifer Villarin.

CHAPTER 14

1. Gloria LaFranchi, author interview.
2. David Villarin, author interview.
3. Lydia Young, author interview.
4. Hazem Belal, testimony given at Justin Helzer's trial.

CHAPTER 15

1. Concord police reports, August 7, 2000.
2. Paul Crain, author interview.

CHAPTER 16

1. Steve Chiabotti, author interview, and a tape recording of the conversation between the detective and Taylor Helzer.
2. Judy Nemec and Nancy Hall, author interviews.
3. Olga Land, author interview.
4. Transcript of search warrant hearing, August 7, 2000.
5. Hal Jewett, author interview.
6. Steve Nash, author interview.

CHAPTER 17

1. This scene was taken from the grand-jury testimony of a woman who came forward after later realizing Dawn Godman was a suspect in the Stineman killings. The woman's mother had been killed eight years earlier and the case struck a chord with her. "These old, elderly people were killed, and this woman's mother. And I just thought, that's not right."
2. *San Francisco Examiner,* June 7, 1996.
3. *San Francisco Chronicle,* August 7, 1998.
4. *Contra Costa Times,* August 10, 2000.
5. *San Francisco Chronicle,* August 10, 2000.
6. *Marin Independent Journal,* August 15, 2000.
7. Lusha Villarin, author interview.

CHAPTER 18

1. *Contra Costa Times,* August 13, 2000.
2. *Contra Costa Times,* August 13, 2000.

3. *Marin Independent Journal,* August 15, 2000.
4. Steve Chiabotti, author interview.
5. U.S. Department of Justice, Bureau of Justice Statistics. In 2000, Contra Costa held fairly steady, with fifty-six murders. Marin jumped from one to five—two of whom were Jennifer Villarin and James Gamble.
6. Gary Yancey, author interview.
7. *San Jose Mercury News,* August 11, 2000.
8. *San Francisco Chronicle,* August 11, 2000.
9. Paula Kamena, author interview.
10. Dale Miller and Gary Yancey, author interviews.
11. Justin Helzer letters written in jail to Dawn Godman and Taylor Helzer.

CHAPTER 19
1. *Contra Costa Times,* September 8, 2000.
2. *San Francisco Chronicle,* September 8, 2000.
3. Paul Crain, author interview.

CHAPTER 20
1. Dr. Stephen Raffle, testimony given at Justin Helzer's trial.
2. Contra Costa Detention Facilities incident and disciplinary reports.
3. The already famous Dietz would garner much more attention after testifying for the prosecution in the 2002 trial of Andrea Yates, the Texas mother who drowned her five children. Dietz mistakenly said that an episode of the television show *Law & Order* aired just before the killings and featured a similar crime. After testifying, Dietz told Court TV that he checked his facts and determined he was in error. He wrote prosecutors and offered to return to the stand in order to correct his testimony. Prosecutors did not call him back. Yates, whose attorneys had asked that she be found not guilty by reason of insanity, was convicted of murder. An appellate court later threw out the conviction because Dietz's testimony could have affected the judgment of the jury. Yates was retried and in July 2006 found not guilty by reason of insanity.
4. Dawn Godman sentencing memo.
5. Contra Costa County Detention Facilities incident and disciplinary reports.
6. Contra Costa County Detention Facilities incident reports. Jail deputies listened in on several of Taylor Helzer's conversations with other inmates and then with his mother during their investigation of his escape plans.

CHAPTER 21

1. Justin Helzer trial juror, author interview.
2. *San Francisco Chronicle,* May 14, 2004.
3. Justin Helzer pro se motion for mistrial, dated October 1, 2004.
4. Justin Helzer trial jurors, author interviews.
5. Justin Helzer trial jurors, author interviews.
6. Justin Helzer trial juror, author interview.
7. Justin Helzer trial jurors, author interviews.

CHAPTER 22

1. I Corinthians 15:40–42
2. Fawn M. Brodie, *No Man Knows My History: The Life of Joseph Smith* (New York: Vintage Books, 1995).
3. Doctrine and Covenants 76:85.